RETHINKING INDIA

THE GREAT INDIAN MANTHAN

STATE, STATECRAFT AND THE REPUBLIC

T0243797

Edited by

PUSHPARAJ DESHPANDE
GURDEEP SINGH SAPPAL

VINTAGE
An imprint of Penguin Random House

VINTAGE

USA | Canada | UK | Ireland | Australia
New Zealand | India | South Africa | China | Singapore

Vintage is part of the Penguin Random House group of companies
whose addresses can be found at global.penguinrandomhouse.com

Published by Penguin Random House India Pvt. Ltd
4th Floor, Capital Tower 1, MG Road,
Gurugram 122 002, Haryana, India

First published in Vintage by Penguin Random House India 2023

ISBN 9780670093038

Typeset in Bembo Std by Manipal Technologies Limited, Manipal
Printed at Replika Press Pvt. Ltd, India

www.penguin.co.in

Contents

Series Editors' Note

Psychologists tell us that the only true enemies we have are the faces looking back at us in the mirror. Today, we in India need to take a long, hard look at ourselves in the mirror. With either actual or looming crises in every branch of government, at every level, be it central, state or local; with nearly every institution failing; with unemployment at historically high rates; with an ecosystem ready to implode; with a healthcare system in a shambles; with an education system on the brink of collapse; with gender, caste and class inequities unabating; with civil society increasingly characterized by exclusion, intolerance and violence; with our own minorities living in fear; our hundreds of millions of fellow citizens in penury; and with few prospects for the innumerable youth of this nation in the face of all these increasingly intractable problems, the reflection is not sightly. Our true enemies are not external to us, not Pakistani terrorists or Bangladeshi migrants, but our own selves: our own lack of imagination, communication, cooperation and dedication towards achieving the India of our destiny and dreams.

Our Constitution, as the Preamble so eloquently attests, was founded upon the fundamental values of the dignity of the individual and the unity of the nation, envisioned in relation to a radically egalitarian justice. These bedrock ideas, though perhaps especially pioneered by the likes of Jawaharlal Nehru, Dr B.R. Ambedkar, M.K. Gandhi, Maulana Azad, Sardar Patel, Sarojini Naidu, Jagjivan Ram, R. Amrit Kaur, Ram Manohar Lohia and others, had emerged as a broad consensus among the many founders of this nation, cutting across divergent social and political ideologies. Giving shape to that vision, the architects of modern India strived to ensure that each one of us is accorded equal opportunities to live with dignity and security, has equitable access to a better life and is an equal partner in this nation's growth.

Yet, today, we find these most basic constitutional principles under attack. Nearly all the public institutions that were originally created in order to fight against dominance and subservience are in the process of subversion, creating new hierarchies instead of dismantling them, generating inequities instead of ameliorating them. Government policy merely pays lip service to egalitarian considerations, while the actual administration of 'justice' and implementation of laws are in fact perpetuating precisely the opposite: illegality, criminality, corruption, bias, nepotism and injustice of every conceivable stripe. And the rapid rise of social intolerance and manifold exclusions (along the lines of gender, caste, religion, etc.) effectively whittle down and even sabotage an inclusive conception of citizenship, polity and nation.

In spite of these and all the other unmentioned but equally serious challenges posed at this moment, there are in fact new sites for socio-political assertion re-emerging. There are new calls arising for the reinstatement of the letter and spirit of our Constitution, not just normatively (where we battle things out ideologically) but also practically (the battle at the level of policy articulation and implementation). These calls are not simply partisan, nor are they exclusionary or zero-sum. They witness the wide participation of youth, women, the historically disadvantaged in the process of finding a new voice, minorities, members of majority communities and progressive individuals all joining hands in solidarity.

We at the Samruddha Bharat Foundation proudly count ourselves among them. The Foundation's very raison d'être has been to take serious cognizance of India's present and future challenges, and to rise to them. Over the past two years, we have constituted numerous working groups to critically rethink social, economic and political paradigms to encourage a transformative spirit in India's polity. Over 400 of India's foremost academics, activists, professionals and policymakers across party lines have constructively engaged in this process. We have organized and assembled inputs from *jan sunwais* (public hearings) and *jan manchs* (public platforms) that we conducted across several states, and discussed and debated these ideas with leaders of fourteen progressive political parties, in an effort to set benchmarks for a future common minimum programme. The overarching idea has been to try to breathe new life and spirit into the cold and self-serving logic of political and administrative processes, linking them to and informing them by grassroots realities, fact-based research and social experience, and actionable social–scientific knowledge. And to do all of this with harmony and heart, with sincere emotion and national feeling.

In order to further disseminate these ideas, both to kick-start a national dialogue and to further build a consensus on them, we are bringing out this set of fourteen volumes highlighting innovative ideas that seek to deepen and further the promise of India. This is not an academic exercise; we do not merely spotlight structural problems, but also propose disruptive solutions to each of the pressing challenges that we collectively face. All the essays, though authored by top academics, technocrats, activists, intellectuals and so on, have been written purposively to be accessible to a general audience, whose creative imagination we aim to spark and whose critical feedback we intend to harness, leveraging it to further our common goals.

The inaugural volume has been specifically dedicated to our norms, to serve as a fresh reminder of our shared and shareable overlapping values and principles, collective heritage and resources.

Titled *Vision for a Nation: Paths and Perspectives*, it champions a plural, inclusive, just, equitable and prosperous India, and is committed to individual dignity, which is the foundation of the unity and vibrancy of the nation.

The thirteen volumes that follow turn from the normative to the concrete. From addressing the problems faced by diverse communities—Adivasis, Dalit Bahujans, Other Backward Classes (OBCs)—as well as women and minorities, to articulating the challenges that we face with respect to jobs and unemployment, urbanization, healthcare and a rigged economy, to scrutinizing our higher education system or institutions more broadly, each volume details some ten specific policy solutions promising to systemically treat the issue(s), transforming the problem at a lasting structural level, not just a superficial one. These innovative and disruptive policy solutions flow from the authors' research, knowledge and experience, but they are especially characterized by their unflinching commitment to our collective normative understanding of who we can and ought to be.

The volumes that look at the concerns, needs and aspirations of the Shudras, Dalits, Adivasis and women particularly look at how casteism has played havoc with India's development and stalled the possibility of the progressive transformation of Indian society. They first analyse how these sections of society have faced historical and structural discrimination against full participation in Indian spiritual, educational, social and political institutions for centuries. They also explore how the reforms that some of our epoch-making socio-political thinkers like Gautama Buddha, M.K. Gandhi, Jawaharlal Nehru and Dr B.R. Ambedkar foregrounded are being systematically reversed by regressive forces and the ruling elite because of their ideological proclivities. These volumes therefore strive to address some of the most glaring social questions that India faces from a modernist perspective and propose a progressive blueprint that will secure spiritual, civil and political liberties for one and all.

What the individual volumes aim to offer, then, are navigable road maps for how we may begin to overcome the many specific challenges that we face, guiding us towards new ways of working cooperatively to rise above our differences, heal the wounds in our communities, recalibrate our modes of governance and revitalize our institutions. Cumulatively, however, they achieve something of even greater synergy, greater import: they reconstruct that India of our imagination, of our aspirations, the India reflected in the constitutional preamble that we all surely want to be a part of.

Let us put aside that depiction of a mirror with an enemy staring back at us. Instead, together, we help to construct a whole new set of images. One where you may look at your nation and see your individual identity and dignity reflected in it, and when you look within your individual self, you may find the pride of your nation residing there.

Aakash Singh Rathore, Mridula Mukherjee,
Pushparaj Deshpande and *Syeda Hameed*

Introduction

Uniting the Nation: Re-engineering India's Hardware and Software

Pushparaj Deshpande

Human conduct is characterized as good or bad, depending on whether it contributes towards building a better world—for ourselves and for each other. But are we really working towards a utopia? Or is all we do ultimately motivated by narrow self-interest? Answering that question unknowingly, anthropologist Margaret Mead was once asked what she considered to be the first sign of civilization.[1] Instead of mentioning hunting tools, grinding stones, clay pots or religious artefacts, Mead surmised that the first evidence of civilization was a human thigh bone with a healed fracture from 15,000 years ago. She went on to explain that without modern medicine, a fractured femur would take about six weeks of complete rest to heal. That would have meant a complete inability to perform any of the basic tasks required to survive in a hostile environment, whether it was hunting, foraging or fighting. The healed femur attested that the injured human was not abandoned and left to die. Instead, someone took the time to ferry the fallen to safety, nurse the wound and tend them through recovery. 'Helping someone else through difficulty is where civilization starts,' asserted Mead.

That impulse, to altruistically further another's well-being (extending to associates and strangers beyond immediate blood relatives) or the greater good over narrow self-interest, is the foundation of human civilization. Even though what the greater good means has evolved to dizzying complexities over the years, the raison d'être of all societies continues to remain the same—to survive and thrive *together*. That is why, in differentiating between the State and a government,[2] Aristotle argued that the State is a union of families and villages, having for its end a *happy, self-sufficing and honourable life* (emphasis added). Much later, Mahatma Gandhi would argue similarly when he defined *praja* as a political community whose basic unit is the individual who is considered to be a bearer of fundamental rights and capable of *swaraj*[3]. What is important is that both Aristotle and Gandhi do not define the State in the narrow, modern sense of an agency possessing a monopoly over the legitimized use of coercive force (the Weberian State[4]). Rather, the State (which Aristotle calls '*polis*' and Gandhi calls '*praja*') is defined by Aristotle as 'an association of citizens in a constitution[5]'.

In this conception, the 'State' means the *body of the people*, and its end is not merely to survive, but to enable each individual to live a happy and good life. In this normative framework, the government contracted to govern on behalf of the State is not an end in itself but merely a means to an end. That end is ensuring fullness of life for each individual, since each individual's worth was intrinsic (and not contingent on a relationship to another). Given this, every citizen has claims upon the government. Additionally, a government must not only observe individual rights and freedoms on the one hand but also actualize those conditions through which citizens can fulfil their aspirations. Unless the government guarantees and delivers on both these, individuals will not be able to act in their own rights (*sui iuris* or of one's own laws). Rather, they would be subject to the arbitrary power of other individuals as well as social, economic or political majorities.

Deeply influenced by the experiences of the freedom struggle, India's founders consciously imagined a nation that strived to strike a balance between these two normative conceptions of the State— as a body of people (citizenry) and as a Weberian State. Unlike most nations,[6] they created India as a complex partnership—of the State and the people. The two were conjoined in constructing the 'noble mansion of free India'[7] and wiping 'every tear from every eye'[8]. In making a radical departure from the procedural understanding of democracy, citizens were urged to look beyond their immediate needs and aspirations, and be mindfully concerned about the suffering of those less fortunate than them.

Consciously borrowing from Mahatma Gandhi, Prime Minister Nehru in his famous 'Tryst with Destiny' speech therefore drew 'a sentiment map that link(ed) proper patriotism to extended compassion'[9] towards all peoples, while Dr B.R. Ambedkar argued that 'democracy . . . is primarily a mode of associated living'[10], which can only be sustained by fraternity or 'what Buddha called *maitree*'[11]. Similarly, *Jana Gana Mana*, India's national anthem, portrays and emphasizes the 'we' as consisting of people from every religion and region. In this radical conception, India's founders were extolling the citizenry to be equally invested in furthering national goals. More importantly, they were also ensuring equality between the citizenry and the State. This was an entirely novel imagining on how a nation and government should be. This positioning also enabled the crafting of a patriotism that was not adversarial (against another nation or militarist). Instead, this patriotism united in advancing progressive national ideals and objectives.

In outlining national goals for the citizenry and the State, India's founders accordingly crafted a progressive charter designed to actualize enabling conditions for citizens to *be*, and *do* well. That charter, that we today know as the constitutional idea of India, guaranteed *socio-economic equality for all* (the right to equality, the right to free speech and the right against exploitation), *religious tolerance and secularism* (the right to freedom of religion) and equally important, *the right to live with human dignity*[12]. The underlying principles of this charter were that each person was accorded equal opportunity to live with dignity and security, had equitable access to a better life and was an equal partner in the nation's growth.[13] It was believed that these conditions would liberate society from the 'graded inequalities of the past'[14].

The product of our founders' collective dreams of and for the nation, India's constitutional charter became *the* political project of the State. Pragmatically recognizing that the greater burden of actualizing this national project would fall on the government, a strong Weberian State was carried forward from pre-colonial India, in which both juridicial and legislative authority was located. The governing structures of the State not only centralized power vertically but were empowered to be maximalist in the application of the rules designed to further the promised social revolution. This was to nudge the polity towards the desired constitutional future by actualizing the State's welfare agenda, socializing citizens to progressive values and keeping pre-existing regressive impulses within society in check.

This was done for three reasons—first, India's founders were very seized of the fierce competition over resources, opportunities and privileges between overlapping religious, caste, gender, linguistic, regional and ideological identities. To avoid the failures of other countries in managing diversity (an imperative that became even more urgent after the horrors of Partition), they accorded primacy to the State and politics. It was felt that only a strong institutional framework could neutrally arbitrate between contending interests, preserve the integrity of the social fabric (without allowing a single interest to steamroll others) and thereby integrate India's constituent units into a common fabric.[15]

Second, all societies struggle with group subordination, wherein a majority (whether religious, caste, class or gender) dominates opportunities and resources, and thereby excludes others, which leads to their marginalization. India's founders were therefore very concerned about cultivating fraternal emotions so that majorities would not just tolerate but also embrace minorities. They were also worried that the State would have to actively inhibit those who weren't particularly motivated by this inclusive imperative. As Dr B.R. Ambedkar famously said, 'Constitutional morality is not a natural sentiment. It has to be cultivated. We must realize that our people have yet to learn it. Democracy in India is only a top-dressing on an Indian soil which is essentially undemocratic'.[16] Given these imperatives, it was felt that a powerful State would maintain a balance between supporting the vulnerable, without compromising on the capacity of the well-endowed for activity.

Third, after a lifetime of colonial exploitation (nearly $44.6 trillion was siphoned away from India between 1765 and 1938[17]), there was an intense suspicion of the foreign private sector. Motivated by the consequent urge to build up self-sufficiency and resilience, an empowered State was created to effectively further India's constitutional promise, while subtly asserting the nation's sovereignty.

However, there is an unresolved paradox that the establishment of a strong Weberian State created—that of an individual as both sovereign (and hence a holder of inalienable rights/freedoms) and the subject of a sovereign State. Since India became independent in 1947, many governments have evolved customs and norms that try to balance these two conflicting ideas. Barring a few historical lapses, they have cultivated space for dissent and negotiating ideological differences. However, the truth remains that this negotiation (and space) is entirely dependent on institutional memories/ informal conventions and not institutionalized mechanisms. This could become especially problematic when the party in power is unwilling to adhere to those informal conventions and is instead more assertive of government sovereignty. When this is taken to its logical conclusion. any act or thought that contradicts the government (or more specifically, the political party in power) could perforce be deemed to be criminal. This could lead to a radical re-conceptualization of the individual and the government, and their relationship with each other.

How the Indian State was envisaged

In their efforts to forge a nation that was free, fair and equal, India's founders were convinced that the State would have to establish itself as the supreme custodian of order and justice; to be autonomous and have institutionalized authority to shape the polity. Only then could it further the nation's constitutional promise, be the protector of the weak and vulnerable, and weave a symphony from the numerous voices of India. Only then could it be an instrument of progressive change, political stability and economic development.

To do this, the State was designed to actively engage with society and yet be above it. It would perforce need to be responsive to the needs and aspirations of society, and yet be autonomous and impartial in policy-formulation. That is why, despite brute electoral majorities, the first few governments of independent India invested considerable time and effort in manufacturing a bipartisan consensus on the fundamental role of the State. It is a testament to their determination that the State has served as a neutral arbitrator between diverse interests by dispassionately negotiating with and managing a plethora of interests.

It was also decided that the arena of interaction between these diverse interest groups should be as layered as possible. That is why, as a federal polity, India has multiple centres of mediation—at the Union, state, district and municipal/panchayat levels. This nationwide infrastructure for mediation was methodically leveraged both for managing competition and building coalitions between groups and parties.

Clash of political projects

Yet, today, the legitimacy and stability of the Indian State is under question. To understand the quagmire the State is in today, it is important to contextualize the historical circumstances in which it operated post Independence. It is well established that the shared dreams of India's founders, which emanated from their experiences during the freedom struggle, were embedded into India's Constitution. These dreams, which have been loosely characterized as an egalitarian stream of thought,[18] have been wrongly argued to mark a rupture from the past. They actually pre-existed in India, under Emperor Ashoka for example, as also the Bengal Renaissance. In that sense, India's founders partly articulated India's civilizational values in a modern language and context, and partly borrowed from the best that the West had to offer. To implement these radical innovations, the architects of modern India reduced their dependence on the Congress Movement[19] and vested their faith exclusively in the State. With no political contenders, and armed with social and political capital because of their body of work in the freedom struggle, they felt secure in moulding the State into a powerful tool to give shape to the political project of creating a free, fair and equal society. A lot of effort was consequently devoted in building up the State so it could serve as the ultimate custodian and executor of this national political project.

While there were legitimate reasons for them doing so, India's founders grossly underestimated the agency, ability and wilfulness of orthodox forces in furthering their ideological interests. This orthodoxy never accepted the legitimacy of the political project that India was embarking on post Independence. It was vehemently opposed to the idea of forging an India on constitutional principles.[20] This orthodoxy's argument centred on the belief that India's cultural, epistemic and civilizational future lay in the social order of the past. While Mahatma Gandhi did partly fall in this tradition, he actively engaged with the egalitarian school of thought and frequently evolved his positions, becoming more and more egalitarian over time.

Yet, there were those who belonged to this orthodoxy (most notably the Rashtriya Swayamsevak Sangh [RSS] and the various outfits of the Sangh Parivar[21]) that refused to brook any kind of engagement or ideological integration with the egalitarian tradition. They began to covertly resist and oppose the national political project,[22] thus setting the stage for a conflict between diametrically opposed political projects. This clash has been understudied, and traditional analyses of the State have tended to look at the shadows, rather than the flames. It is this clash that would lead to irreconcilable contestations on *what was, what is*, and most of all, *what should be*. These have played out over the past seventy years and very substantially explain the crisis of the Indian State today.

Because the State was controlled largely by the Indian National Congress (INC) for the first few decades after Independence, and because the Sangh had been banned briefly in 1948, the latter remained on the political and institutional margins for a long time. It was therefore compelled to spearhead a multifold guerrilla campaign. Firstly, it fashioned an alternative political project to rival the one the State was championing. In providing the ideological framework for this political project, M.S. Golwalkar, the Sangh's key ideologue, began by first critiquing the normative basis of the State and its political project. In repudiating the conceptual basis of the Indian State, he argued that '. . . [we] have almost completely lost sight of our true Hindu Nationhood, in our wild goose chase after the phantasm of founding a "really" democratic "State" in the country'. Instead, he went on to posit that 'we [the RSS and the Sangh] stand for national regeneration and not for that haphazard bundle of political rights—the state'[23] nor for the civic nationalism enshrined in India's Constitution.[24]

In providing an alternative, Golwalkar argued that the nation *preceded* the democratic State (since the nation was a 'cultural unit', while the 'State was a political unit'). In his view, this nation consisted of people who lived in India with 'uniformity of outlook, a common range of ideas, a common way of thinking and common preferences',[25] as well as a 'distinctive characteristic culture . . . (including) a common cultural language and a common cultural literature which regulate and govern their life even in minute details'.[26] Given this, the State was wrong in trying to synthesize a nation out of diverse cultures with 'different racial, religious and cultural differences'[27] since '. . . we began to class ourselves with our old invaders and foes under the outlandish name—Indian . . . [and] have allowed ourselves to be duped into believing our foes to be our friends and with our own hands are undermining true Nationality'.[28] V.D. Savarkar, another key ideologue of the Sangh Parivar, had similarly argued that 'we are a *jati*, a race bound together by the dearest ties of blood'.[29]

Accordingly, citing the example of Nazi Germany (which reportedly 'has also shown how well-nigh impossible it is for races and cultures, having differences going to the root, to be assimilated into one united whole, a good lesson for us in Hindusthan to learn and profit by'[30]), Golwalkar went on to argue that the nation has to be purified and preserved by cleansing it of impurities. Towards this end, he proposed 'a para-militarist tendency towards national discipline . . . [that] will ensure that the nationals of that nation behave properly as nationals, or else they can be disciplined or punished'.[31] To him, it was imperative to repudiate the project of national integration that the State had embarked on, since it integrated various cultures and religions into one composite whole and inspired a patriotism that celebrated that belief. Inspired by Golwalkar, the Sangh took upon itself the role of preserving the nation by waging war against the values that the Indian State stood for, since they could potentially destroy the 'true nation'.[32]

In an effort to stymie the State's political project, the Sangh again took inspiration from Golwalkar's *We or Our Nationhood Defined*, which asserts that 'the democratic State shall be under the sovereignty of the nationality to which majority of the people in the State belongs'.[33] Accordingly, State institutions were either infiltrated by those who were ideologically aligned to the Sangh,[34] or pre-existing agents within the State were gradually co-opted.[35] These have since been a vital source of information for the RSS and useful agents in circumscribing the State's welfare programmes. While it could be a case of correlation not always being causation, it is noteworthy that the higher the percentage of rural-based Scheduled Castes (Dalits) in a district population, the lower the level of public services.[36] These regressive elements within the State have actively worked to exclude Scheduled Castes (Dalits), Scheduled Tribes (Adivasis), women, minorities (especially Muslim) and LGBTQ+ communities from employment (both public[37] and private[38]), land holdings, access to essential public services such as healthcare, sanitation, etc. It has been well documented[39] that equality of opportunity and status was, and is, a norm followed more in the breach.

Most importantly, the Sangh built up a vast network of non-State social, cultural and religious institutions that worked to further its political project at the grassroots. As the current *Sarsanghchalak* (RSS supremo) said, 'The Sangh's primary task is to effect a transformation in each individual. Any individual thus socialized will then work in creating a likeminded environment, and thereby alter the fundamental nature of society'.[40] It found fertile ground for its work because constitutional principles were not deeply embedded in the collective consciousness of India. This is because India has always been more organized around its culture rather than its politics. As it has been argued, 'In India, there exists a *law of the land*, which the Constituent Assembly and later various governments spearheaded and implemented [with varying degrees of success] . . . Covertly resisting and opposing this supra framework are various dominant communities and organizations . . . who religiously adhere to the *laws in the land*, which are sometimes diagrammatically opposed to the norms enshrined in the Constitution of India'.[41]

It is a matter of record that in submitting the draft of the Constitution to the Constituent Assembly, Dr B.R. Ambedkar had presciently warned that 'rights are protected not by law but by social and moral conscience of the society. If social conscience is such that it is prepared to recognize the rights which law proposes to enact, rights will be safe and secure. But if the fundamental rights are opposed by the community, no Law, no Parliament, no Judiciary can guarantee them in the real sense of the word.'[42] His bitter experiences with discrimination had taught Dr Ambedkar that deliberately inhumane conduct towards others is never by accident but always the result of deep-rooted prejudice and hatred. He was therefore very aware of the urgency in both understanding why societies behave badly, and crafting solutions to transform them into more compassionate and mindful ones.

That is why Mahatma Gandhi and Prime Minister Nehru assiduously reshaped patriotic emotion from an abstract love for the nation as a territorial entity to the body of people (which comprised diverse cultures and peoples). In doing this, *Bharat Mata* (Mother India) was portrayed as constituting the people[43] who had suffered adversities together in the past, and who had to now work together to create a better future. Leveraging cultural values and symbols, citizens were continuously exhorted to transcend narrow self-interests and join in forging a just and compassionate society. Nationalism was thus transformed into *maanavnishtha Bharatiyata* (humane Indian nationalism).[44]

Despite this forewarning, after Gandhi and Nehru, the architects of modern India did not sufficiently invest in shaping the hearts and minds of the people, in what has been theorized as the 'political cultivation of emotions'.[45] Doing this would have meant influencing social consciousness through soaring political rhetoric, social and political symbols, popular culture (films, songs, art, literature and folklore) and public education. It would have also meant inspiring social morality by giving meaning to development and welfare projects (what Rousseau famously called inventing a 'civil religion'[46]). Every nation needs to invest in this, simply because societal compassion and concern for the other tends to diminish with the passage of time. These emotions need to be reinvigorated periodically (and for every generation), so that citizens pledge themselves to something larger than their individual selves. Furthermore, without this encompassing and compassionate ethic, institutions and laws cannot sustain themselves.

While the Constitution did undoubtedly create a theoretical edifice of a liberal, just and free society, the onus of embedding these values in society was on the State. The State did not mould constitutional principles in the common man's tongue, so it could inspire, enthuse and drive. The State also did not create institutions to uphold and further constitutional values, relying instead on a pre-colonial architecture of the State, which was designed to be extractive and coercive. Instead, governments relied exclusively on a doctrinaire of modernism and charismatic/enlightened leaders to further progressive values. Unfortunately, many lacked the missionary zeal, political maturity and power to do so. This continues to be the biggest challenge of politics in India even today.

This historical oversight by the architects of modern India meant that they failed in creating systems (exemplified by strong, independent institutions) to socialize Indians to constitutional values and create a constitutional patriotism. Consequently, the State's ability to gauge what the broad masses of the unpolitical population thought and felt was severely diminished. This gave the Sangh space to cultivate public emotions that questioned the moral authority of the State, delegitimize its political project and vilify certain communities. To put it simply, while the State focused on transforming society through structural policy interventions, the Sangh focused on transforming the individual through structural socio-cultural interventions. It is because of their tireless efforts that large sections of India have been socialized to conservative norms and believe that the State's political project is a diabolical instrument of subversion (of 'Indian' society). It is no coincidence that India's youth is today deeply conservative (socially), very religious and driven by caste norms, as a 2017 Centre for the Study of Developing Societies (CSDS) and Konrad Adenauer Stiftung (KAS) study[47] highlighted.

This was reiterated by a 2021 report by the Pew Research Center,[48] which damningly highlighted that an overwhelming majority of Indians prefer to live near, marry and engage with their own castes or creeds. Worryingly, 65 per cent of Hindus believe a true Indian has to be a Hindu, while 50 per cent believe that a true Indian has to be both Hindu and a Hindi speaker. Left unchecked, this will ultimately undercut India's hyphenated civic identity[49] (Indians ascribe to multiple regional, linguistic, religious and caste identities, while also being proudly Indian[50]).

Flash point: How the State was delegitimized

Even though India's Constitution was (and remains) progressive, in striving to secularize society, the State steamrolled and flattened 'diverse visions of a desirable society . . . into a single monolithic vision'.[51] This invariably caused 'serious economic, social and cultural disruption in the lives of . . . the social fabric of the communities'.[52] The State did not adequately invest time in understanding the social, cultural and psychological effects of these changes and consequently did not address them. This was primarily a *political* failure and political parties must shoulder the blame for their inability to negotiate with sectional interests.[53] This failure of executing the State's *raj-dharma* led to a number of India's constituent units becoming either dissatisfied with, or insufficiently invested in the State and its political project.

This was exacerbated by the collapse of the Congress System,[54] the second democratic upsurge and the tumultuous decade of the 1990s (which saw socio-economic upheavals, the sharpening of communal and caste divisions as well as the first government led by the Bharatiya Janata Party [BJP], the political wing of the RSS). Firstly, upon finding that the State was unable to satisfy their interests, a number of interest groups (Other Backward Classes, upper castes, dominant sections of the Dalit communities, socialist forces, religious groups, etc.) formed new political parties. Amplifying sectional interests, these new parties replicated the Congress's State-centred politics to better represent community interests and to establish themselves in their respective spheres of influence. This created intense political competition and temporarily re-established negotiations between diverse interest groups (even if the State was increasingly engaging with, but not entirely above interest groups).

However, the 1991 economic liberalization dramatically altered the State's ability to perform its welfare functions. The locus of the State's focus shifted from directing production to regulating the economy as well as balancing the private and public sectors. At the same time, some other State-driven functions were outsourced or scaled back, while transnational conglomerates pressurized governments to reduce taxes and enhance corporate tax breaks (thus leading to an outward flow of revenues and reduced government revenues). These inter-linked processes significantly shrank the State's ability to effect radical socio-economic change. In doing so, the State moved further away from its constitutional *raj-dharma*.

This was exacerbated by the fact that there has not been sufficient investment in enhancing State capacity or institutionalizing robust systems for the implementation of government policies. Therefore, because the State didn't evolve sufficiently, its core institutions were unable to adequately respond to the dynamic economic, social, political or geopolitical challenges that every nation inevitably faces. The bitter reality was that by the late 1990s, the Indian State faced a deep-rooted rot, which some governments tried to address piecemeal by unsustainable political centralization and by the outsourcing of essential state functions to private players. This was compounded by a series of capitulations by progressive parties (either for political expediency or incremental gains), the judiciary and even the administration.

Vast sections of India adversely impacted by the State scaling back its welfare functions mobilized against the government of the day. Benefiting from this civic upsurge and deeply sensitive to one part of the problem, the Congress Party-led United Progressive Alliance (UPA) government spearheaded a two-fold strategy when it came to office in 2004. It tried to accelerate growth and development on the one hand and strived to ensure it was inclusive through the rights-based paradigm on the other. The latter was especially a reassertion of the nation's original political project and sought to give citizens a greater ownership of their rights and civil liberties through acts such as the Right to Information, the Mahatma Gandhi National Rural Employment Guarantee Act, the Right to Food, the Forests Rights Act, etc. The paradigm was a brave recognition of the fact that while the 1991 reforms had created prosperity, the benefits had not accrued to all equitably. It was thus a bold and imaginative State-sponsored programme to ensure justice—social, economic and political.

The net result of this successful strategy was that 271 million Indians came out of poverty[55] and aspired for more. Many found a better life in India's cities, which boasted of an entirely different set of norms and cultures. When these people returned to their villages and towns occasionally, they brought back the seeds of an aspirational revolution. This led to social mobility and a class transformation, which contributed to an aspirational bulge. This new class (the middle class) no longer saw the State as its *mai-baap* (be all and end all) and wanted the State to support them by providing for basic public infrastructure, but 'get out of the way'[56]. Their self-image was no longer that of being weak or vulnerable. They were increasingly confident of their ability to pull themselves up out of poverty and chagrined at their characterization as being in need of a helping hand. They expected the State to provide conducive systems and an environment that would empower them to do, and be, better.

Despite this, a large number of Indians remained poor and outside the economic mainstream. These co-existed alongside the aspirational new India, but remained on the margins. For example, sub-caste Dalits and sub-caste Other Backward Classes felt that both India's traditional social welfare paradigm as well as the new schemes of empowerment continued to exclude them from the promise of the nation. They (like many other Indians) were not just yearning to be equitably included but also empowered. Instead, they remained unheard and unseen because almost all political parties were winning elections 'on the strength of a social pact that links corporate and landed interests to a broadening middle class'[57]. It is this inadvertently excluded India that was eventually channelized against the system.

This fundamentally altered Indian politics, which the Congress Party (just as it was crystallizing into a traditional social democratic party like the European parties) did not sufficiently understand. In fact, the Congress fell into an intellectual coma that has been characterized[58] as the 'politics of inevitability'. It allowed itself to think that the terms of reference on which politics would be conducted was exclusively developmental and economic, and hence lowered its defences to the brewing cultural war underneath. This unleashed an unparalleled crisis which has had grave consequences for the Indian State.

Partly because of its historical legacy, the Congress remained focused on alleviating poverty and empowering the most vulnerable. However the rise of a large, ever-expanding middle class meant that the appeal of the poverty alleviation paradigm was significantly lessened. Additionally, this class's anxiety about its place in society (partly because of a fear of slipping back into a lower economic strata and partly because of its disconnect from its original roots) meant that it increasingly identified with the nation and nationalistic rituals. Numerous other factors buttressed this self-image. The forces of globalization, technological innovations, the arrival of corporate capital and later social media platforms changed how middle-class Indians saw themselves. Faced with accessible and affordable new technologies within their reach, and increasingly connected with the world, the middle class was aggressively aspirational and vehemently impatient with the old, 'backward' India. Hyper-individualistic, their privileges (caste, income, education, etc.) enabled them to move up, but they were impatient of the others not being able to take advantage of the opportunities that the 1991 reforms had opened up. Their sense of responsibility was no longer to society but to themselves and their families.

Yearning for *samman* (respect and dignity), *samruddhi* (progress and prosperity) and, most of all, *vikaas* (development)[59], this new class was progressively anxious of its place in society and increasingly began displaying a 'mixture of *rebellious* emotions and *reactionary* social ideas'.[60] They felt angry at being *left out* (because of seemingly inadequate prospects of socio-economic advancement) and even angrier at being *held back* (because of nepotism, corruption and supposedly unfair State patronage towards minorities and historically marginalized communities). There was a pervasive belief that most establishment political parties (that had been in governments until then), civil society organizations, the intelligentsia and sections of the media were colluding to exclude ordinary Indians from the fruits of development and delaying the restoration of Bharat (India) to its past glories. It was also believed that democracy's complex trials and processes were a conspiracy against the nation. The importance of this irrational mass psychosis in ordinary citizens should not be underestimated, since it paved the way for a frontal attack on the governing structures of the State.

It is this mass psychosis that the Sangh was well positioned to instrumentally exploit. It has been widely alleged that the India Against Corruption movement[61] was a politically organized expression that the Sangh engineered. This movement was coupled with a multi-pronged strategy that discharged an undemocratic upsurge against the political system and thereby delegitimized the entire democratic super-structure. As it has been argued:[62]

Firstly, establishment parties were attacked in the media and on social media platforms for their inability to transform their respective nations into utopias. Many public intellectuals joined in this chorus. Secondly, this cacophony was exacerbated by the mind-boggling claims of corruption by an anti-corruption crusader holding a high post within the state. This was soon followed by a complete policy paralysis with the RSS' political outfit arbitrarily disrupting legislatures and breaching customary parliamentary norms. All of this was magnified by the misuse of social media platforms, which mercilessly mocked the senior-most politicians of the establishment parties. And amidst this chaos emerged a knight in shining armour (the leader). Dismissive of democratic niceties and gradualist approaches, he was methodically positioned as a silver bullet to the nation's problems.

This 'knight' was projected as the fulfilment of the aspirations of all classes. This was possible because the narratives of the freedom struggle (that conjoined citizens immediately after Independence) no longer resonated with a generation that had no memory of that struggle. Therefore, the new narrative of suffering that the Sangh manufactured is that India has not progressed or prospered in the past sixty years, and that the mainstream political parties are primarily responsible for that backwardness. What the Sangh therefore did is capitalize on individual anxieties and weaponize them in their pursuit of State power.

The de-institutionalization of the State

What began as a cultural insurgency has now morphed into a full-fledged political one. Since it assumed office in June 2014, the BJP has initiated a 'gleichshaltung'[63]-like policy to seize control of all political, economic and social institutions in India.[64] As the twelve essays in this volume attest, almost every institution by which the State stood its ground since Independence has been ambushed or hijacked to further the Sangh's political project.[65]

The President of the Indian National Congress, Mallikarjun Kharge, in his essay titled 'The Cabinet: A Check on Authoritarianism' masterfully leverages historical evidence to assert that the cabinet system is ideal to govern a diverse nation like India, since it has in-built checks and balances. He painstakingly illustrates how the principle of collective responsibility moderates authoritarian and unconstitutional impulses. Leveraging his unique vantage point, he goes on to explain how the undermining of the cabinet system and the concomitant transformation of the Prime Minister's Office (PMO) as the de facto decision-making body has adversely impacted good governance and India's national interest.

In explaining the rationale and operational methodology of the National Advisory Council (NAC), the Chairperson of the Congress Legislative Party Sonia Gandhi's essay serves as a yardstick to gauge all advisory councils to the Prime Minister. The essay asserts that advisory councils are deliberately designed to be multi-stakeholder consultative bodies so as to make policymaking more responsive to the needs of citizens. However, the BJP government has eschewed the advice of experts and grassroots organizations, and instead spearheaded policies that benefit select crony capitalists at the expense of poor and middle-class Indians. The essay goes on to demonstrate how this has compromised civic rights and freedoms, as well as welfare schemes meant to empower the most vulnerable.

In 'Reimagining Parliament: Hopes and Perils', India's former Vice President Hamid Ansari alludes to numerous shortfalls in the Parliament's functioning as an instrument of control over the Executive. Consequently, he alludes to the fact that Parliament is being misused to rubber stamp the Executive's policies. The essay also poses some structural solutions to restore Parliament's functions and primacy.

Former Governor Margaret Alva's provocatively titled article 'The Partisan Role of Governors in New India' strongly contends that Governors are constitutional statesmen whose actions (and inactions) directly impact federal relations. In stark contrast, as her essay methodically illustrates, apart from appointing partisan individuals beholden to the prime minister (and not the Constitution), the Union government has empowered Governors to seize the powers of states, interfere in the functioning of elected state governments, engineer defections from Opposition parties and impose unconstitutional policies on to states.

In 'Reimagining, Reforming and Transforming India's Judiciary', Madan Lokur contends that the Supreme Court and the entire judiciary has been on a collision course with the political Executive. The essay goes on to assert that the Executive occasionally exerts control over the appointment of judges, their transfer and perhaps roster management through the Chief Justice. Additionally, there is a pervasive impression of a compromised judiciary because crucial cases (including constitutional cases) have been in abeyance by the Supreme Court and because of post-retirement benefits to judges. That is why he feels compelled to propose revolutionary procedural and systemic changes to India's justice delivery system.

Similarly, in his essay on the Election Commission of India (ECI), former election commissioner Ashok Lavasa contends that the foundations of a functional democracy rest on the ECI enabling free elections and asserting itself when anything impinges on the electoral process. However, the ECI's authority is diminished if political leaders persist in deteriorating political behaviour that violates the Model Code of Conduct (including communal and casteist statements, offering inducements for garnering votes, reporting to abusive language), with 'invisible' support for parties in the form of so-called opinion polls, doctored panel discussions on television channels, political propaganda in entertainment channels or films and electoral bonds (which enables secret transactions with tax relief, both for the donor and the beneficiary). What the essay subtly suggests is that the playing field is not just imbalanced but also stacked unfavourably in the ruling dispensation's favour.

Highlighting structural faultiness in the institutional architecture that manages India's federalism, Kerala's former finance minister Dr Thomas Isaac systematically shows how these gaps have been misused by the BJP government to undermine the powers of state governments. For example, he demonstrates how the Union government has fiscally constricted states by subverting tax devolution (resorting instead to surcharges/cess), delaying compensatory transfers of the Goods and Services Tax, withholding funds for central schemes, etc. These are being insidiously leveraged to undermine states governed by Opposition parties, which has an adverse impact on the people's welfare.

In 'Patronage and Professionalism in the Indian Bureaucracy', Dr N.C. Saxena argues that the Indian bureaucracy has been methodically captured both ideologically and politically, and deployed to further the ruling dispensation's ideological goals. Providing a plethora of examples, he shows how the breaching of this firewall between civil servants and the political class has led to undesirable outcomes—in policy design, programme implementation as well as in the neutrality of public institutions. Consequently, either talented officials are opting out of senior postings with the Union government or compelled to resign from the services well before their prime. As a career bureaucrat well versed with India's steel frame, Dr Saxena strongly argues that the rot that has been introduced in the last decade is crippling India's ability to compete with the most developed nations or provide for its citizens.

Similarly, India's first Chief Information Commissioner Wajahat Habibullah, in his magisterial essay analysing the performance of the Central and state information commissions since their inception, posits that they were meant to be formal mechanisms to further transparency and accountability in governance. However, the BJP government has circumscribed the Right to Information (RTI) Act by circumscribing it, gerrymandered the appointment process of information commissioners and declined disclosing information previously accessible under the RTI. The essay decries this iron wall of secrecy which had not just reduced citizens to subjects (rather than equal partners in the nation's development) but also covers up all malfeasance in government.

On the other hand, although political coalitions and civil society are not formal State institutions, both are critical to managing the government better and making it more accountable. Towards that end, the General Secretary of the Communist Party of India (Marxist) Sitaram Yechury's essay titled 'The Centrality of Coalitions to Statecraft' posits that political parties are platforms for conversations and negotiations between India's constituent units. Given this, he decries the RSS-BJP's efforts to force India's diversities into a unitarian religious, cultural and political straitjacket that he argues harms the national interest. In making this assertion, Yechury contends that coalitions between political parties ensure governance is more democratic and people-centric. In doing so, the essay proffers an agenda for the functioning of successful coalitions.

Finally, even though civil society is outside the formal ambit of the State, it is undoubtedly the State's conscience-keeper. In that spirit, Prof. Ingrid Srinath's 'An Agenda for Policy Reform for Civil Society in India' is an important addition to the volume. She argues that civil society is the social basic of a mature democracy since it allows citizens to hold up a mirror to the government, oversee service delivery of government schemes, amplify the under-represented and vulnerable and objectively scrutinize legislation and policies. However, in the last decade, the State has methodically circumscribed civil society by limiting access to funding, cancelling licenses arbitrarily and clamping down on any dissenting voices. Collectively, these suppress India's vast silent majority and represent an existential threat to democracy itself.

These are not the only institutions that are central to governing India. However, they are among the most crucial. All of them rest on a broader political culture, and the capture and misuse of one institution leads to a domino effect. In the last decade, these institutions (along with many others) have been deployed to coerce the India's constituent units into accepting one ideology, one people and one leader. It is a matter of record that Nazism had also actively implemented the theory of 'Ein Volk, ein Reich, ein Führer'[66]

(One People, One Nation and One Leader). This twofold process that the BJP has initiated is to systematize a 'controlling statism that disciplines the members of the organic nation to act as, for and in the organic nation'.[67] Consequently, in place of a State, India has a vigilante paramilitarist organization masquerading as the State.

In the pursuit of reshaping India into a mono-faith, mono-lingual and mono-cultural nation, the nation (as imagined by Golwalkar and Savarkar) has been systematically prioritized over the State and the people. Because the nation is positioned as supreme, it has been subtly proselytized that citizens have duties exclusively towards it and not to constitutional values, the institutions of the State or even all of India's constituent groups. Since everyone in the nation is not yet invested in this notion, the paramilitarist custodians of the 'true nation' have been given free rein to discipline errant citizens and thereby restore India to an imagined time of cultural and racial purity.

Consequently, instead of negotiating with India's constituent units, the State apparatus has been appropriated to accelerate the war[68] against all those Golwalkar classified as enemies. This has meant a dramatic reconceptualization of the citizens' relationship with the State in India. First, the modern State has a monopoly on legitimate violence, taxation and delivery of essential services. The BJP government is partially outsourcing the first and third functions of the State to its ideological parent. Second, given India's founders envisioned India as a social democracy, they saw the government's primary duty as guaranteeing and delivering those conditions that would actualize fullness of life for *every* citizen regardless of their caste, gender, religion or class. This included guaranteeing social rights (access to the basic conditions of life such as health, primary education, food, shelter and work) as well as political, civil and cultural rights (freedoms of speech, expression, association and religion). However, today, India has strayed from this consensus (and both anecdotal and empirical evidence[69] suggest we already have). Rather than viewing *all* citizens as holders of inalienable rights, the State is increasingly excluding citizens on the basis of their religion and ideological inclination (following Golwalkar's exhortation to 'purge' all impurities from the body of the nation). This has been exacerbated by the State's withdrawal from its responsibility to provide life-equalizing opportunities (such as universal education, healthcare and dignified jobs) and unilateral decision to mortgage the instruments of service delivery through the National Monetization Pipeline.[70]

This extraordinary situation has had two grave consequences. On the one hand, this breakdown of negotiation between various interests has created strong centrifugal forces in some places. Citizens and state governments are faced with the bitter reality that their constitutionally guaranteed political, civil and cultural rights and freedoms are being methodically undermined, both by State and non-State actors. While the State has leveraged draconian laws[71] to suppress freedom of expression of speech, and cracked down on students, farmers, activists, public sector employees, journalists, etc.,[72] non-State actors have imposed rigid norms with regard to food, clothing, language, mobility, religion and free speech on Dalits, Bahujans, Adivasis, women, as well as ideological and religious minorities.[73] In successfully spreading fear and cultivating anger, these non-State actors are drowning out the best in us and amplifying the worst in us.

On the other hand, because the State has either actively spearheaded, ignored or weakly responded to these attacks, many of India's constituent units have erupted in protests over the past few years. Citizens no longer feel as if they belong to the same nation and bound by a 'consciousness of kind' as Dr Ambedkar put it. There is a pervasive belief that the State has been partisan in the application of the rule of law,[74] which increasingly seems to be contingent on conformity to the ruling party's ideology. This impression is exacerbated by the fact that the State has either delayed arresting perpetrators, or arrested journalists[75] who have reported on uncomfortable facts and because legislators affiliated to the ruling party have intervened positively on behalf of perpetrators.[76] In some cases, the State has also allied with non-State actors in intimidating and attacking minorities.[77] Consequently, an ever-widening catchment of the disenchanted are opting to migrate out of the nation (as the Global Wealth Migration Report of 2020 has pointed out[78]).

This escalating spiral of State-sponsored terrorism and concomitant abdication of civic/welfare functions not only destabilizes the social fabric of the nation, but also delegitimizes the sovereignty of the State, which no longer enjoys a monopoly on force. It also negates the State's painfully learned practice of creatively absorbing dissent within the mainstream so as to create a new consensus without disrupting the status quo. This has created a pervasive distrust of many State institutions. Far from being seen as the ultimate moral authority, today the State is viewed as just another contending stakeholder, untethered from both constitutional and institutional values.

In fact, in reimagining the State's primary duty to serve as a neutral upholder of law and order, the BJP government has quietly buried the notion that the State will further a constitutional consciousness. Unlike previous governments, the BJP has delinked development (*vikaas*) and modernism, and promised the former as a technocratic service without making any claims on citizens to abide by constitutional norms (and hence become modern). Consequently, citizens can be casteist, communal, patriarchal or xenophobic, but the State would no longer make any demands on citizens to shed these atavistic tendencies nor would it penalize them were they to flout constitutional values. No longer is the State making any demands from people—to be tolerant of differences; to be just; to suppress regressive and violent tendencies. These ideological expectations have been vilified as elitist, outdated and alien to India. Purportedly promoting the notion of being comfortable with our cultural selves, society is constantly being partitioned on community lines by the Sangh Parivar's myriad institutions who have repeatedly propagated the flawed notion that religious communities have divergent political, economic, social and cultural interests (and that these will inevitably lead to clashes).

This has unleashed chaos at an unprecedented level, which constantly reminds people of their human vulnerabilities and powerlessness. This has created a Hegelian dialectic in that it has generated mass hysteria and fear amongst the silent majority, which is not just accepting of solutions that limit their rights but actually finds them desirable. Mirroring Aldous Huxley's *Brave New World*, this national nihilism is characterized by citizens being tricked into embracing their own enslavement on the one hand. On the other hand, this situation is being methodically leveraged by the Sangh to deepen ties with the people and thus gain legitimacy and power. In fact, it is possible that in ceding ground to non-State actors (who prioritize the social order over constitutional values), the ground is laid for dissidents to be vilified as subversive enemies of society (and not just the State).[79] This naturally paves the way for scrutinizing and circumscribing individual freedoms (that are seen as natural threats to the social order).

This use of violence as the first and last resort to deal with India's constituent units belies logic. After all, even the colonial government believed that the use of violence against peaceful protestors would delegitimize its rule. Why then does this government, which uses suppression so freely, not seem to be too concerned about the loss of legitimacy? Why also has it ramrodded controversial decisions incompatible with constitutional principles[80] without batting an eyelid? One reason for this is that the ruling dispensation no longer looks beyond its own narrowly defined core constituencies for electoral or political support. Equally, the ruling dispensation feels very secure in its ability to manufacture consent and hence its electoral future. It is therefore not especially worried about imposing controversial decisions that could adversely impact citizens and the nation. This distinguishes it from other governments, which always keep one eye on the electoral consequences of any decision they take, whilst also considering what would best serve the national interest. A government that doesn't feel the need to customize its policies to the sensitivities of interest groups or be discursively accountable to them is no longer responsive to the needs of either of those groups, as well as society at large.

That is why, weakening transparency and accountability in governance, the Right to Information Act has been undermined[81] and the Chief Information Commission (CIC) has been circumscribed.[82] Similarly, the number of audit reports by the Comptroller and Auditor General of India (CAG) have plummeted by 75 per cent[83] and investigative agencies are being misused to conduct motivated witch-hunts.[84] Moreover, rather than selecting subject matter experts as lateral entrants into the bureaucracy, reportedly individuals whose ideological proclivities are aligned to the Sangh are being selected, as Dr N.C. Saxena's essay in this volume suggests. Additionally, it has been pointed out[85] that the current ruling dispensation has abandoned established protocols and is bringing back/promoting officials as secretaries on the basis of their ideological loyalties, even though they were originally rejected for 'empanelment'. Consequently, officials have flouted the Civil Service (Conduct) Rules, 1968, and openly spouted xenophobic, racist and communal views just to pander to the ruling dispensation.[86]

That is why, in ignoring the sensitivities of interest groups, responsibilities that were traditionally disbursed and delegated in multiple centres of mediation have been centralized to an extreme degree in the Prime Minister's Office (PMO).[87] The Prime Minister no longer functions as the first amongst equals. In fact, cast in the mould of a potentate, it is the Prime Minister (and not the State) who is portrayed as the ultimate source of moral and legal authority. It is the Prime Minister who directly engages with (even though he is above) society. He does this while assiduously refusing to engage in or resolve an ever-escalating cycle of hatred, violence and social tension. Yet while power is absolute and unshared, accountability is dispersed and shared. The powers of other institutions of the State relative to the PMO are greatly diminished. This de-institutionalization has created 'a sole, tutelary, and all-powerful form of government, but elected by the people',[88] in which citizens have been 'reduced to nothing better than a flock of timid and industrious animals, of which the government is the shepherd'.[89] It is no coincidence that V-Dem classifies India as an 'electoral autocracy'[90] while Freedom House downgraded India from a free democracy to a 'partially free democracy',[91] and the Economist Intelligence Unit called India a 'flawed democracy' in its Democracy Index.[92]

This political centralization of power has also led to three major structural shifts in India's politics and political economy. Firstly, it has long been recognized through trial and error that the normative requirements of the nation–state have to overlap with the pragmatic aspirations of the political class. However, by centralizing powers in the PMO, by depending on bureaucrats (and bureaucrat-ministers) and by promoting stakeholders for their loyalty to the party leadership rather than ideological clarity or proven capabilities, the BJP government is ironically delegitimizing the political party as a concept. By monopolizing political initiative, the BJP stifles entrepreneurship and innovation. No longer does India boast of creative geniuses such as Homi Bhabha, Durgabai Deshmukh (who led the Central Social Welfare Board), S.K. Dey (who spearheaded community development projects) who are empowered to experiment with disruptive ideas and build institutions. That freedom to experiment had made Indian talent very attractive to other nations. As it has been argued, 'Indians were counselling and advising countries on building everything, from multipurpose dams to democratic institutions'.[93] Sadly today, excessive centralization, micromanagement and prioritizing personal loyalty over competence has resulted in the triumph of mediocrity in governance.

The BJP has compounded this by a concerted attack on other political parties (exemplified by the vilification of career politicians, engineered defections,[94] sabotaging of elected governments[95] and circumscribing legislators by undermining the MPLADs[96] and Parliament[97]). This has fostered structural implosions within political parties as well as a pervasive distrust of political organizations. This has unfortunately been exacerbated by political parties themselves, who have myopically pushed out stakeholders with divergent views and ambitions on one hand and not undertaken disruptive programmatic or normative innovations on the other. Given that the BJP has been instrumentally increasing its catchment area by accommodating diverse stakeholders (many of whom are ideologically discordant), India's political parties today face an existential crisis. In manufacturing this, the BJP is clearly refashioning itself as *the* umbrella party. Only time will tell whether the BJP seeks to remould itself like the Congress System of yore or strives to herald a China-like one-party State. Given the BJP has blurred separation between the party and government and increased the powers of the party, the possibility of it striving to actualize a one-party State is a very real possibility. This is dangerous for a diverse and federal polity like India. After all, political parties are indispensable given they act as pressure groups for diverse sections of society, including the most marginal groups. In fact, the proliferation of political parties in India is proof of the deepening of democracy in India. This will inevitably be diminished in the face of a monolithic party headed by a centralized leadership.

Second, India is also witnessing unprecedented levels of corporate-controlled capitalism,[98] wherein large conglomerates strongly influence policymaking. Preferring to negotiate with one unitary actor at the Centre (rather than multiple state governments), a few conglomerates have created oligopolies and cornered national public assets such as airports, highways, railways, mines, etc. It is no coincidence that nearly 70 per cent of all corporate profits in 2019 accrued to the top twenty firms (as compared to less than 50 per cent in 2011).[99] It is also no coincidence that in September 2019, the BJP government reduced the corporate tax rate from 34.61 per cent to 25.17 per cent. This tax cut means a revenue loss of Rs 1.45 lakh crore to the public exchequer. However, 99.3 per cent of India's companies have a turnover of less than Rs 400 crore per annum; in effect, the tax cut benefits only 0.7 per cent of large corporate companies.

This economic centralization and State-capital Gordian knot has had major socio-political implications. Unlike laissez-faire capitalism[100] (where the State minimally intervenes in markets and companies negotiate with the government in a 'decentralized' fashion, responding to incentives of market competitiveness), in the corporate-controlled capitalism that India is witnessing today, the State doesn't really feel the need to respond to firms apart from the largest conglomerates. This is also because conglomerates with 'national' preferences offer the financial support for political centralization as a quid pro quo for various concessions/commissions (it is telling that the BJP cornered 76 per cent of total electoral bonds[101] in 2019–20,[102] and received more than 78 per cent of its funding from unknown sources,[103] or 3.5 times higher than funding for all other national parties combined).

Why is this problematic? After all, it has been argued that private capital would be more effective than governments in managing the levers of a nation's economy, in delivering growth and consequently influencing societies. However, this understanding fails to adequately acknowledge that the primary aim of any corporation is profit and not socio-economic welfare or human development. Corporations do have a role in a nation's development and can be leveraged to further a nation's economic and foreign policy goals. But they need to do so in a partnership with the State (which necessitates reimagining the public-private partnership model, which unfortunately devolved into a public-private contracting model, wherein the State would contract private corporations to implement projects). But it needs to be acknowledged that by themselves, corporations cannot create a more equitable or just society. Nor can they redress critical socio-political problems facing a nation. So when a government allows corporations (or any other non-State stakeholder for that matter) disproportionate access and say in how a nation's affairs should be conducted, it is effectively abandoning its constitutional responsibilities.

This has already had a profound impact on India. On the one hand, apart from a focus on the largest conglomerates, the BJP government has mostly ignored the need to create a nurturing policy environment for a vast majority of companies, thus constricting their potential for national development. On the other hand, while corporate profits have mushroomed for less than 1 per cent of corporate firms,[104] dignified jobs in manufacturing have plummeted.[105] Therefore, contrary to the prevalent view on inflation (wherein inflation is macroeconomic in origin), burgeoning corporate profits have directly contributed to overall price increases,[106] since large firms have unchecked market power (and little State regulation) to hike prices. Consequently, the kind of economic distress India is now facing is unprecedented. Inflation is at record levels[107] partly because the government has slashed strategic price controls (such as allocations to the Price Stabilisation Fund which was cut by 642 per cent[108]) leading to high volatility in food prices. Furthermore, the State has chosen to depend on indirect taxes as its principle source of revenue[109] at a time when consumption (which contributes to 58.4 per cent of India's GDP[110]) is at a historic forty-year low. Unemployment is at a forty-five year high[111] because the government has chosen to focus on a microscopic number of large conglomerates rather than micro, small and medium scale enterprises (that generate 40 per cent of total employment[112]). Consequently the incomes of 84 per cent Indian households have fallen[113] and the average household debt has ballooned.[114] This has created acute socio-economic distress.

Third, casting civil society as a frontier for war and foreign interference,[115] the ruling dispensation has spearheaded a structural adjustment of India's civil society landscape, as Prof. Ingrid Srinath's essay highlights. On the one hand, most governments (Union and state) no longer listen to Civil Society Organizations (CSOs) or movements, either in the pre-legislative stage or in redressing lacunae in the implementation of government schemes. On the other hand, activists, journalists, academics and students have been targeted by a plethora of the State's governing instruments, as well as by non-State actors (who have resorted to violence and abuse, both online and offline). This has been further exacerbated by restricting CSOs' access to resources (including cancelling Foreign Contribution Regulation Act registrations[116] and revoking 12A/80-G licences[117] and anecdotally, pressurizing private companies and philanthropists to redirect funding to a plethora of institutions affiliated to the Sangh Parivar, etc.). This is partly because the BJP government has re-conceptualized *vikaas* (development) as the furtherance of large projects rather than citizens' well-being. Consequently, civil society is vilified as disruptive to India's development trajectory and therefore anti-national.[118] This portends a grave threat to the system's integrity because civil society (arguably the fifth pillar of Indian democracy) is an indispensable safety valve for societal tensions in a polity. History teaches us that in the absence of systemic safety valves, tensions mature into conflicts and eventually revolutions.

What India is witnessing today is a negation of the core presuppositions of a functional democracy. Inclusive and consultative policymaking, debate and mutual respect for differences, the right to dissent, the notion that citizens have rights over their government are all norms that have been continuously undermined. These norms are all premised on an assumption of good faith on all sides, especially from the State. Just to cite one example, both the political Opposition and civil society depend on the State to protect the right to dissent. However, when good faith is missing, each of these principles can be (and are being) abused. This is a mortal threat to any democracy.

Transforming the State

Today, India is rapidly becoming the world's largest flailing democracy. For various reasons, the governing structures of India's

State no longer have the resilience to tackle the unprecedented pressures they face. On the one hand, they have not evolved sufficiently to respond to 'the multiple challenges India faces— ranging from its rapid urbanization to low agriculture productivity, from security threats to weak human capital, and from widespread corruption to environmental degradation'.[119] On the other, India's institutional framework has been systematically undermined, from within and without. While the political leadership has restructured power and spearheaded an attack on democratic norms in the name of democracy, we have witnessed unusual institutional cowardice in safeguarding the integrity of institutions.

The State is the central binding agent in both the substantive and symbolic unity of India. Given this, it would be expedient to effect drastic structural changes, both to sanitize compromised systems and to make the State more responsive to new problems. Actualizing this would mean urgently rethinking existing social, economic and political paradigms. Today, there is little clarity on what India should be in the year 2047 (when India turns 100), let alone in 2147. Since there is no clarity of thought on the *why*, there is little vision on *what* needs to be done and *how* it can be effected. Just to give one example, one of the reasons that China's economy has reached dizzying highs is that its development model is partly predicated on the State driving both private and state-owned enterprises on the basis of a larger political/geopolitical goal, especially in strategic sectors that are critical for national development and security.[120] In stark contrast, India has spearheaded a wanton and ill-advised fire-sale of nearly 300 public sector units (PSUs)[121] (that Prime Minister Nehru famously called the temples of modern India) along with thirty-one airports, twenty-three ports, 26,700 kms of highways (20 per cent of the nation's road length), 400 railway stations, 1400 kms of rail lines,[122] etc. This will result in mass layoffs and severely compromise the State's capacity to secure (let alone guide) India's national security as also its human development, energy, space and economic goals. Instead, India should recalibrate the policy of selling PSUs to generate revenue and leverage them for global diplomatic and economic statecraft. After all, India needs to fast establish herself as a strong and robust global player, not just an aligned client-state.

Additionally, it is critical that we institutionalize innovative disruptions in government processes to make the State more responsive to the needs and aspirations of the citizenry. For example, in India, the State boasts of a robust vertical accountability system (where officials are accountable to their superiors) but no horizontal accountability systems (wherein the State is accountable to the citizenry or even set performance parameters). This outdated system rewards inertia and lethargy, not innovation and dynamism. That is why it has been argued that there is negligible management capacity in the Indian State.[123] This can be redressed by transforming the management paradigm in government (by ensuring longer tenures for specialists, streamlining processes and minimizing transfers).

Likewise, contrary to the pervasive belief that India's bureaucracy is ineffective and inefficient (prompting Prime Minister Modi to bat for 'minimum government, maximum governance[124]'), India's bureaucracy is bloated at the senior levels and lean at the lower levels. The bitter reality is that India's population to doctors,[125] population to judges,[126] population to teachers,[127] population to municipal workers and population to nurses[128] ratios are amongst the worst in the world. It is because of this that delivery of essential goods and services is dismal. Yes, India needs to be freed from the shackles of bureaucratic controls. However, it is only by deploying a vast army of highly trained personnel at the panchayat and urban local body levels that India can very substantially enhance last-mile connectivity. If these are sourced from dynamic and well-connected activists from local areas, this will have the added benefit of kick-starting a social revolution from below since public sector jobs provide a means for upward socio-economic mobility. Given these multiple benefits, the Indian State should expand employment at these levels rather than greater contractualization.

We also have to insulate the governing structures of the State from political and ideological interference, so they can remain custodians of India's constitutional promise. This would mean, for instance, making the Enforcement Directorate, the Central Vigilance Commission and the Central Bureau of Investigation truly independent. Similarly, the Press Council and Election Commission should ideally be given more teeth so they can perform their duties freely and fairly. This would also mean revisiting the procedures for appointments to the judiciary, to the Election Commission, to tribunals, to the Comptroller and Auditor General, etc. Today, there are unwarranted discretionary powers with the government of the day. As Dr N.C. Saxena's essay in this volume points out, officials desirous of post-retirement jobs are more than willing to oblige any ruling dispensation (even if it means compromising on their oaths of office). This needs to be redressed, and a mandatory cooling-off period must be institutionalized. Furthermore, given that the appointment of numerous fourth branch institutions require the participation of the Leader of Opposition (LoP) in the lower House of Parliament, it is important to have an LoP irrespective of the numerical strength of the Opposition parties. Without oversight by the Opposition, it is that much easier for the Executive to appoint pliant officials.

This would also mean insulating the State's human resources from unconstitutional influences and motivations. A vast majority of India's bureaucrats subscribe to and function within the framework of the constitutional idea of India. Yet, borrowing from Arendt,[129] some routinely surrender their very humanity, either for self-interest or fear or driven by some deep-rooted prejudice. In doing this, they refuse to be persons with agency and blindly follow orders that discriminate and penalize. As the Milburn and Asch experiments[130] demonstrated,[131] this has sparked a tsunami of violence in India, as ordinary people either take up arms to enforce what they deem right because authority figures direct them to do so, or turn a blind eye to violence. Admittedly, there is no tailor-made answer on how this can be checked. However, this can be mitigated partially by periodic trainings, more transparent evaluations (either by an independent bureaucracy-watchdog along the lines of the Election Commission or through greater parliamentary scrutiny over departmental functioning) and stricter penalties for violations, as well as carefully defined limits on the individual authority of the political Executive and senior bureaucrats. The union bureaucracy *has* to be truly national in its outlook for it is the ultimate strategic instrument of the State's power. This can be achieved by robust institutional checks and balances on the Executive, by further empowering the legislature and the judiciary. After all, a popular mandate cannot be construed as an absolute one. If the political Executive's ideology/actions are incompatible with constitutional and democratic norms, it can successfully flatten India's democratic super-structure (ironically, in the name of the people). Consequently, instead of constructively arbitrating between contending interest groups, such a political Executive can misuse a brute electoral majority to ramrod atavistic policies.

That is why we must acknowledge that executive power is still personalized and find ways to redress this structural shortcoming. Although there are procedural checks and balances on how this power is exercised, these are mere norms. It takes individual courage (within the cabinet, within the bureaucracy, within other governing institutions of the State and most of all, within political party organizations) to activate and give meaning to procedural checks. Sadly today, India is rife with examples where procedural checks have been rendered impotent. How can this be effectively redressed? To do this, an out-of-the-box informal innovation will have to be collectively institutionalized by India's political parties. While retaining partisan differences (a sine qua non in a parliamentary democracy), there has to be a consensus cutting across party lines on at least where the nation should be heading. The leadership of every party must recognize that subverting Parliament, the cabinet and other consultative processes with non-

State stakeholders undermines both governance and reform; that governance and reform are processes, not events. In the national interest, there has to be consensus and continuity in the *why*, *what and* how of socio-economic, political and cultural reform.

That is why the leadership of every party must build bridges and institutionalize an informal political caucus of sorts. This bipartisan caucus must carefully identify and meticulously groom political stakeholders for advancement. These stakeholders should be those who are guided foremost by constitutional values, have a certain vision for the future and do not resign individual and organizational agency to charismatic leaders with no affinity to democratic or constitutional norms. This has become even more critical when one sees the future of the BJP, where current leaders have seemingly abdicated their powers to a select few and future leaders are unfortunately being inoculated against constitutional and democratic values.

What would be expected of such leaders that the caucus identifies (or indeed any future leaders)? Firstly, conjoined in furthering the constitutional idea of India, they would consciously unsubscribe from the argument[132] that a nation can be characterized as a democracy merely if it conducts elections periodically or if it delivers material benefits and political stability. A good democracy is more than that. Future leaders would stay true to the belief that a good democracy is morally obligated to uphold in letter and spirit the concept of 'one person, one vote' (and what that entails in terms of corresponding civil rights/liberties and entitlements). These leaders must also recognize that it is their solemn duty to also create enabling conditions for social, economic and political plurality. If India is to remain a functional democracy, these future leaders will also have to recommit to upholding the stated and unstated conventions of parliamentary democracy. This means respecting fundamental rights and freedoms, ensuring the rule of law and guaranteeing space for political opponents and elected state governments.

Breathing life into such an informal caucus will invariably be contingent on both the political Executive's initiative and the active collaboration of key Opposition leaders. Together, they can both legitimize and institutionalize such a mechanism. But to do this, it is critical for the political Executive to respectfully accommodate political opponents. This is because on the one hand, the cabinet system operates on the principle of collective responsibility and can moderate authoritarian and unconstitutional impulses. On the other hand, accommodating the Opposition is critical because political parties are also important democratic institutions that serve as 'transmission belts for public opinion and group interests . . . [as well as] instruments of change.'[133] Rather than viewing them as adversarial 'instruments of individual power',[134] the State must treat them as partners in nation-building. This is equally predicated on a consensus on what and where India should be moving towards and therefore a consociational notion of democracy.

Nations are ultimately built on stories. That is why it is imperative that a new story is woven, drawing from India's rich legacy. This means infusing new life into India's civilizational values and imagining a brighter and inspiring future. To do this, apart from re-engineering India's *hardware* (redressing structural flaws in India's existing institutions, creating new institutions equipped to address fresh challenges and re-engaging all of India's systems), progressive forces must also radically reinvent their political strategies and operational methodologies to socialize Indians to constitutional values. They need to reimagine politics as more than a mere electoral battle. This would mean investing time, effort and resources in re-engineering both India's *software* (culture, values and attitudes) and *hardware* (economy, institutions and systems).[135]

Re-engineering India's software would mean creatively reshaping social consciousness by disseminating liberal, plural and democratic values through films/serials, books, news, social media, educational systems and religions. It would mean rebuilding organic relationships with the people at every level—from the panchayat to the Parliament. It would also mean a dramatic social engineering of political parties, so they are truly representative of the vast diversities of India. Most of all, it would mean re-articulating a vision for India in a manner that resonates with different sections of society. We need to learn that exhortations to protect the Constitution or democracy, which are extremely important, do not enthuse people with extremely individualistic aspirations. We will have to weave their multiple stories into a national one and wield them to counter those who seek to impose a unitary story on India.

This necessitates forging a principled coalition with all of India's existing systems—its bureaucracy, community stakeholders, the media, civil society, interest groups, including corporate India, the diaspora, etc. All of these exercise a powerful influence on the State and on society. Therefore, they are equal stakeholders in the business of nation-building and must share the responsibility of (re)building India along progressive values. It is incumbent on the political Executive to collaborate with these systems to forge an alternative vision of and for India. This shared vision will have to find ways to ensure that both the nation and its people thrive. It would also need to find sustainable solutions to expand the size of the pie, while ensuring that the manner in which it is sliced is just. In fact, special efforts will need to be made to forge a bipartisan consensus on distributional questions—both among India's constituent units and among nations. This entails balancing different interests and values in our plural society.

A seemingly unsurmountable problem is the issue of generating an equilibrium between contending value systems/political cultures. Some of India's progressive parties have responded to this clash of political cultures by 'resorting to the same semantics and idioms that the BJP leverages cynically. To the RSS, this is a welcome rightward shift in public discourse, which is probably why the RSS's General Secretary can posit that the BJP singly does not alone represent Hindu society and that opposing the BJP does not mean being at odds with Hinduism'.[136] Fighting the battle on the terms set by the BJP-RSS does not further India's constitutional project, nor does it offer an inspiring alternative.

As it has been argued earlier,[137] 'the challenge for progressives is not mobilising those Indians who already feel affinity with the core values enshrined in India's Constitution and already believe in a liberal, secular, and democratic India. The challenge is to convince the silent majority of India who are either not unduly bothered about the threat posed by Hindutva or feel (however misguided that notion may be) that the constitutional values somehow undermine their identity and culture.' While it may be impossible to reconcile the two clashing political cultures in India, there is room to accommodate different value systems that regressive forces have co-opted and appropriated.

This demands that the custodians of India's constitutional project (especially progressive parties) truly accommodate the values and aspirations of different narratives, and not push out those who do not conform to the prevailing dominant perspective. Only with a dramatic shift in cognitive and normative attitudes can we begin to convince our fellow Indians that India is built not on discrimination (and clashing community interests), but on *maanavnishtha Bharatiyata* (humane Indian nationalism).[138] Only then can we foster a herd immunity to extremism of all kinds. Progressives need to therefore give life to what Jawaharlal Nehru once exhorted, 'In a democratic country, one has to take the vast masses of the people into confidence. One has to produce a sensation in them that they are partners in the vast undertaking of running a nation . . . this is the essence of democracy'.[139] Only collectively can we effectively redress the kaleidoscopic challenges India faces today.

This is an even bigger imperative because of the nature of the Indian economy. India is a consumption-driven economy. But we will have to dramatically rethink this model because of the adverse effects of climate change and the inevitable shrinkage of resources and opportunities. This will eventually enhance competition and exacerbate social and psychological tensions. Without a doubt, the future wars of major powers will not be over lines in the sand but will be a long drawn-out competition for sustainable growth. The key question then is—how will the Indian State manage these in the future? Driven by political imperatives, can it continue to govern India by creating enmity among India's constituent units? Will it pit the haves against the have-nots? Or will it find a way to bind them together fraternally, so they can all enhance their capabilities and fulfil their functionings?

Far too many people never get the chance to be all they can be, from which we all miss out. That is why the State must enable everyone to flourish, so we can all gain. That is why progressives must expend effort to convince citizens that our best future is in a constitutional democracy, that our leaders must uphold a certain set of principles that we all agree on and that in order to retain our regional power and flex globally, we must set a high standard. Both political parties and the State need to therefore constantly reinforce that if we adhere to progressive values, we will progress and prosper.

Conclusion

India, imperilled as it is today, is on the cusp of a major reorientation. It will require visionary leadership that can steer the nation towards her manifest destiny. Given the limitations of the current leadership, it will be incumbent on a new leadership to heal the nation's wounds, instil a constitutional patriotism and institutionalize innovations that ensure that the nation's political project can never be derailed again. This leadership will have to steel itself not only to battle those who make war against the nation but also to reconcile with *all* Indians, irrespective of their ideological proclivities. They will have to collectively re-found India and rebuild a better world. This new world must be more cooperative, compassionate and equitable, and has to conceptualize prosperity differently.

Doing that would perforce necessitate convincing our people that along with rights, we also have national duties—to each other and to the founding ideals of our nation. Malice will undoubtedly attack these ideals. But given that our destinies are inevitably bound together, this future leadership will need to make people realize that their freedoms and rights can never be at the cost of another; that how we adhere to, and live up to our moral code—our bedrock of values—is the ultimate test of our patriotism. This means planting in each individual a devotion to the central principles of the nation.

It will also mean creatively reimagining how the nation is governed. To comprehensively further India's constitutional promise, India's future leadership needs to not just engage but actively leverage both State and non-State institutions. On the one hand, this would mean better politico-bureaucratic human resources (more normatively, competent and entrepreneurial) and better statecraft (aligning institutions to work towards one aim, as well as streamlining and deploying them more effectively). On the other hand, it would also mean a parallel non-State network of systems, both within and outside India, that complement the implementation of the State's national project.

This won't be easy, and multiple visions will collide, collapse or collude until they forge a new national order. But what's critical is understanding and committing ourselves to the inevitable reality that we are united in a great and common cause—of building the noble mansion of an India built on the ideals of liberty, equality, fraternity and justice. Thomas Paine once argued,[140] 'These are the times that try men's souls. The summer soldier and the sunshine patriot will, in this crisis, shrink from the service of their country; but he that stands it now, deserves the love and thanks of our men and women. Tyranny, like hell, is not easily conquered. Yet we have this consolation with us, that the harder the conflict, the more glorious the triumph.'

The Cabinet: A Check on Authoritarianism

Mallikarjun Kharge

Introduction

It is precisely because plurality is the hallmark of India that India's founders chose parliamentary democracy as the system of governance for the nascent republic. Motivated by their experiences during the freedom struggle (of having to consistently struggle with authoritarian viceroys, governors and the district magistrate or the resident), the architects of modern India adopted the 'daily assessment of responsibility',[1] eschewing the American system's 'periodic assessment of responsibility'.[2] Accordingly, India's first prime minister, Pandit Jawaharlal Nehru's cabinet accommodated divergent and ideologically eclectic voices, including two staunch critics of the Indian National Congress. Five non-Congress members were included in a cabinet of twelve, including Dr B.R. Ambedkar (who established the Republican Party), John Mathai, C.H. Bhabha (who was a businessman), Shanmukham Chetty (from the Justice Party) and S.P. Mookerjee (who founded the Jan Sangh). While this was largely a testament to Nehru's consensual style of politics, it more importantly established a sound precedent for future governments. After all, great care was taken to ensure

1

that India's many diversities—religious, caste, gender, regional and political—found a place in the first cabinet. In its very composition, Nehru's first cabinet became a north star to future governments.

Since Pandit Nehru's first government, the functioning of the sanctum sanctorum of India's democracy—the cabinet—has undergone tremendous changes. Swinging to one extreme, the cabinet's powers have been circumscribed and highly centralized in the Prime Minister's Office (PMO). On the other hand, other cabinets have been consensual and collaborative. All through, the cabinet has shaped (and continues to shape) the life of every Indian. Yet, few people (even in government) know how the cabinet works; fewer understand how it is actually meant to function. It is, therefore, only fair that the cabinet form of government not be so shrouded in mystery as it is today.

I

Evolution of the Cabinet System

In India, unlike in Britain and the settler dominions such as Canada, Australia and New Zealand, the prime minister and the cabinet are explicitly mentioned in constitutional articles (articles 74 and 75(3) of the Indian Constitution). Since the council of ministers (cabinet) was to counsel, guide and control the prime minister (who Pandit Nehru famously said was to be the nation's *pratham sevak* or first servant), care was taken to ensure that the cabinet was a reflection of (and negotiation between) India's diverse constituent groups. To deepen this negotiation and make governance more inclusive, a key convention that was consciously borrowed from the British system was the Bagehotian buckle of the cabinet—fastening the Executive with the legislature. Both the cabinet and the prime minister were to be collectively responsible to the legislature— the House of the People.[3] This was explained most lucidly by Dr B.R. Ambedkar, who not only laid down two prerequisites for the smooth functioning of a democratic Executive (namely, that it must be a stable Executive; and that it must be a responsible Executive[4]) but also emphasized that the 'cabinet should work on the basis of collective responsibility and the only sanction through which this is to be imposed is through the Prime Minister'.[5]

Yet, both the parliamentary form of government and the cabinet system developed on the basis of rules and norms that lay outside the body of the Constitution. Given that India's Constitution is silent on the executive powers of the cabinet, multiple interpretations of the cabinet system have evolved over the decades since Independence. This evolution is the outcome of the interplay between the prime minister, the council of ministers, the bureaucracy and even the political party. It continues to be a dynamic process, leading to particularist developments that haven't always been conducive to the health of the nation. However, by and large, I must agree with the assessment that the 'cabinet system, far from being unable to provide leadership to the nation in an effective manner, seems better adapted to the requirements of modern liberal-democratic government than other systems in that, it is more flexible and it ensures better co-ordination among the various elements of the political chain'.[6]

The Prime Minister and the Cabinet

The lack of clear demarcations of the role and executive powers of the cabinet meant that the initial ten years of government, and especially the first five years, witnessed a keenly fought tussle.[7] Through trial and error, the role of the cabinet, its relation with the legislature as well as intra-executive relationships between the ministers themselves and between the prime minister and the cabinet, were continuously defined and redefined. There were two discernible streams of thought that emerged through this interplay. On the one hand, Deputy Prime Minister Vallabhbhai Patel was of the opinion that while the prime minister's position was certainly pre-eminent, he was merely the first among equals and had no overriding powers over his colleagues. He argued that if the prime minister were supreme, 'a Cabinet and Cabinet responsibility would be superfluous'.[8] Patel's conception of the cabinet relied on the argument that ministers had the 'entire responsibility' of implementing cabinet decisions in their ministries and that 'the Prime Minister should influence by way of consultation' and not by an edict.[9] On the other hand, Prime Minister Nehru subscribed to the notion that since the prime minister binds the cabinet together, that office had 'a special function to perform, which covers all the Ministries and departments and indeed every aspect of governmental authority'. This, he argued, was necessary 'otherwise there will be no cohesion in the Cabinet and the Government and disruptive tendencies will be at work'.[10] As experience shows, in the initial day-to-day functioning, it was Patel's understanding that played itself out—more so because the cabinet comprised towering titans.

Nevertheless, since executive power and decision-making in essence flowed from the cabinet, Nehru tried hard to ensure that as an institution, it was ideationally diverse and representative. He even included ministers of different ideologies, some of whom had political moorings outside the Congress Party.[11] Furthermore, four ministers were nominees of the powerful counterweight and party boss Sardar Patel, while four others represented non-Congress political groups. Additionally, to ease the suspicions of the rulers of the princely states, whose integration into the new Indian political community the government wanted desperately to facilitate, care was given to appoint ministers who had held responsible administrative positions in those states before Independence.[12] The consequence of these pressures and concerns was the creation of a cabinet far more conservative in inclination than the prime minister, whose radicalism perhaps would not have stood the test of the times that the nascent nation was going through. This had an inadvertent effect, in that the cabinet (and often the Congress Party itself) played a role in constraining prime ministerial autonomy. Both the Congress Party president and the newly appointed President of India often presented diametrically opposite viewpoints to the prime minister on crucial legislations.[13]

Despite this, Nehru took great pains to institutionalize the cabinet system, working consensually with ministers. The prime minister was rarely found stifling opposition within his cabinet and functioned like the first among equals. He insisted that all important matters should at some stage be brought up in cabinet; there were numerous cabinet committees and consultation was frequent. Many of these often resulted in delayed decision-making, and cabinet ministers often differed over crucial policy and political decisions.[14] However, although the stability of the government was questioned over frequent resignations from the cabinet due to differences, the alibi of political stability was never allowed to supersede discussions and deliberations on differing points of view. It was in these formative years that the procedures of collective policymaking were established firmly as a precedent. Pandit Nehru leveraged the strengths of ministers such as Sardar Patel, G.B. Pant, Maulana Azad, T.T. Krishnamachari, Amrit Kaur (who were all towering personalities with large constituencies, both in the formal and non-traditional sense) and deliberately left the minutiae of policymaking and policy implementation to them. He consciously did not create an omnipotent Prime Minister's Office that ran roughshod over his ministers and the bureaucracy. A case in point is the debate over the establishment of the Planning Commission. The Union government announced the decision to institute a Planning Commission to the interim Parliament on 28 February 1950. However, it began functioning less as a mere advisory body and more as a body formulating and driving government policies. This sparked a reaction from within the cabinet, most notably by the then finance minister, John Matthai, who argued the Planning Commission was beginning to function like a 'super-cabinet'[15] and that 'cabinet responsibility has definitely weakened since the establishment of the Planning Commission'. Nehru promptly issued statements assuring that the Commission would not diminish ministerial powers[16] and ensured that by the time it was established in March 1950, its powers were limited to devising plans and making recommendations to the cabinet.

This democratic self-restraint that Nehru exercised enabled ministers to build a national profile independent of the prime minister. Additionally, considerable time and latitude were afforded to individual ministers to develop expertise in particular policy areas and to attend to the administrative requirements under their charge. To a large extent, this hastened the process of ministers, as indeed the PM himself, overcoming their previous confrontational and hortatory political proclivities (a sine qua non during the struggle for independence). This gave essential training for ministers-to-be on how to run an administration, engage with diverse interest groups within the framework of the State, govern consensually and most crucially, it institutionalized the cabinet system. This ensured that the cabinet did not morph into an agency designed to maintain support to the prime minister at any cost and perpetuate his hegemony; rather it also became an effective check against any dictatorial tendencies that a prime minister might display. An unrecognized by-product of this painstaking process was that it curbed most centrifugal tendencies in India (since there were multiple points of contact in government for India's constituent units to engage with), thereby avoiding the missteps that panned out in Pakistan. This contributed substantively to India's resilience as a parliamentary democracy.

An important lesson that one gleans from the experience of the first cabinet is the centrality of the prime minister to a decentralized and empowered cabinet and vice versa. A 'good' prime minister can empower ministers and constructively drive a government while adhering to a large normative goal. She/he will consciously accommodate political heavyweights in the cabinet to ensure it functions more effectively. Like Pandit Nehru did,[17] a good prime minister will transfer his/her political supremacy and clout to the cabinet and institutions of government. A prime minister can just as easily impose his/her writ on the council of ministers and on the bureaucracy, shunning diversity of views and visions. Used judiciously, the former approach can be extremely beneficial to the nation. The latter approach may perceptively yield some short-term gains but will invariably be detrimental to a nation as large and diverse as India. Ultimately, the biggest lesson that can be learnt from Prime Minister Nehru's cabinets is that 'in Cabinet government . . . both in theory and to a large extent in practice, ministers and prime minister form part of a common enterprise in which they have a share'.[18]

II

In addition to the centrality of the prime minister's position within the cabinet, the concerns of the possibility of abuse of executive powers bestowed on ministers are very real. G.V. Mavalankar, the first Speaker of Parliament, raised this issue on several occasions and wanted the Parliament to be an independent institution, not an extension of government or of party. Prime Minister Nehru held this view as well and as early as 1937, had argued that 'it is not possible or desirable to interfere in the day-to-day work of the ministries, or to call for explanations from them for administrative acts, unless some important principle is involved. Even when such explanations are necessary, it is not always easy to discuss them in a public forum like that of the All India Congress Committee'.[19] Much later, he would reiterate that to hold the prime minister accountable to the party would be a mockery of parliamentary democracy.[20] And so, he continuously asserted the Executive's independence and agency from the party (clashing with the party president Purushottam Das Tandon on numerous instances). In parallel, to ensure that the cabinet did not exceed its brief, he made considerable efforts to support an alternative ministry (a shadow ministry of sorts) within the Opposition in the Parliament.[21]

However, while significant attention was paid to carving out a system of separation of powers between the legislature, Executive and judiciary, and to creating a system of checks and balances on the government as a whole, the possibility of the abuse of centralized executive power did not receive much consideration either in the constituent assembly debates or in parliamentary debates. Commenting on this, the Supreme Court of India observed that

> 'the Indian Constitution has not indeed recognized the doctrine of separation of powers in its absolute rigidity . . . In the Indian Constitution, therefore, we have the same system of parliamentary executive as in England and the Council of Ministers consisting, as it does, of the members of the legislature is, like the British Cabinet, a hyphen which joins, a buckle which fastens the legislative part of the State to the executive part . . . The Cabinet enjoying, as it does, a majority in the legislature, concentrates in itself the virtual control of both legislative and executive functions'.[22]

Sadly, the nature of relations and horizontal accountability of the prime minister and the cabinet to the legislature and judiciary were left entirely to the reasoning and good intentions of political leaders.[23] This ambiguity led to confusion and paved the way for conflict between prime ministers and the cabinet on the one hand, and imposed an unrealistic burden on the occupant of the chair of the prime minister (to make the structure function properly) on the other. Consequently (and especially after Pandit Nehru's demise), the cabinet transformed into a dominant institution in government. There was an excessive centralization of power by ministers who were either party stalwarts themselves or working in tandem with each other. They even engineered the successions of two prime ministers, namely, Lal Bahadur Shastri (1964) and Indira Gandhi (in 1965 and 1967). This diminished the office of the prime minister. Consequently, rather than focusing on ushering in a constitutional social transformation, the government for a brief period was losing focus. Matters came to a head when powerful party leaders tried to gain supremacy over the government and the party by propping up their own candidate for the presidential poll.

Prime Minister Indira Gandhi resolved this untenable situation both within the party and the government. While the developments within the party have been well documented and lie beyond the scope of this paper, what she did in government was to create a powerful PMO (then known as the Prime Minister's Secretariat), building upon the fledgling steps taken by Prime Minister Shastri. In fact, an interesting side note is that it was Shastri who expanded the scope of the PMO and empowered bureaucrats and advisers to exert considerable influence in decision-making.[24] Faced with a similar political situation as Shastri, Mrs Gandhi felt it would be politically expedient to create an institutional arrangement that guaranteed the perpetuation of constitutional values and ideological goals, indeed the political agenda of the government and the prime minister. Needless to say, she felt this was perforce predicated on her consolidating powers. As a result, the departments of revenue intelligence and enforcement, as well as intelligence agencies such as the Intelligence Bureau, Central Bureau of Investigation and the Research and Analysis Wing were shifted from the ministry of finance and the ministry of home affairs and placed under the PMO and the cabinet secretariat (again an adjunct of the PM), respectively.

Nevertheless, her PMO-driven form of centralized governance struck a unique compromise. Serving as both party president and prime minister, she exclusively focused on expanding the party's base and mass politics. It was not that ministers could not expand their political profiles; but they could not do so at the expense of the party. At the same time, Mrs Gandhi expanded the prerogatives of her ministers. Ministers such as R. Venkataraman, G. Zail Singh, P.V. Narasimha Rao and Pranab Mukherjee were empowered by her to grow and assert themselves within the government. They were given the freedom to focus on the nuts and bolts of administration and orient the government's policies with the party's larger ideological goals. They were constantly prodded into gaining mastery over statecraft, which to her mind was critical to effectively executing the party's ideological and welfare agenda. Contrary to popular belief, Mrs Gandhi methodically and personally groomed many bright and dedicated youngsters who went on to serve the nation and the party for decades.

It has been argued that under Mrs Gandhi, the cabinet was reduced to an advisory council to the prime minister. However, the cabinet *collectively* decided the government's direction. While the prime minister undoubtedly constructed the broad ideological goalposts, every minister had the freedom to voice his/her views and was ultimately responsible for the implementation of the policy, once the cabinet decided collectively. Each one was encouraged to be vocal and consider the political, economic and social implications of every policy. And when they decided on something collectively, they stood by it—both to the Parliament and to the media. Every minister knew and adhered to the principle that the council of ministers was *collectively responsible* and *accountable* to the legislature. Notwithstanding her decision to create a centralized form of governance, Mrs Gandhi was acutely conscious that ignoring opinions and disempowering ministers (who were political agents in their own right) would negate the foundation of India's parliamentary democracy.[25] That is one of the reasons why she purposefully circumscribed the role of the PMO in her last term, which operated much more cautiously and professionally. No minister got instructions from the 'PMO' on anything and if at all, it was from the prime minister herself.

III

Shakespeare's adage 'uneasy lies the head that wears a crown' most appropriately describes the position that India's prime ministers find themselves in. The prime minister is burdened with steering the ship of the State, of delicately balancing the nation's manifold interest groups, of ensuring the nation is sailing towards a desirable social, economic, geo-strategic and political goal, and of being the political face of the party she/he represents. Most importantly, the prime minister is the chief spokesperson of the country when dealing with all international State and non-State actors. Amidst all this, they have to also be connected to the people. Consequently, a lot rides on the prime minister, for she/he is both 'a political as well as an executive leader'.[26] The overall state of the nation is reflective of the functioning of the PM and his/her administration.

Even though the moral authority to govern vests with the prime minister, unless the cabinet and the political party are supportive of the PM, she/he cannot function effectively. The prime minister simply cannot afford to be embroiled in wars with cabinet ministers, for that imposes a high opportunity cost. While cabinet ministers should, and must, assert their agency in debating nuances of policymaking, governance and its impact on the overall politics of the nation, they should not diminish the prime minister. Doing so not only weakens the prime minister but also undermines the government. Ministers will only wilfully do so at the behest of their party leadership, for their personal ambitions or for vested interests. Like Prime Minister Indira Gandhi faced in her first term, Atal Bihari Vajpayee and Dr Manmohan Singh also had to face strains that appropriated executive functions from the PM's domain. Because of coalition compulsions, they were forced to decentralize powers to ministers, at times untenably. Ministers were beholden to their respective party bosses and sometimes breached the Common Minimum Programme, which was a solemn agreement among all coalition parties conjoined in the government—both the National Democratic Alliance (NDA) and the UPA.

Dr Manmohan Singh, in whose cabinet I had the honour of serving, navigated this situation masterfully. This was most evident in cabinet meetings, where Dr Singh intervened strategically. He would tactically forge consensus with various ministers before cabinet meetings and let ministers take the lead in stating positions that he endorsed. He also institutionalized this consensus-building process through Empowered Groups of Ministers or Groups of Ministers (GoMs).[27] Even though Dr Singh involved himself deeply in the mechanics of policy formulation, he actively empowered ministers to negotiate with diverse interest groups and learn to balance political compulsions. This self-restraint by the prime minister facilitated the creation of a strong pool of future political leaders. In doing so, Dr Singh limited himself to decision-making on the basis of larger administrative, geopolitical and policy variables. Consequently, a historic sixty-eight GoMs and fourteen EGoMs were constituted during the UPA government to consider various issues. All the issues discussed in these were usually placed before the full cabinet for deliberations and a final decision.

Furthermore, Dr Singh strived hard to work cooperatively with the cabinet as a whole, as well as with individual ministers. He also strived to save the coalition on multiple occasions. Issues were discussed and debated threadbare, and he invariably nudged us to remain within a framework. His gentle interventions were like the proverbial roar—episodic but always valuable. I have no hesitation in stating that he was the inheritor and practitioner of the best traditions and qualities of leadership that India is proud of.

Unlike what has been proselytized today, these are essential to the core principle of a cabinet system and have deepened the principle of collective responsibility. However, it must be conceded that while this freed the prime minister to focus exclusively on furthering the national interest, it opened up problems in coordination between ministers and synergy in programmes (especially towards the end of UPA-II when the prime minister was exceptionally occupied with external pressures).

A Brobdingnagian PMO

While PM Singh was striving to balance coalition pressures, especially in the second half of UPA-II, a concerted campaign was undertaken by the Opposition with the help of the 'deep state' to portray him as 'weak'. The key levers of power suddenly stopped functioning. The reasons became clear when many joined hands with the Bharatiya Janata Party (BJP), which subsequently rode to power under Narendra Modi. Even though he publicly promised to correct the perceived (and frankly manufactured) flaws that had crept into the institution of the cabinet and the prime minister, it soon became clear that the new dispensation was not correcting mistakes but taking them to the other extreme. The principles of collective responsibility in government have sadly been ignored. Precedents that were established so painstakingly since 1947 have been flouted. One glaring indicator of this is the dismissal of EGoMs and GoMs as soon as the ruling dispensation assumed power in 2014.[28] This was purportedly done because they contributed to the much touted 'policy paralysis'. This logic was flawed because EGoMs and GoMs provided the cabinet with detailed information on subjects entrusted to them and in the process, enabled better policymaking. In abolishing EGoMs and GoMs, the NDA government has undermined informed and inclusive decision-making.

This was exacerbated by the merging of ministries such as corporate affairs with finance on the one hand, and housing and urban poverty alleviation with urban development on the other. Purportedly done to further the goal of 'minimum government, maximum governance', this seemingly innocuous move centralized powers in the PMO. In a less publicized statement released by the NDA government, it was explicitly mentioned that 'wherever the Ministries face any difficulties, the Cabinet Secretariat and the Prime Minister's Office will facilitate the decision-making process'.[29] The rationale given for this was that it would 'expedite the process of decision-making and usher in greater accountability in the system'. Interestingly, the portfolio allocation for the council of ministers lists 'all important policy issues' among others against the name of the prime minister. This is an unprecedented first, and the locus of power has effectively shifted from the cabinet to the PMO.

This has been exacerbated with the appointment of bureaucrats and technocrats as ministers, eschewing the earlier practice of having political heavyweights as ministers. While it could be argued that this infuses technical expertise within government, this has grave implications for India's social contract. Earlier, ministers were chosen because they had deep ties to specific groups—to communities, to sectoral interest groups, to academics/think tanks, to the diaspora, to civil society, etc.—apart from administrative experience. Their connections were leveraged to engage in a sustained dialogue with India's diverse interest groups, to ensure that governance was more people-centric. Today, only the PMO is permitted to engage with all of India's interest groups. In this construct, the Prime Minister is no longer first among equals, but the sole Chief Executive, like that in the United States of America.

The morphing of the PMO into an independent Executive force is a perversion of the cabinet system. When individuals who cannot otherwise get elected begin to disproportionately influence governance, it leads to an oligarchic control of the State apparatus. Today, the PMO is a de facto super cabinet, that plans, directs and monitors major policies and projects, while the cabinet rubber-stamps decisions. That is why laws are moved that are not responsive to the true needs and aspirations of the people.

This appropriation of ministerial prerogatives and functions has been extended to other spheres of governance as well. For example, it is true that India's foreign policy uniquely depends on the political and strategic acumen of the Prime Minister, who has to consider all geopolitical, economic and tactical variables that could best further India's interest. Nevertheless, the PM is advised by the External Affairs Minister, the entire foreign service and numerous advisers who provide considered inputs based on their expertise and experience. Eschewing this, PM Modi has spearheaded a highly personalized form of foreign policy, drawing from past precedents. A case in point is his decision to stop over in Lahore in December 2015 to greet then Prime Minister of Pakistan Nawaz

Sharif on his birthday.[30] This effort, supposed to be out-of-the-box thinking, ended up undermining years of patient and skilful diplomacy through which India had cornered Pakistan. Similarly, that a Prime Minister would go to campaign for the leader of another nation (Howdy Trump rally in Texas, USA[31]) and again host a foreign leader in India for a rally (Motera rally in Gujarat[32]) is highly questionable. It goes against every principle of foreign policy and diplomacy, for it is tantamount to interference in the internal affairs of another nation. Likewise, after the devastating earthquake in Nepal, there was no need to be so roughshod with Nepal over the Madhesi issue. Given our ancient cultural, religious and political ties, the earthquake was an opportunity for India to help our dear friends in need and thereby deepen ties with the Nepalese people. Instead, by blockading Nepal on the Madhesi issue, the NDA government has pushed Nepal (the only Hindu nation in the world) into China's arms.[33] Likewise, with China, PM Modi also made excessively personalized overtures to President Xi Jinping (as exemplified by meetings in Ahmedabad in 2014, Wuhan in 2018 and Mahabalipuram in 2019). Yet, his efforts have done little to stop China's efforts to undermine India's territorial sovereignty. Worse, PM Modi's personalized diplomacy has lulled him into passivity.[34] He has refused to condemn and counter Chinese aggression in Ladakh, Doklam and Arunachal Pradesh. In personally displaying weakness, PM Modi has compromised India's standing and image. Therefore, it must be said, every Prime Minister needs to remember that friendships are between nations, not leaders. Personal political interests can never supersede the national interest.

Coalitions, Cabinets and the Prime Minister

Parliamentary democracy places authority in the hands of the cabinet, which is expected to steer the government while adhering to an overall normative goal. That is why cabinet formation is one of the most important tasks in forming a coalition government. The allocation of cabinet portfolios is much more than a mere payoff to be determined by coalition bargaining. In that sense, Prime Minister Nehru's first cabinet gave a workable template for future governments. It contained prominent non-Congressmen such as Dr B.R. Ambedkar, S. Chetty, John Mathai and S.P. Mookerjee as well as influential and towering Congressmen such as Rajendra Prasad and Maulana Azad who were known to be ideologically opposed to Nehru.[35] This cabinet was not just representative of diverse ideologies but also laid the foundation of how prime ministers ought to conduct themselves. First, the cabinet was not expected to be a one-man show and second, the onus of building consensus among the constituent parties of a coalition largely falls on the prime minister. The prime minister is thus meant to be the keystone of the cabinet arch; in the words of Harold Laski, the prime minister is the 'centre to the life and death of the Cabinet'.[36]

Consequently, the prime minister perforce has to be sincere, thoughtful, consensual and firmly wedded to the national interest. Each prime minister brings to the table a style of governance that is unique to them. While some tend to dictate positions, others arbitrate. Some prime ministers adopt a competitive attitude towards the junior parties and/or rival factions within their own parties, while others seek to bridge differences among political groups. These differences in leadership styles directly impact the quality of governance and have profound ramifications. Although prime ministers can stifle differences in coalitions, forcefully advocating a position or a competitive orientation towards coalition partners could stifle good decision-making procedures and alternative perspectives. In fact, research has pointed out that leaders who adopt the role of an arbitrator may contribute to slow policymaking, but such leaders (and the coalitions they head) score high on legitimacy and representative criteria.[37]

Prime ministers also have to work with the reality that in multiparty cabinets, coalition partners are independent actors, electoral competitors, and frequently disagree on policy matters and issues facing the nation.[38] However, disagreements within governments are not unique to coalition cabinets. The dynamics of negotiation and decision-making require a very nuanced approach by the prime minister or whichever cabinet minister she/he empowers. Even though the mechanics of resolving such disagreements are laborious, the resultant middle path is the best way forward. Such inclusive policy decisions invariably stand the test of time. For example, in 1995, under the terms of the World Trade Organization (WTO) agreement, India was to amend the Indian Patents Act, 1973, to allow product patents. We couldn't get the bill passed within the stipulated five years due to opposition from the Left and the BJP. When the government changed at the Centre, Prime Minister Vajpayee's government moved the same legislation again, despite having opposed and stalled the same when we were in power, only for political reasons. At that time, Prime Minister Vajpayee spoke to Dr Manmohan Singh, then leader of the Opposition in the Rajya Sabha, and sought the support of the Indian National Congress to have the bill passed. Accordingly, Dr Singh discussed it with Congress President Sonia Gandhi first and then the Congress Parliamentary Party. Eventually, with the Congress Party's support, the bill was passed.

Such precedents and norms were something that Prime Minister Vajpayee tried hard to emulate. During his tenure, over half a dozen central leaders and coalition partners were involved in deliberations and decision-making. In matters relating to particular states, important state leaders (including from Opposition-ruled states) were also taken into confidence.

However, sometimes, even with the best of intentions and efforts, governments are unable to convince coalition partners. There is no guidebook on how a prime minister should navigate such situations. An apt illustration is the Indo-US nuclear agreement, where Prime Minister Singh tried hard to take all allies along. However, when the credibility of the government began to be affected because of a perceived veto by coalition partners, the prime minister acted decisively. Not only was he prepared to resign, but he also faced a no-confidence motion (and was thus prepared to stake his government in the pursuit of India's national interest).[39] Despite this, Dr Singh never lost sight of the protocols that all parliamentarians and ministers are expected to follow. He reached out to former prime minister Vajpayee, who reportedly agreed on the issue but was helpless in convincing the BJP (which inexplicably opposed the bill publicly).[40] Dr Singh also reached out to former President A.P.J. Abdul Kalam, who convinced the Samajwadi Party to support the UPA government on the issue. And throughout the long and hard process, PM Singh never resorted to mudslinging or any petty politics (as has been unfortunately happening today). Along with the then Congress President, Sonia Gandhi, Dr Singh firmly and skilfully navigated resistance, convinced coalition partners and even reached across the aisle since they were convinced the issue would best serve India's national interest.

Sadly today, these high principles and norms of ministerial conduct have been assigned to the dustbin of history. Eschewing their *coalition-dharma*, the BJP issues dictates to coalition parties on controversial laws and policies (like the three farm laws).[41] Many policy decisions are reportedly merely conveyed to Union ministers and chief ministers. Consequently, there is no partnership with either coalition parties, Union ministers or chief ministers. Given how it has routinely undermined its supposed allies, the BJP has gained a reputation of being a predatory coalition partner.[42] But even more worryingly, these developments will have far-reaching and adverse consequences for India.

Conclusion

In high office, one inevitably thinks of those who came before us. Giants like Jawaharlal Nehru, Dr Rajendra Prasad, Vallabhbhai

Patel, Dr Ambedkar, Indira Gandhi and many others have illuminated the paths we tread on. It is difficult to articulate, but that realization bestows a certain sacredness and gravity to the task we embark on. We discharge our duties not for ourselves or our parties alone; we do so for something bigger than all of us. That is why our fidelity must be to our Constitution and this great nation that is India. We have to zealously protect the norms and customs that underpin our democracy.

Unlike dictatorial, authoritarian and even presidential political systems in which a single leader sits at the apex of a hierarchy, parliamentary democracies explicitly place authority and responsibility in the hands of the council of ministers. This is not to bestow excessive powers in the hands of a few but to ensure the smooth functioning of the legislature and the Executive. Not only does this cabinet advise the prime minister in crucial decision-making, it was also conceptualized as a check on the excesses of the prime minister. That is why it is essential that every competent minister be allowed time to learn the ropes, gain administrative experience and flourish publicly. This process takes at least seven to eight years. To change ministers every year or so is counterproductive to the national interest, even if it may be politically advantageous for the leaderships of parties to deliberately disallow leaders to become popular and cement themselves. Moreover, only politically strong ministers (both from within a party and from allied parties) can be an effective balance against an authoritarian prime minister or extra-constitutional authorities like the Rashtriya Swayamsevak Sangh (RSS), which purportedly interfere in governance.[43] But only a truly big leader can be generous enough to empower new talent and share the limelight.

I want to reiterate that whenever the PMO has become the de facto decision-making body in India, sans any accountability or transparency, cabinet ministers are reduced to rubber stamps with no real authority or agency, and governance in India has suffered. Leaders across the political divide keep falling into this restructuring-by-stealth of India's parliamentary democracy towards a presidential form of governance. Many have publicly and myopically advocated for a presidential system of government for India. In positing this, such leaders are invariably driven by personal ambitions rather than the furtherance of the national interest. I have no hesitation in saying that the presidential form of government is thoroughly unsuited to governing a country as vast and diverse as India.

As Prime Minister Jawaharlal Nehru once said, '. . . this is too large a country with too many legitimate diversities to permit any so-called "strong man" or "iron lady" to trample over people and their ideas'.[44] Given India's diversity and pluralism, only a democratic structure that recognizes the aspirations of all Indians can aid the process of nation formation. India's successful parliamentary democracy has proved that this system is ideal for a pluralistic society with a largely heterogeneous population. It is important to encourage dialogue among competing interests to ensure adequate opportunities for equal participation and self-expression as well as the evolution of a national consensus. Only the cabinet system of government can ensure informed and reasoned public engagement and the warm embrace of divergent stands in public discourse. Thus, it is our legal and ethical obligation to ensure that no cracks develop in this mighty democratic structure that India's founders have built brick by brick. Only then can we ensure that our core civilizational values remain vibrant and the nation achieves its rightful place in the comity of nations.

As narrated to Pushparaj Deshpande.

Enhancing Peoples' Rights and Freedoms: The NAC Revisited

Sonia Gandhi

Introduction

For the Indian National Congress, politics has always been a vehicle for transformation—first to gain independence and then to make India more just, equitable, liberal and democratic. Drawing on India's rich civilizational legacy, the Congress Party has consistently strived to deepen human freedoms and weave multiple voices into a national symphony through *maitreya* (camaraderie), *karuna* (compassion), *satya* (truth) and *ahimsa* (non-violence). The Congress did this because we firmly believe that we have a stake in each other, and we must unite in the common quest of 'building the noble mansion of free India'. It is because of this framework that India has grown to be a progressive polity that accommodates all aspirations, has overcome impossible odds and evolved into one of the world's leading nations.

As a nation grows, so do the needs and aspirations of the people. That is why it is critical to ensure that India's nurturing framework, which sustained the nation for many decades, is renewed through a new socio-political compact. This compact would perforce need to deal decisively with economic inequalities, bring greater integrity to the economy and society, and widen opportunities and freedom for all. Therefore, when the Congress Party-led United Progressive Alliance (UPA) won the 2004 general elections, it was strongly felt that the new government should forge a new disruptive paradigm that meaningfully addresses the nation's dynamic needs and aspirations. To give shape to this vision, the National Advisory Council (NAC) was constituted by the UPA government twice, first from 2004 to 2008 (NAC-1), and subsequently in 2010 to 2014 (NAC-2). Serving as a voice of the common man, the NAC was mandated to advise the Prime Minister of India on issues related to the social sector.

The NAC consistently strived to suggest policies and legislations that *extended* and *enhanced* the rights and freedoms that were guaranteed to each Indian citizen. This was to not only check economic, social and political inequalities but also enhance the quality of life for every Indian by providing the basic preconditions of a meaningful life. In doing so, special focus was given to Article 41 of the Directive Principles of State Policy which posits that 'the State shall, within the limits of its economic capacity and development, make effective provision for securing the right to work, to education and to public assistance in cases of unemployment, old age, sickness and disablement, and in other cases of undeserved want'. Over the course of its tenure, the NAC recommended a progressive Rights Based Paradigm to the UPA government, which has substantively deepened India's constitutional promise.

The Normative Basis for the NAC

The crafting of the NAC as a platform to advise the government on social developmental issues stemmed from the Congress Party's unambiguous intent to place welfare and social development at the centre of governance. This was based on the belief that along with focusing on economic growth, the State must also enrich people's freedoms, rights and opportunities. This is essential because markets by themselves cannot ensure that growth is inclusive, which is why public institutions must intervene positively to ensure citizens who are *free from want*. Firmly committed to this, the UPA government dedicated itself to delivering those conditions that would actualize fullness of life for all.

That is why the UPA's National Common Minimum Programme (NCMP)[1], which was jointly created after extensive consultations with the allies of the UPA, emphasized on the need to create enabling conditions such as pro-people policies, laws and public infrastructure, which would equitably share the benefits from sustained growth amongst all sections of society. In doing so, the NCMP took inspiration from Mahatma Gandhi's famous adage that has by and large shaped the actions of governments since India gained independence:

'I will give you a talisman. Whenever you are in doubt, or when the self becomes too much with you, apply the following test. Recall the face of the poorest and the weakest man whom you may have seen, and ask yourself if the step you contemplate is going to be of any use to him. Will he gain anything by it? Will it restore him to a control over his own life and destiny? In other words, will it lead to swaraj for the hungry and spiritually starving millions? Then you will find your doubts and your self melting away.'

Accordingly, the NCMP's thrust was to ensure that economic growth would be accompanied by equity and social justice. The NCMP's key objectives were to further inclusiveness—social and economic, and to provide for full equality of opportunity to each citizen. As Prime Minister Dr Manmohan Singh said in his address to the nation on 24 June 2004, 'The essence of the National Common Minimum Programme is the recognition that policies that are aimed at promoting economic growth must also advance the cause of distributive justice . . .' Based on this normative understanding, the NAC strived to formulate a policy framework for the Prime Minister's consideration that would further uplift and empower citizens.

Precedents to the NAC

It was consciously decided that the NAC should be modelled on existing institutional and democratic paradigms. Consequently, borrowing from the experience of other advisory bodies to the Government of India, such as the Prime Minister's Economic Advisory Council and the National Innovation Council, the NAC was designed as a multi-stakeholder body of individuals and organizations advising the Prime Minister.

The NAC also sought to replicate and systematize the rigour of the pre-budget consultations that the Ministry of Finance undertakes prior to formulating the union budget. It actualized this by systematically consulting with subject matter experts and stakeholders. This was to ensure that policymaking was more inclusive and responsive to the needs of citizens.

The imperative of ensuring policy formulation is inclusive and pro-people is something that the Congress Party has scrupulously adhered to even before Independence. In fact, an earlier precedent to the NAC was the National Planning Committee (NPC) set up by the then Congress President, Subhas Chandra Bose, in December 1938[2]. Chaired by Jawaharlal Nehru, the NPC consisted of twenty-nine sub-committees[3] and included a wide range of stakeholders ranging from scientists, industrialists, economists, workers, farmers and politicians. In enhancing the role of citizens in shaping governance, the NPC adapted from the consensual and decentralized culture of the Congress movement that steered India's freedom struggle. It is this rich democratic tradition that enabled India's founders to forge a plan that would constructively inform the first elected government of independent India, and eventually facilitate India to emerge as one of the world's foremost economies.

Constituting and Composition of the NAC

It was consciously decided that the NAC's mandate would be limited to developing a policy and legislative framework on social policy and the rights of disadvantaged groups, by seeking expert opinion and public feedback and forwarding detailed recommendations to the Prime Minister of India with stated rationales and evidence. It was also tasked with reviewing flagship legislations, policies, schemes and programmes of the government, and suggesting measures to address constraints in their implementation.

Given the NAC was designed to advise the Prime Minister of India, the members of the NAC were handpicked by the Prime Minister in consultation with the chairperson. In choosing the composition of the NAC, great care was taken to identify conscientious and meritorious individuals who could give independent feedback, propose innovative ideas based on credible knowledge of the grassroots to further India's welfare paradigm and constructively critique policy on the basis of constitutional principles. This was based on the belief that the government should enter into a consultative relationship with individuals and organizations that had been thinking about issues of well-being, so that it could benefit from their expertise and experience.

It was ensured that a wide range of academics, activists, professionals or former policymakers, as well as those from the country's most marginalized regions, communities and issues were equitably represented as members of the NAC[4]. These included stakeholders from the North-East, Scheduled Tribes (STs) and Scheduled Castes (SCs). Finally, representatives of mass-based peoples' organizations, movements and campaigns representing a cross section of issues, including social security, developmental economics, administrative reforms, environmental governance, agricultural reforms, corporate governance, minority protection, etc., were also selected.

Given the element of public service involved in the NAC, none of its members received any monetary compensation. However, as with other advisory bodies within the government, members were reimbursed for any travel or accommodation they undertook on behalf of the NAC.

Functioning of the NAC Working Groups

The NAC had constituted working groups to holistically study and consult on thematic issues, and nominated one member as the convener of each group. Each group was guided by a specific mandate and time frame that they would evolve themselves. These working groups were mandated to undertake dedicated analysis and reflection on issues, and consult with a wide array of experts from research organizations, academic institutions, non-governmental organizations and representatives of ministries and departments of government. The stakeholders to be consulted and time frame for the working groups were evolved by the members themselves.

The groups also conducted consultations throughout India[5], which included open dialogues (with citizen groups, campaigns, academic bodies, think-tanks, activists, stakeholders and representatives of organizations likely to be affected by the proposed policy), public hearings, field visits, brainstorming with subject matter experts and eliciting public responses by posting specific proposals on the NAC website.

Great care was taken to ensure that the agendas, proceedings of and recommendations stemming from these meetings were widely publicized in the public domain so as to enable ordinary citizens to actively participate and communicate their feedback. In doing so, the NAC also leveraged its website[6] to proactively disclose information as per section 4 of the Right to Information

Act, 2005. This process gave centrality to plurality and enhanced peoples' participation in the formulation of policies and legislation.

Given the guiding principle of the NAC was openness[7], any feedback stemming from these public hearings and consultations was first discussed within the thematic groups and then submitted as recommendations for wider discussions with the entire council. This was to ensure that each recommendation was sensitive and reflective of the concerns raised by stakeholders and affected communities.

Setting the Agenda for Discussions

Following the above-mentioned process, NAC members would suggest specific agenda items for discussion with the whole council, usually thirty days in advance. However, matters that were required to be brought to the urgent attention of the council would be suggested for inclusion in the agenda at shorter notice. The list of suggested items would be circulated to the members and the final decision regarding inclusion (or otherwise) of suggested items and their prioritization would be taken collectively by the council and the chairperson. Issues for discussion with the full council were also selected on the basis of 'petitions' that any individual or organization in India could send to the NAC via post and email[8].

Council Meetings

The NAC would meet once a month and more frequently, if needed. Dates for NAC meetings would ordinarily be firmed up and announced for at least two following months. The NAC Secretariat would send notices as well as relevant background documents via email to the council members well in advance. Furthermore, a brief note listing the action taken on the minutes of the last meeting and outlining any other activities undertaken in between NAC meetings would also be circulated in advance of every meeting.

The final decision regarding inclusion (or otherwise) of suggested recommendations and their prioritization was taken collectively by the council based on how pressing and important the issues were. The approved recommendation would then be communicated by the chairperson to the government for their consideration and further action.

Once the recommendations were submitted to the government, members of the NAC sometimes interfaced with the policy process, but not on behalf of the NAC, and only in their public and personal capacities. For example, when draft legislations tabled by the UPA government were referred to standing committees of the Parliament, NAC members and peoples' organizations would make representations to those committees.

Secretariat[9]

The NAC was also ably supported by a secretariat in its functions. This secretariat facilitated the functioning of the working groups and minuted the meetings of the NAC and the working groups. The secretariat also facilitated consultations of working groups with government representatives from both the state and Centre, and followed up with the appropriate ministry on the recommendations that the NAC submitted. Finally, it also submitted a Secretariat Report at every meeting of the council as well as a Quarterly Action Taken Report, which detailed the follow-up action taken by the government on the recommendations of the NAC.

This entire process went a long way in demonstrating that a consultative pre-legislative and policy process is the only way the Indian polity can absorb and be strengthened by diverse views and interests that exist in India. In fact, this function eventually became the NAC's most creative contribution, and resulted in a wide range of stakeholders routinely appealing to the NAC to demand for public consultations on proposed policies and laws, where they felt decisions were being taken without consequences being adequately considered.

Problems faced by the NAC

Despite the fact that the NAC was to function purely as an advisory body to the Prime Minister, it was uncharitably caricatured publicly as a separate power centre because the chairperson happened to be the president of the Indian National Congress.

First, the only rationale for the NAC's existence was to ensure that issues of concern to the weakest and most vulnerable sections of society were studied exhaustively and championed as vigorously as other sectoral issues. This was especially imperative given that governments the world over were reorienting their policies to focus on enhancing growth rates, while globalization and other related processes were exacerbating increasing inequities and constricting people's access to socio-economic and environmental resources. Therefore, it was strongly felt that a more interventionist approach was needed to reduce social and historical deprivations on the one hand and to empower people on the other. This was based on the belief that our government had a moral obligation to provide basic goods so that citizens are able to pursue projects of their own choice, participate in society as equals and live meaningful lives.

Second, the NAC and its members never enjoyed the privileges of policymaking that are accorded to the Executive, legislative and judiciary. Its role was limited to submitting recommendations to the Prime Minister. The final decision regarding whether and how to operationalize any recommendations submitted was left to the discretion of the Union government. The NAC did not get involved in shaping the Executive's decisions or in operationalizing the final decisions.

In fact, numerous recommendations submitted by the NAC were not taken up by the Executive, further underscoring its advisory role. For example, the NAC submitted detailed recommendations proposing a national legislation to ensure that a portion of the budget equal to the population proportion of SCs and STs was allocated to support schemes to bridge the gaps in the development of SCs and STs when compared to the rest of society. Similarly, the NAC also proposed instituting a framework of social security for the unorganized sector. However, the government could not take up either of the two issues.

It is extremely ironic that the NAC was vilified, when the current National Democratic Alliance (NDA) government has routinely deposed before, and taken direction on policy and legislation from the unelected and unaccountable Rashtriya Swayamsevak Sangh (RSS), most visibly in September 2015 when Union ministers gave detailed presentations explaining their policies, and sought their *marg darshan* (guidance), as Prime Minister Narendra Modi put it. Furthermore, in my view, there has been an excessive centralization of power and functions in the Prime Minister's Office, while ministries have been reduced to rubber stamps. Both these developments make a mockery of India's parliamentary democracy, while the former undermines the sovereignty of the State itself.

Achievements of the NAC

It is on the basis of the idea that humans beings are the penultimate ends of any development that a progressive welfare architecture was proposed by the NAC to the Prime Minister of India and subsequently institutionalized by the UPA government. As former prime minister Manmohan Singh aptly pointed out, 'Growth is not an end in itself. It is a means to generate employment, banish poverty, hunger and homelessness and improve the standard of living of the mass of our people'[10]. The welfare architecture that the NAC proposed therefore sought to guarantee socio–economic entitlements through enhanced social sector expenditure and legally enforceable rights for the most marginalized and vulnerable sections of society. A wide array of issues were exhaustively studied by the NAC[11], of which some of the more notable ones include:

1. The passage of the Right to Information Act (RTI) set out a practical regime for people to secure access to information and enable maximum disclosures, making government more accessible. Fourteen years subsequent to the passage of the Law, the RTI Act stands tall as the strongest tool in the hands of people to hold power to account. Between 40 to 60 lakh RTI applications are filed in India[12], with more than 80 per cent of the applicants being from rural areas. People have effectively used RTIs to gather information on issues dearest to them, ranging from rations, pensions, housing, teacher appointments in government schools, to larger issues affecting society, including contracts to corporate conglomerates, funds spent on road maintenance, etc. This has dramatically enhanced transparency and accountability in governance and empowered people by giving them the right to information at par with members of Parliament and members of Legislative Assemblies.

2. To ensure basic financial security and reduce distress migration, the UPA government instituted the Right to Employment (the Mahatma Gandhi National Rural Employment Guarantee (MGNREGA) Act, 2005, making access to employment a legal right. The Act provides 100 days of employment at minimum wages, especially to the poor and the marginalized. It has been instrumental in financially empowering the poor. Between 2006–07 and 2013–14, MGNREGA provided around Rs 1,55,000 crore as worker wages mostly to poor, landless and distressed villagers[13]. Further, between 2011–12 and 2013–14, a total of 616 crore person days of work was provided for close to 14.3 crore families[14]. In addition, it has created sustainable assets (3.15 crore sustainable assets in just three years between 2011–12 and 2013–14)[15] that have enhanced the quality of

living in villages. Today, one of three rural households seek work under MGNREGA, and it is the largest workfare legislation in the world with 11.2 crore workers, out of which 57 per cent are women.

3. The passage of the Forest Rights (the Scheduled Tribes and Other Traditional Forest Dwellers [Recognition of Forest Rights]) Act, 2006 recognized the rights of STs and Other Traditional Forest Dwellers (OTFDs), correcting a historical injustice. Since the operationalization of the Act in 2008, over 25,03,161 claims have been settled and 16,54,431 titles (individual and community) have been distributed across India (as of 31 May 2015)[16]. Even in states affected with left-wing extremism, large numbers of tribals have secured legal rights over their land. Nearly 87 per cent of the claims have been settled, with 15,80,513 titles distributed (individual and community)[17]. In spite of poor implementation and adverse judicial interventions, the FRA remains one of the strongest means of protection for more than 200 million STs and OTFDs in over 1,70,000 villages of the country.

4. The passage of the National Food Security Act (NFSA) provided subsidized food grains to approximately two-thirds of India's 1.2 billion people through multiple interventions such as fair price shops, mid-day meal schemes, anganwadi centres, maternity allowances, etc. Besides expanding coverage of the targeted public distribution system, the NFSA conferred legal rights to receive quality food grains at subsidized prices (of Rs 3/kg for rice, Rs 2/kg for wheat, Re 1/kg for coarse grains) for up to 75 per cent of the rural and 50 per cent of the urban population all over India. In addition, it also provides healthcare and educational support to girls and adequate pensions to senior citizens.

5. The consultative process followed by the NAC ended up creating a blueprint for a rigorous pre-legislative process. The Pre-Legislative Consultative Policy (PLCP) that the

NAC suggested strived to enhance transparency, public participation and consultation in law-making prior to any bill being introduced in Parliament. It was hoped that the PLCP would manage to further transform our democracy from a representative democracy to a more participatory and deliberative democracy. This was especially necessary given that the formulation of policies and legislations is currently the exclusive preserve of the Executive.

It is because of the welfare architecture spearheaded by the UPA that India witnessed the fastest-ever decrease in the percentage of its population below the poverty line between 2009 and 2011, as the 2015 Human Development (HDI) Report[18] pointed out. Similarly, between 2000 and 2014, India's Human Development Index value went from 0.462 to 0.609 (which is a much higher increase than the previous fifteen-year period). Focused government interventions also led to improved life expectancy (because of improved healthcare) and enhanced capabilities (because of improvements in educational outcomes).

Conclusion

The NAC's advice to the Prime Minister substantively deepened India's social and political rights. Its advice was based on the steadfast belief that development should be inclusive, something which has always been an article of faith for the Congress Party. This meant ensuring that the growth of the Gross National Product was coupled with continuously enhancing human contentment by provisioning for social and physical infrastructure for development. This also meant ensuring resources and opportunities flow to all citizens equitably, at a time of rapid growth and concomitantly, rising inequality. This is in stark contrast to the proselytized myth of the market as the exclusive driver of social welfare and provider of goods and services. Helping people directly is surer and faster, compared to the uncertain hope that the spending on large capital-intensive projects will eventually trickle down to the people at large. In fact, the contention that free markets can automatically remove social and historical deprivations has been empirically disproven elsewhere, most notably in East Asian economies, where the quality of life for ordinary citizens improved dramatically only because of 'heavy doses of government involvement'[19] which led to 'relative equality, education, and health, along with industrial planning and coordination'[20].

Despite this, the NDA government in India is systematically withdrawing from its core responsibilities. It is reshaping the relationship between the State and the citizens, who are no longer viewed as *holders of inalienable rights*. Driven by its ideological imperatives, the NDA has systematically undermined India's radical rights-based paradigm that sought to enhance human wellness. For example:

1. Amendments to the Land Acquisition and Rehabilitation Act and the Mines and Minerals (Development and Regulation) Act by the NDA have enabled corporations to acquire Adivasi and forest land without the free and informed consent of *gram sabhas*. In fact, Adivasis and forest dwellers can now be arbitrarily evicted without any compensation, rehabilitation and resettlement. This has led to the diversion of over 10,000 hectares of forest land every year since 2014.[21]

2. The NDA government has also diluted the RTI Act in July 2019 by giving the Executive the power to determine the tenure and stature of the Central and State Information Commissions. Earlier, by deliberately not appointing eight of the ten Information Commissioners, 3,14,323 RTI requests were pending in 2021. In October 2019, eleven information commissions had a waiting time of more than one year, with some taking over five years[22]! This deliberate weakening of the Information Commissions, which were instituted to check

arbitrary application of power, is a direct attack on transparency and accountability.

3. The National Food Security Act (NFSA) was to deepen the State's commitment to resolving issues of food security, malnutrition and ensuring nutritious food for the most needy. Despite this, the implementation of the NFSA was delayed three times (through executive orders, without going to the Parliament) by the NDA. The Act was finally implemented in 2016. Even then, expenditure on NFSA as a percentage of GDP has dropped to 0.5 per cent in 2019–20 (down from 0.8 per cent of GDP in 2013–14)[23]. This is problematic because while the population of India has increased since 2011 (when the last census was conducted), the NFSA's coverage has stagnated. This has been exacerbated by the fact that the NDA government has also put pressure on state governments to shift to Direct Bank Transfers in PDS[24] and to make Aadhaar[25] mandatory. Many families' services were discontinued as they were not linked with Aadhaar[26]. Given that the 2017 National Health Survey suggests that approximately 19 crore Indians were compelled to sleep on an empty stomach every night, such disruptions are extremely problematic.

4. Violating the core principles of the MGNREG Act, the NDA has been consistently trying to convert it into a supply-driven programme. It has done so by imposing exclusionary technical fixes such as the Aadhar-Based Payment System (ABPS), which inordinately delays time wage payments and adversely impacts attendance at work)[27], withholding financial support to state governments which impacts federalism[28] and constricting it through declining budgets (funding for MGNREGA has been reduced by a third, bringing it below 2018–19 levels). Consequently, even though the Act guarantees 100 days of employment, the average number of days of employment from 2016–17 to 2020–21 has been forty-eight days[29]. Similarly, the Act mandates that if employment is not provided by the state

government within fifteen days of application, it has to pay an unemployment allowance. Yet the total unemployment allowance paid by eleven states in 2017–18 was Rs 2.82 lakh and has now dropped to Rs 12,000 in 2019–20 (paid by four states)[30]. This yet again demonstrates a lack of intent and commitment to implement the MGNREGA in letter and spirit.

5. Equally worryingly, of the 186 bills that the NDA introduced in Parliament between 2014 and 2019, 142 have seen no consultations[31]. Only forty-four bills were placed in the public domain for comments, of which twenty-four did not adhere to the thirty-day deadline. This excludes citizens from the policymaking process and makes a mockery of India's parliamentary democracy.

Over and above these, the rights and protections guaranteed to SCs and STs, to minorities, to women, to the media, to civil society, to organized labour among numerous other sections of society have been systematically circumscribed by the NDA. Funding for the rebranded *Sarva Shiksha Abhiyan* has remained stagnant for three years in a row[32], rations to the poor have been halved since the 5 kg of free food grain under the PM Garib Kalyan Anna Yojana has been arbitrarily stopped[33], and the rise in prices over the past four years means that every rupee buys about a quarter less than it did in 2018[34]. Along with attacking social and economic rights, the NDA government has primarily worked for the benefit of select crony capitalists at the expense of poor and middle-class Indians. This has led to continuous disasters—from demonetization to a badly-designed GST hurting small businesses, to the failed attempt to bring about the three farm laws and the subsequent neglect of agriculture. Furthermore, destructive privatization has handed over priceless national assets to selected private hands cheaply, leading to unemployment, especially for the SCs and STs. Even the hard-earned savings of crores of poor and middle-class Indians are threatened as the government forces trusted public institutions like the LIC and SBI to invest in poorly-managed private companies. This collectively compromises the well-being of our people and portends grave consequences for us as a country.

The promise of independence was of a good life for every Indian, not only to satisfy their basic needs but to have equal opportunities to empower themselves socially, economically and politically. The rights-based legislations spearheaded by the UPA government was designed to actualize those goals and thus improve people's lives by providing work, meals, better learning, affordable healthcare or cash in their hands. Rights-based laws empower citizens and ensure the government delivers—on education, food, work and nutrition.

If India is to take her rightful place in the comity of nations, we need to address the attacks on India's Rights-Based Paradigm urgently, and thereby return to its noblest ideals, the spirit of its Constitution. We also need to expand the rights and freedoms enshrined by the Rights-Based Paradigm. As Prime Minister Jawaharlal Nehru once said,

'The future is not one of ease or resting but of incessant striving so that we may fulfil the pledges we have so often taken and the one we shall take today. The service of India means the service of the millions who suffer. It means the ending of poverty and ignorance and disease and inequality of opportunity . . . And so we have to labour and to work, and work hard, to give reality to our dreams. Those dreams are for India, but they are also for the world.'

Reimagining Parliament: Hopes and Perils

Hamid Ansari

I

The creation of a rule-based accountability system, and the formulation of the rules themselves, is as old as the first human groups who concluded that living together is preferable to separate individual existence. Down the ages, this has been the rationale of village councils and of bigger bodies. Experience has taught humanity that accountability is an essential ingredient of the exercise of authority, and the latter without the former is not conducive to public good. Thus has evolved the institution known today as the Parliament or the Legislative Assembly.

Since human beings desire to live in freedom, it is but natural that this legislative-cum-accountability organization should reflect their own choice. This is what Gandhiji meant when he said in 1922 that 'swaraj would not be a gift of the foreign rulers but spring from the wishes of the people of India as expressed through their freely chosen representatives'.[1] It found expression in the programme of action of the Indian National Congress as also in the debates of the Constituent Assembly. From this emerged the principle that the power and authority of the sovereign people of

India 'are derived from the people'. This was enshrined in our Constitution, prefaced by its rousing Preamble.

Democracy as a system of governance based on a constitution limits the majority and protects the minority. It thus has wider moral implications than mere majoritarianism, which is likely, sooner or later, to degenerate into elective despotism. Pluralism therefore is the soul of democracy. 'A true democracy', it is said, 'is surely one in which the existence of the power of the many is conditional on respect for the rights of the few.' There is no place for 'a crude statistical view of democracy'.

Our Constitution prescribed universal adult franchise on the first-past-the-post system, and the first general election of 1951–52 was held on this basis. The voter turnout was 44.87 per cent. The two Houses commenced their work in May 1952. Since then, seventeen elections for the Lok Sabha have been held, and the voting percentage in the last one, in 2019, was 67.4 of whom 68 per cent were women. It is evident that the Indian voter has embraced democratic processes wholeheartedly. The electoral process was further embraced by the Indian people when elections were deepened by the 73rd and 74th amendments to India's Constitution, which ushered in democracy at the village and urban local body levels.

It is evident that the democratic system has settled in, and the Indian voter is participating in these elections in increasing numbers. Over decades, the electoral machinery under the charge of the Election Commission of India has done a commendable job of organizing these elections at all levels. The process has been helped by extensive use of technology to simplify the nuts and bolts of the electoral system.

On the positive side, therefore, the scorecard makes good reading. The institution of electoral democracy has been put in place, has been tested periodically and found to be fundamentally efficacious. No less relevant are the changes in the participatory profile of the electorate and the impetus given to it by the social awakening of the 1990s. These have deepened the process of both participation and representation; more on this count, however, needs to be done to ensure better representation of women and some deprived segments like religious minorities.

Parliamentary democracy and the Parliament of India in its two Houses and the state legislatures are the creations of the Constitution. They are entrusted to discharge within their prescribed domains the responsibilities of: (i) accountability of the Executive; (ii) law-making; (iii) controlling the national finances and approving taxation proposals; and (iv) discussion of matters of public interest and concern. In addition, the Parliament has some electoral and judicial functions.

The experiences of seventeen general elections have also brought to light some drawbacks of the system and on the basis of experience gained, the need for correctives has also been felt. Particularly relevant is the 255th Report of the Law Commission of India in 2015, which focused on election financing, paid news, political advertising, and introducing internal democracy and transparency within political parties. On the functional side, some questions do arise: How well have parliamentary institutions, beginning with the Parliament of India, functioned? Have the functions of executive accountability, law-making and public debate been discharged in adequate and requisite measure? Is the voting public satisfied with the performance?

The answer to the first question must be empirical as well as qualitative. What is it that the Parliament is required to do? What has been the frequency of meetings of the two Houses of Parliament, and of the state legislatures? How effectively have they, as instruments of accountability and legislation, delivered? What has been the response of the legislatures to matters of public concern in normal and abnormal times?

The constitutional provisions, and statistical data, tell the story in good measure. The Constitution provides that sessions of Parliament should not be separated by more than six months at a time. It is also stipulated that sessions and their duration are decided by the President of India on the advice of the government of the day and other political parties; individual members have no say in the matter.

The record shows that the frequency of meetings of Parliament has declined progressively. In the 1950s and 1960s, the Lok Sabha met for an average of 121 days a year; the average for the Rajya Sabha in this period was ninety-four. This figure declined to an average of seventy-two in subsequent decades. The data for state legislative assemblies, often in single digits, makes dismal reading. Allowance must also be made for time lost due to 'disruptions' that have now become endemic. In both the fourteenth and the sixteenth Lok Sabhas, for instance, about 24 per cent of time was lost through disruptions. The functioning of the Rajya Sabha was no better.

The malaise was described by former Speaker of the Lok Sabha the late Somnath Chatterjee 'as politics of intense confrontation (gaining the) upper hand with the result that disruption of the proceedings of the House through sloganeering, coming into the well of the House, walk-outs, etc., have greatly eroded people's faith in the efficacy of this great institution'.[2] 'Petulant children' is how the then finance minister Pranab Mukherjee described the disrupters. On the other hand, eminent parliamentarians in both Houses sought to justify disruptions as valid parliamentary tactics.

Recommendations of the Committee on Ethics in both Houses have suggested correctives but with little success. In the realm of rules, the presiding officers of both Houses have the authority to ask an unruly member to withdraw for the day; they can also ask a defaulting member to 'withdraw for the remainder of the Session' provided a motion to this effect is carried in the House. In addition, the Lok Sabha through its Rule 374A (made in December 2001) gives the Speaker the authority to expel a member for five days for causing 'grave disorder' by coming into the well of the House. The desired results, however, have not been forthcoming because these rules were premised on individual defaulters, not groups. A meaningful recourse to parliamentary etiquette thus becomes an essential corrective.

The first challenge, then, to restore the sense of purpose of Parliament is to restore the duration of its sittings to around 100 days a year and make its members imbibe in word and deed the purpose for which they are elected by their constituents. The primary responsibility for this rests with party and group leaders, without whose knowledge and consent disruptions do not take place.

The legislative functions of Parliament are substantive rather than pro forma. In the nature of things, a great majority of legislative proposals emanate from the Executive and embody its collective wisdom and experience. The need, nevertheless, to subject them to the scrutiny of legislators cannot be dispensed with nor can their right to seek wider scrutiny through expert and public opinion. This was the rationale of having Standing Committee scrutiny, a device that is now being resorted to with declining frequency.

Close observers of the functioning of our Parliament have opined that over the years there has been a decline in its effectiveness as an institution of accountability and oversight. One simple reason is the availability of time. The fact that in earlier years sessions were of longer duration meant that more time could be given for each of the primary functions of the Houses. Legislative proposals emanate from the Executive, and their impact on different segments of society needs public inputs both from elected representatives and from different segments of civil society. Hasty legislation inevitably results in faults or oversight that lead to legal or political challenges.

Since one of the primary functions of Parliament is accountability of the Executive, its mechanisms become a matter of critical importance. The first among them is the use of the question hour. It is an individual right and can be exercised on a daily basis within the framework of procedures. Questions can be starred or un-starred; the former, to be answered orally, allows follow-up supplementary questions. They quiz the Executive on a wide range of policy matters as also on specifics. Notices of these are given in advance and are answered in the form of written replies. In actual practice, this form of accountability is often diluted by verbosity in oral answers. The prescribed procedure requires both questions and answers to be 'short, crisp and to the point' and should not be an occasion for making statements. Both, regrettably, are observed in the breach with the result that the efficacy of the hour as an instrument of accountability is diluted. This is in sharp contrast to the efficacy of the question hour in other parliaments. There have nevertheless been occasions when 'innocent' questions have opened the door for wider investigations.

The British House of Commons, since October 1961, has followed the practice of a weekly Prime Minister's Question Hour. Its effectiveness has been commented upon favourably. Biographical accounts of some incumbents of that high office have shed interesting light on the efforts made by the individuals to seek 'a crutch' before facing the House. Our own Parliament has not been tempted to risk this innovation and often, but not always, questions relating to the head of government's portfolios are answered by junior ministers.

Apart from the daily question hour, there are a great many other procedural devices through which the Executive's accountability is ensured. Short duration discussions, calling attention and special mentions are admissible procedures that can be resorted to given the time and inclination of the Executive of the day to allow other viewpoints to be voiced.

The Parliament has a set of standing committees to facilitate its work. These are: (i) committees to inquire (on privileges and petitions); (ii) committees to advise (business advisory committees and the Committee on Rules); (iii) housekeeping committees; and (iv) committees on scrutiny and control (committees on public accounts, estimates, government assurances, subordinate legislation, public undertakings, welfare of Scheduled Castes and Scheduled

Tribes, and the departmentally-related standing committees). In addition, ad hoc committees are set up to report on bills and motions.

One of the functions of Parliament is to scrutinize the functioning of the departments of the government in the context of their budgetary demands. In 1993 and taking note of the need for it, the system of departmentally-related standing committees was instituted and twenty-four such committees (twenty-one from the Lok Sabha and ten from the Rajya Sabha) were instituted. These examine bills, budgets and specific matters referred to them pertaining to the work of the department. Their work pertaining to proposed pieces of legislation has been somewhat uneven. While 60 per cent of the bills introduced in the fourteenth Lok Sabha were referred to them, the same figure for the fifteenth Lok Sabha was seventy-one but declined to twenty-seven for the sixteenth Lok Sabha.

The proceedings of the two Houses of Parliament are controlled and guided by the Speaker in the Lok Sabha and the Chairman in the Rajya Sabha. Both are elected offices whose holders do not require rare qualities 'but common qualities in a rare degree'.

Do the legislatures at the Central and state levels function enough? Do they spend sufficient time on deliberation, legislation and accountability of Executives? Is their functioning in keeping with established norms and in line with public expectations? Do they by their functioning, set a model or a pattern of behaviour for the public especially the youth to emulate? Are correctives possible, or has the system irretrievably lost its way? This can be done only if the number of working days in Parliament and in State Assemblies is increased in good measure, as was the case in the first two decades or so.

The record shows that the notional time allocation is different from time actually utilized for the conduct of business. A uniquely Indian contribution to parliamentary practice known as 'disruption' has contributed to this, and data is available about the time so lost.

It reflects poorly on our seriousness as a people to adhere to agreed norms of behaviour.

II

Debates on our democracy have also focused on the meaning of political representation and the paradox emerging from it. Who represent? Who is represented? How can the system be made more representative? How should we ensure that every segment of our very diverse society is reflected in the elected body? This can only be done by the political parties in their normal functioning.

Apart from the less than satisfactory score on functioning within the prescribed procedures, students of Indian polity have raised questions about (a) the social composition of Parliament and (b) the changing concepts of representation. The first is reflected in the community/caste-wise composition, the educational and occupational background of the members and in the decisive transformation of the social base post–1990. Available statistical data and academic studies sustain it. The second, no less relevant, is the changing public perception of what constitutes representation.

A modern democracy is representational in nature, and hence determining the modes of representation and making it operational become critical. In the aftermath of Independence, we chose adult franchise and the first-past-the-post system; the data of the electorate's participation in early general elections tells its story candidly. The political discourse subscribed to 'unity in diversity', but the intent in the early period was on the former rather than the latter. It has been opined that 'the first two parliaments were dominated by men who were quite patriarchal . . . and felt that their social background did not affect their views and perceptions and sense of responsibility as representatives.' The nature of representation started changing in the 1970s and underwent drastic transformation in the post-1990s. Greater public awareness of their rights in a democratic polity led to greater participation in the political system. This is evident from the change in the nature of representation in the 1970s and particularly in the post 1990s period. Questions of representation of diversity, and of federalism, came to the fore and cannot be wished away.

Alongside are questions about whom the representatives represent. Since 'caste remains a key variable' of our social structure and has been a vehicle of socio-political change, many studies have been undertaken on the caste and community backgrounds of state-level elected representatives to examine how caste-based representation has translated into politics in a dynamic perspective. They indicate a distinctive 'evolution of the caste profile of the Hindi belt MPs' and 'the growing politicization of the OBCs, [which] was the direct consequence of the Mandal Commission's Report, largely due to their mobilization in favour of reservations resulting in a transfer of power from upper castes to OBC politicians'; '[which] process is even more pronounced at the state level among some of the larger states of the Hindi belt.'[3] The outcomes vary since the arithmetic of caste varies from state to state. The caste/class transfer of socio-economic democratic power, however, remains an existential reality of Indian polity.[4]

A rival claimant to representative power is civil society. This is a global phenomenon of recent origin and has emerged as both complementary and antithetical to questioning or supplementing the representativeness of Parliament. It has manifested itself in both forms in our polity. An obvious reason for this is that 'while Parliament has become increasingly representative in descriptive terms, it has also simultaneously become unresponsive in terms of legislation and governance and has tended to avoid accountability by closing ranks.'[5]

The situation with regard to the Parliament has been summed up by an eminent political scientist: 'Our democratic sensibilities have become so weak that more and more metaphorical instances of such steamrolling of norms and principles emerged every day. A stark example of this can be seen from legislative functioning.

The reduced recourse to parliamentary committees to vet bills, the ramming of legislation without enough discussion, the sleight of hand in converting ordinary bills into Money Bills, are various techniques of bulldozer governance that are practised more and more frequently. To add to that, the instruments of suspending members of legislatures for long and indefinite periods and muting their mikes when they are speaking in the House are other strategies that are fitted into the armoury of this genre of governance.'[6]

III

It would be fair to measure the Parliament's functioning on three counts: (i) as a legislative institution in terms of its functioning; (ii) as an instrument of control over the functioning of the Executive; and (iii) in terms of present-day realities and the role of civil society organizations and institutions. A decline in terms of its assigned responsibilities is much too evident, and credible observers have opined that we are now more a symbol than substance of a vibrant democracy.[7] There are also shortfalls in the Parliament's functioning as an instrument of control over the Executive. Particularly noticeable is the tardiness in galvanizing the functioning of the departmentally-related standing committees. The responsibility for both principally, but not wholly, rests with the Executive of the day and can be induced through collective action of the political parties combined with public pressure.

Similarly, the attendance of ministers in meetings of the standing committees should be made obligatory and should not be confined to Secretaries of the government; the two Houses of Parliament should revert to the earlier practice of sitting for 90 to 100 days; there should be a binding mechanism to check disruptions and time lost should be recouped within a specified period; and to accommodate civil society concerns, rules and procedures for the functioning of the petition committees of the two Houses should be reviewed.

The imperative to retrieve the institution is evident to adherents of democratic values and of the Constitution. The apprehension that a dormant Parliament could become the first stage to its oblivion is real and lends credence to allegations of India becoming 'the world's largest illiberal democracy'. The primary objectives of proposed correctives should be to induce Parliament to accommodate in its functioning the realities of our times, restore its primacy in the functioning of institutions of the Indian State, and convince a younger generation that it remains relevant.

The Centrality of Coalitions to Statecraft

Sitaram Yechury

Introduction: The Importance of Political Diversity to the Idea of India

India is on the cusp of history. Threatened by a hegemonic force that is steamrolling India's colourful diversities into a unitarian religious, cultural and political straitjacket, all secular forces committed to the constitutional idea of India will necessarily have to safeguard Bharat, which is the union of states. This historic fight is both political and ideological.

Some people have (perhaps deliberately, to foment discord) argued that the political vigour of this historic battle might be weakened because the Opposition's plurality can prove to be a structural weakness. This is a fallacy and needs to be critically dissected. I am reminded of 1996, when I was on an NDTV interview talking about the results of India's 1996 general elections. I was asked: 'As the mandate is fractured with no party coming close to obtaining a majority, does this constitute a regression of democracy in India?' I disagreed, arguing instead that this actually reflected the maturing of Indian democracy. Even though some have myopically argued that India should ideally be a presidential or single-party polity, the vast social diversities and immense plurality of India simply cannot be constricted in a political monolith. In fact, India's rich history attests to the fact that the nation's social diversity is repeatedly reflected in political diversity.

The next question that was posed to me on NDTV was: 'How will a government be formed?' I asserted that it will necessarily have to be a coalition government and that coalitions are inherent in a country with such a rich diversity. Soon after this interaction, former prime minister of India V.P. Singh, in a way, endorsed my observations by positing that India itself is a grand coalition. Indeed, the political history of modern India is a history of building and forging coalitions for advancing causes to achieve a political objective or for governance.

In fact, the 'Idea of India' was itself a reflection of how India not merely accepts but celebrates its diversity and rich pluralism. India as a country has perpetually negotiated its immense diversities (in a sense transcending them) by forging social and political coalitions. These coalitions enabled the fostering of a substantially inclusive unity of the Indian people, which has time and again been leveraged constructively to further national interests. This point is best illustrated by the lessons that India's freedom fighters learnt from the experience of how the British crushed the first war for independence in 1857. The pervasive unity that emerged during this glorious 1857 uprising was best summed up by contemporary British chronicler Thomas Lowe, who lamented that 'the infanticide Rajput, the bigoted Brahmin, the fanatic Musalman joined together; cow killer and cow worshipper, the pig hater and the pig eater had revolted together'[1]. In order to prevent any recurrence of such unity being reforged, the British adopted their notorious policy of 'divide and rule'. By the early twentieth century, India's freedom fighters deeply internalized the belief that this divide and rule policy had to be structurally challenged and overcome to achieve India's freedom. That is why forging a unity of hearts and minds was imperative.

Mahatma Gandhi painstakingly forged this pan-India socio-political coalition. The solidarity he extended with the workers' struggle in Ahmedabad[2]; the solidarity he proffered with the peasantry in the Champaran struggle[3], the support to the Khilafat movement[4] and the Poona Pact with Dr Ambedkar[5] are just a snapshot of how carefully he stitched together a powerful peoples' coalition. One may agree or disagree with the operational aspects of the issues that Gandhi undertook, but at their foundation, each of these were designed to unite India's diversities with the express purpose of attaining freedom. Gandhi's efforts also had emotional appeal to different sections of people—the coinage of the term 'Harijan' as an expression against untouchability and caste oppression; invocation of 'Ishwar–Allah', etc. It is this inclusive unity of our people that provided the foundation for the 'Idea of India'.

Post independence, the Congress Party, a party of the Indian ruling classes[6], which dominated as the single party governing the country for nearly two decades, was itself a coalition of various social groups, inheriting the unity forged during the freedom struggle. However, as a consequence of policies of capitalist development, many political developments erupted post-Independence. One such development was the formation of class divisions over pre-existing caste divisions, which is an interesting aspect worth studying, but which lies beyond the scope of this essay. The forging of alliances with the vested feudal interests in rural India that resulted in the perpetuation of the caste divisions, etc., need not detain us here in our present discussion on the centrality of coalitions under a federal democratic political system.

However, what is relevant to note is that by the mid-1960s, many regional interests had emerged in India. On the one hand, there was a strong opposition built through popular struggles by the communists that led to the formation of communist-led governments in states such as Bengal, Kerala and Tripura. On the other hand, many regional parties emerged following the collapse of the Congress 'System'[7] with the formation of non-Congress governments in some states. The domination of a single party rule virtually ended, thus paving the way for forging various coalitions, both at the state and at the Union levels. Following the defeat of internal emergency in 1977, the first coalition government at the Centre emerged (even though it was called the Janata Party government, the party itself was a coalition of different political forces). All of these coalitions were a product of, and reflection of the diversities in India. The concept of federal solutions through coalitions in diverse societies has already been deeply theorized.[8]

These experiments in political coalitions (or it would be more accurate to characterize them as a resurgence) directly negate the flawed assumption that political plurality is a regression of democracy. As it has been rightly argued, 'Democratic accountability is best achieved in plural societies through parliamentary federalism. Those who bemoan the costs of coalition governance ignore similar deals clocked in the secrecy of dominant party discipline. The multiplicity of partners and sub agendas will obviously bring about greater transparency, but the policy outcomes are not necessarily different or even inferior to those emerging from single party dispensations'.[9]

Key Principles of Successful Coalitions

The experiences of multiple coalition governments clearly demonstrate the centrality of the *commonality of purpose* for forging coalitions. Commonality of purpose is crucial not just for a government's electoral success but also for the national well-being. In the absence of a normative glue, coalition partners may work at odds with each other, and governments are unable to function effectively and to act decisively, fearing a collapse.

Following the defeat of the Congress Party under Prime Minister Rajiv Gandhi, a minority government headed by Prime Minister V.P. Singh was formed in December 1989 with the outside support from the Left Front on the one hand and the Bharatiya Janata Party (BJP) on the other. The elections were contested around the issue of alleged bribes taken in the purchase of Bofors guns.[10] The popular sentiment against corruption in high places dominated the election campaign. However, there were different agendas that were pursued by the National Front and the BJP. With its commitment to advance social justice, the V.P. Singh-led National Front moved to implement reservations for Other Backward Classes (OBCs) in accordance with the Mandal Commission recommendations.[11] The BJP feared such *mandalization* would create cleavages within large sections embracing the Hindu order, whose unity the BJP was trying to forge to advance its objective of converting India into a Hindu Rashtra. The BJP therefore withdrew its support, forcing the government to fall.[12] The BJP leader L.K. Advani soon embarked on his infamous Rath Yatra from Somnath to Ayodhya championing the building of a Ram temple at the disputed site.[13] This yatra eventually left behind a trail of bloodshed and conflict, and its consequences injected communal poison in the body politic of India.

The second important factor for a successful coalition government is a steadfast *commitment to the purpose of the coalition* of various parties. No coalition government can succeed if it is forged merely to share power and the spoils of office. A classic instance of this is the experience of the United Front government that came into existence in 1996. Following the tragic assassination of former PM Rajiv Gandhi during the 1991 election campaign, the Congress formed a government under Prime Minister Narasimha Rao in June 1991. It was under this government's watch that the Babri Masjid was demolished. Consequently, that government faced the closest ever no-confidence motion.[14] It defeated the motion by a mere fourteen votes with the help of certain parties that led to the infamous JMM corruption case[15]. Though the Rao government lasted its full term, the general mood in the country was anti-Congress for a combination of various reasons.

In the 1996 June general elections, the Congress Party could not muster a majority and since it lost its sitting government, it did not stake any claim. The BJP under Atal Bihari Vajpayee staked its claim as the single largest party. Given the role of their ideological parent[16] in the demolition of the Babri Masjid, their overall regressive agenda and for a host of other reasons, a number of secular national and regional parties came together to constitute the United Front[17] in order to prevent the BJP from forming the government and carrying forward their agenda of the Hindu Rashtra. The Congress extended outside support to the United Front. Though this combination had more parliamentarians than the BJP, the then President Shankar Dayal Sharma invited Vajpayee as the leader of the single largest party to form the government. That government failed to win the trust vote and had to quit on its thirteenth day.[18] The United Front government under H.D. Deve Gowda then assumed office. This government was rendered unstable and the prime minister had to be changed midway with I.K. Gujral taking over. However, the Congress withdrew support from this government as well on the grounds that though it was the largest party supporting the United Front, it had no share in the government or the power structure.

A similar lack of commitment by certain other parties led to the fall of the BJP-led minority government, which assumed office after the United Front government fell in 1998, but it lost the trust vote in 1999. However, the BJP then formed the NDA, won the subsequent elections and formed the government. It is noteworthy that the choice of the prime minister and the functioning of the government based on the concept of coalition-dharma was a testament to the need for broad principles of understanding and functioning, even for a party like the BJP. There are those who argue that these principles moderated the BJP, perhaps. However, as time proved, a leopard cannot change its spots.

Following the five years of BJP government under PM Vajpayee, various secular democratic opposition parties came together because of the perceived threat that even the supposedly moderate Vajpayee government was posing to India's Constitution. Deeply concerned that changes in the character of the Republic would be brought about by an overt communal agenda, these parties coalesced on to a common platform. This common platform was methodically built on the basis of a commonality of purpose and the commitment was to ensure the defeat of a communal-oriented government and the formation of a secular government.

In the 2004 general elections, the BJP was exuding confidence with high-pitched campaigns of 'India Shining' and the 'feel-good factor'. The BJP, pursuing the Rashtriya Swayamsevak Sangh's (RSS) political project, always favours a unitary state structure as opposed to the federal structure that India's Constitution prescribes and that has been laboriously built since 1947. Consequently, the BJP always seeks to convert parliamentary elections into a presidential form of elections. In 2004, the question posed was that there was no alternative to Vajpayee, something the BJP is again posing today vis-à-vis Narendra Modi. Nevertheless, the secular parties fought the elections together and defeated the Vajpayee-led BJP.

When the BJP failed to secure a majority, the secular parties forged the United Progressive Alliance (UPA) with the support of the Left parties from outside. The Left parties had won sixty-one Lok Sabha seats, defeating the Congress candidates in fifty-seven constituencies. Yet, they extended support to the UPA government on the basis of a Common Minimum Programme[19] in the national interest. This brings us to the third critical aspect of coalition politics.

The third important factor for the success of a coalition government is the *forging of a Common Minimum Programme (CMP)*. A CMP is always worked out after the formation of the government as a blueprint of the policy direction for the government. Prior to the elections, allied parties may have a common set of issues to campaign on. Many, if not all of these, will ultimately find place in a CMP. The commitment of all parties of any coalition to such a programme defines the *degree of cohesion*.

However, any deviation by the leader of the coalition, hence the government, from the CMP, which is perforce a consensual declaration of intent, will lead to ruptures and consequent instability. This unfortunate circumstance is precisely what occurred when the UPA-I government under Dr Manmohan Singh entered into a civilian nuclear deal with the US. This was an issue that was not part of the CMP, and so the Left Parties withdrew their outside support reducing the UPA government to a minority. The government, however, survived the trust motion. It went on to win the next elections in 2009, ensuring that the UPA government lasted two full terms.

Similarly, the United Front government also had a CMP, but the uncertainties and instability it faced due to the outside support of the then Congress gave little time for it to be implemented, though some important new initiatives were rolled out and are still in place.

When the commitment to the commonality of purpose based on a CMP is strong, then it really doesn't matter if the coalition arrangement was a pre-poll alliance or a post-poll one. All coalition governments beginning from the 1977 Janata Party were forged post-poll. Though the Janata Party was formed earlier, the government could only be formed when Jagjivan Ram's Congress for Democracy joined the Janata Party post elections. There have been only two exceptions: in 1999 after it lost the trust vote, the BJP forged the NDA as a pre-poll alliance, and in 2009, when the UPA contested as part of a pre-poll alliance.

The fourth important issue determining the success of a coalition is about *how it functions*. A successful coalition should ideally have either a steering or a coordination committee that meets periodically to review the implementation of the CMP, as well as to iron out differences in the style and functioning of coalition partners. When situations like UPA-I exist where Left parties provided outside support, a separate Left–UPA coordination committee was constituted, which met regularly.

Usually, an issue that often causes discord and tension in the running of a coalition is the public expression of disagreements by some coalition partners. The government has the doctrine of collective responsibility of the cabinet. When such instances occurred during the United Front government in 1996, it was collectively decided to adhere to certain ground rules. The principle followed for the functioning of the government should also be followed by the coalition alliance and hence, the British guidelines for the conduct of government affairs was communicated to all Cabinet offices by the United Front government in July 1996, a month after assuming office. These guidelines read: 'The internal process through which a decision has been made, or the level of Committee by which it was taken, should not be disclosed. Decisions reached by the Cabinet or Ministerial Committees are binding on all members of the Government. They are, however, normally announced and explained as the decision of the Minister concerned . . . Collective Responsibility requires that Ministers should be able to express their views frankly in the expectation that they can argue freely in private while maintaining a united front when decisions have been reached. This in turn requires that the privacy of opinions expressed in Cabinet and Ministerial committees should be maintained.'

While there are numerous other variables that contribute to a coalition's success, these four factors—commonality of purpose; commitment to pursue this purpose; a concrete set of policies to guide the coalition government, that is the CMP, and the ground rules by which the coalition must function both as a government and as an alliance are critical to the success of the coalition.

A Principled INDIA Coalition of and for every Indian

The situation facing the Indian nation and the Indian people is indeed grave today. Manipur has been burning for over three months.[20] The PM and the Union government have done little to control the situation, and are therefore complicit in allowing the situation to move into greater anarchy.

At the same time, the aggressive pursuit of the Hindutva agenda of the Sangh Parivar continues to unfold. PM Modi has raised the issue of a Uniform Civil Code[21], and the Sangh is directly fomenting polarization[22] in the run-up to the 2024 elections. The worsening communal situation is evident from the methodical targeting of the minorities, particularly the Muslims, by lynchings, engineered riots and intensifying hate campaigns leading to hate crimes.

On the other hand, many hold the view that there is gross misuse of investigative agencies against Opposition leaders[23] and misuse of the office of Governors and Lt. Governors against non-BJP governments[24]; that these attacks on federalism are accompanied by the continued undermining of the foundational pillars of the Constitution and institutions. It is felt that Parliament has been reduced to a rubber stamp while the BJP government enacts legislations passed through the din without any discussion.[25] The inauguration of the new Parliament building was perceived to be indicative of the Executive's insidious efforts at undermining the Legislature with Hindutva fanfare.[26] Likewise, the negation of verdicts of the Constitution benches of the Supreme Court through legislations passed on the strength of a brute majority in Parliament reflects the undermining of the Judiciary by the Executive. The Constitutional scheme of separation of powers between the Executive, Legislature and the Judiciary is sought to be obliterated with the Executive assuming supremacy over the other two wings of our democracy.

What we witness today is the aggressive pursuit of the RSS/BJP objective of replacing the secular democratic modern Indian republic with their political project of a Hindu Rashtra.[27] This is a total negation of the inclusive idea of India. The exclusionary and authoritarian Hindutva majority state of the RSS–BJP not only subjugates religious minorities to foster 'Hindutva nationalism', but is vehemently opposed to 'Indian nationhood'.

The RSS–BJP's vision for India seeks to destroy the unity and integrity of our country. India's unity can only be consolidated by strengthening the bonds of commonality that run through our diversity and not by imposing any form of uniformity— religious, linguistic, ethnic or political, which will only implode our society. This must be prevented. Therefore, the principal objective of a coalition of all secular democratic-minded Indian patriots represented by various political parties *must* be forged to achieve the objective of safeguarding the character of our secular democratic republic.

It is with this explicit objective that twenty-six parties have come together under the grouping of the Indian National Developmental Inclusive Alliance (INDIA). The success of this effort lies crucially on building a national level political campaign on issues centring on the defence of the Indian Constitution, safeguarding the guarantees, freedoms and fundamental rights it provides to the Indian people and in defending the economic sovereignty of our country from the mega loot of our national assets. A national campaign by all the parties is essential on pro-people issues to build a national narrative in the defence of the 'Idea of India'.

This becomes imperative because of the unprecedented socio-economic crises that the Indian people are struggling with, including historic unemployment levels, galloping price rise, particularly of food and essential items, cuts in social welfare expenditures and draconian measures that curb civic rights and freedoms. These must be aggressively taken up through the launching of popular struggles of the working people, and by forging fresh coalitions with all sections of society.

Undoubtedly, efforts must be made at the level of every state to arrive at electoral arrangements—alliances, understandings or seat adjustments so as to not allow the BJP to gain from the division in Opposition votes. The situation varies from state to state. In many states such arrangements are already in place, such as in Tamil Nadu, Bihar, Maharashtra, etc. In many others, such arrangements still need to be worked out. In some others, an all-in unity of the Opposition may not work out. In fact, it will not work out in Kerala where the main contest is between the CPI(M)-led Left Democratic Front (LDF) and Congress-led United Democratic Front (UDF). It is this contest that ensures that the BJP cannot even get a single legislator elected, both to the Assembly or Parliament. Likewise in states such as West Bengal, Telangana, Andhra Pradesh, Odisha, etc., such arrangements may not work out as total adjustments for one-to-one contests.

It is crucial for us to remember that electoral politics is not mere arithmetic. Mere additions cannot ensure victory. There are many studies of electoral results that demonstrate that multiple cornered contests have been less beneficial for the BJP than straight contests in terms of seats. Taking all these factors into consideration, INDIA will have to work out the electoral chemistry.

Conclusion

There is a fundamental difference in how the RSS-BJP see India and Indians, and how secular forces committed to the constitutional idea of India see India and Indians. The latter are committed to negotiating with India's diversities in a democratic, equal and inclusive manner, so that the consensus forged is the best charter for our collective interests. In this vision, political parties are also platforms for this conversation and negotiation. And coalitions are a platform for a conversation and negotiation between political parties. A unitary party with a vision to steamroll India into a mono-religious, mono-political, mono-cultural and mono-ideological construct simply cannot allow a negotiation between India's diversities. And because it won't allow this negotiation, it cannot govern well or in the people's/national interest. The multiple economic, political, social and governance failures of the decade are a proof of this.

That is why a broad set of principles on how this negotiation should be conducted, and how a coalition should be run is essential. Inheriting from India's rich political history and the best practices of our freedom struggle, every partner in INDIA is recalibrating itself in the national interest. Its political vision is exclusively oriented to ensure the empowerment of all Indians—irrespective of their religion, caste, gender, sexual orientation, ethnicity or ideological inclination.

Reimagining, Reforming and Transforming India's Judiciary

Madan Lokur

Introduction

The conventional expectation from the judiciary in India is that it will impartially resolve disputes in accordance with the law of the land. However, it is sometimes forgotten that our courts are not only courts of law, but also courts of justice. For this reason, laws are subject to judicial review, a basic feature of our Constitution, which permits an unjust law being declared ultra vires the Constitution, or simply unconstitutional. This is usually on the grounds that the law violates a fundamental right guaranteed by our Constitution or the legislature lacks the constitutional competence to enact the law. For doing complete justice, Article 142 of our Constitution also confers jurisdiction upon the Supreme Court to 'pass such decree or make such order as is necessary to for doing complete justice in any cause or matter pending before it . . .'

Therefore, while law and justice go hand in hand, they are sometimes distinguishable. However, the State prefers to overlook the distinction, integrate and fuse law and justice and is consequently critical of judicial review. The State believes that every law is just and, indeed, there is a presumption of its constitutionality. Yet, when constitutional court declares a law unconstitutional in the exercise of its power of judicial review, this sometimes upsets the State, which then is critical of judicial review, equating it with judicial overreach and invoking the separation of powers doctrine. The oft-repeated argument of the State is that laws are made by the legislature and given that the legislature comprises elected representatives of the people, it is really the people who make laws; hence, laws made by the people cannot be unjust. These advocates of legislative sovereignty forget the existence of a higher law—the Constitution of India, a law that is also made by we, the people, a law undoubtedly just and embodying the basic structure of our democratic republic.

This debate is age-old. The first few years of our independence laid the foundations of the struggle for supremacy in interpreting the Constitution between the judiciary and the State, represented by the political Executive. The seeds of the struggle were sown by a few decisions delivered by the constitutional courts, which were unacceptable to the political Executive. This resulted in the State attempting to curtail judicial review through the first amendment to our Constitution, effectuated in 1951. The first sentence of the Statement of Objects and Reasons for the amendment reveals the State's recalcitrance at what it considered judicial interference: 'During the last fifteen months of the working of the Constitution, certain difficulties have been brought to light by judicial decisions and pronouncements specially in regard to the chapter on fundamental rights'.[1] The Statement was even more critical when it referred to agrarian reforms promoted by the State, but struck down by the constitutional courts: 'The validity of agrarian reform measures passed by the State Legislatures in the last three years has . . . formed the subject-matter of dilatory litigation, as a result of which the implementation of these important measures, affecting large numbers of people, has been held up.' To secure the constitutional validity and acceptance of zamindari abolition laws in general and some State laws in particular, the first amendment to the Constitution introduced, among other provisions, the Ninth Schedule, which protected specified laws included therein from being declared void or unconstitutional on the grounds of violation of any fundamental right.

Basic structure doctrine

The tussle for 'supremacy' between the legislature and the judiciary, which began in the early 1950s, continued into the early seventies, but did not end there. However, the split decision of the Supreme Court in the case of *Kesavananda Bharati versus State of Kerala* is noteworthy in this regard for it gave birth to the basic structure doctrine. Simply stated, this doctrine made it clear that our Constitution was the supreme law of the land and that its basic structure could not be amended even by Parliament. As a result, the fundamental right to property, not being a part of the basic structure of the Constitution, could be taken away by an amendment to the Constitution. Over the years, the courts have identified some 'components' of this basic structure which include, among others, an independent judiciary, the power of judicial review, the secular character of the polity, separation of powers and free and fair elections.

The basic structure doctrine, an extremely significant contribution to jurisprudence, gave birth to a contrasting theory propounded by the political Executive—that of a committed judiciary. The political Executive desired a committed judiciary so that it would interpret socio-economic laws enacted by the legislature (representing the will of the people) in a manner consistent with the goals intended to be achieved. The political Executive expected the views of a committed judiciary to be in sync with its socio-political objectives and that such laws would not be declared unconstitutional. The immediate fallout of this theory led the government of the day, in 1973, to supersede the three senior-most judges of the Supreme Court constituting the bench in the Kesavananda Bharati case for appointment as the Chief Justice of India[2] who would be, in a sense, their saviour—dark days for the independence of the judiciary. This was followed by another supersession in 1976 after the decision of the Supreme Court in the ADM Jabalpur case.[3]

The committed judiciary theory is not dead with the government still expecting the judiciary to align its views with that of the government. This has manifested itself in the government delaying and sometimes stalling the appointment of judges recommended for appointment to the high courts by the collegium of the Supreme Court. This is ostensibly due to a perception that the recommended persons hold views that might not be palatable to the government. The dangers of a 'committed judiciary' and now the 'same page' theory is perhaps the greatest challenge facing India's independent judiciary today.

A resurgent judiciary

The post-Emergency years saw a surprisingly resurgent Supreme Court—completely uncharacteristic of a court that had caved in just a year earlier in the ADM Jabalpur case. Through this decision rendered during the Emergency era, the Supreme Court denied the right of an aggrieved person to access the courts for redress of a violation of a fundamental right. A person could, therefore, be preventively detained without recourse to a court of law and without being permitted to challenge the preventive detention order through judicial review. In reasserting itself post the Emergency, the Supreme Court swung the pendulum in the other direction and expanded the doctrine of locus standi or legal standing to litigate through some path-breaking judgments—the first among them being the famous case of *S.P. Gupta versus Union of India*, which concerned the independence of the judiciary and a threat of transfer of judges. S.P. Gupta was a lawyer, not a personally aggrieved litigant, and yet the Supreme Court entertained a petition filed by him (and several other lawyers) holding that they had the legal standing to litigate, even though they were not personally aggrieved or directly affected. This decision also opened the door for access to justice to any indirectly aggrieved person and introduced public interest litigation, or PIL, into our jurisprudence—another significant contribution to justice delivery.

Some inhuman excesses by State functionaries helped fortify the relaxed locus standi rule enunciated earlier by the Supreme Court. A third party could access the constitutional courts for and on behalf of disadvantaged or underprivileged persons. For example, in what has come to be known as the Bhagalpur Blindings case, the eyes of suspected criminals were pierced with needles and acid poured into them by State functionaries. They could not access the courts for obvious reasons. The Supreme Court was apprised of newspaper reports by a third party, and it accepted the reports as information received and sought to redress the grievances of the suspected criminals and hold the State accountable. Similarly, the case of *Bandhua Mukti Morcha versus Union of India* related to the freedom of bonded labour.[4] Their plight was brought to the notice of the Supreme Court by a social activist organization headed by Swami Agnivesh, a public-spirited person. The Supreme Court intervened and released the labour from their bondage. These and other such progressive decisions were possible through a relaxation of locus standi and the introduction of what is today popularly known as public interest litigation or PIL.

Socio-economic justice through PILs

The role of PILs in enhancing administrative accountability cannot be overstated. For the first time, searching questions were asked of the government by public-spirited individuals on a variety of issues. For example, the rights of under-trial prisoners, in general, came up for consideration in the Supreme Court in the Hussainara

Khatoon series of orders. The Supreme Court highlighted the importance of Article 21 of the Constitution, which guarantees the life and personal liberty of every person. It held that under-trial prisoners have a right to a speedy trial, the needy have a right to free legal aid and advice, and deprivation of personal liberty must be through a procedure that is reasonable, fair and just. The rights of convicted prisoners in general and prison conditions came up for consideration in *Sunil Batra versus Delhi Administration*. In the Sunil Batra case, a convicted prisoner approached the Supreme Court through a letter petition highlighting the torture of an inmate for money by a warden and the terrible conditions in Tihar Jail. It was held that even prisoners have rights—'It behoves the court to insist that, in the eye of law, prisoners are persons not animals, and to punish the deviant "guardians" of the prison system where they go berserk and defile the dignity of the human inmate.'

The development of PIL jurisprudence in India is truly fascinating. It began, as mentioned above, with interventions by the Supreme Court on petitions filed by individuals and non-governmental organizations (NGOs) on social justice issues. Later, environmental jurisprudence was given recognition and importance through the decision in *Rural Litigation and Entitlement Kendra versus State of Uttar Pradesh* in which the focus was on air pollution. Environmental jurisprudence through PILs reached its zenith in the M.C. Mehta set of cases, followed by cases relating to water pollution and forest degradation. As the jurisprudence developed, it invited an unfortunate and adverse reaction from the State, which posited that PIL jurisprudence demolished the barriers between Executive and judicial functioning and impinged upon the separation of powers (a part of the basic structure of our Constitution).

The question underlying PILs was (and continues to be) how do marginalized and disadvantaged sections of society have access to justice and exercise their constitutional rights.[5] A representative suit is of course one such process, but the law's delays in India are legendary. Add to this the cost of litigation, which the weak, poor and disadvantaged sections of society can ill afford. Coupled with difficulties in physically attending courts, accessing justice is daunting for a daily wage labourer or a slum or street dweller whose home is likely to be bulldozed at any time. Should any citizen be denied their constitutional rights because of their poverty? Isn't it morally incumbent on the justice system to evolve an alternative mechanism to redress their grievances? This was unambiguously answered through several decisions of the Supreme Court.

The Supreme Court threw its doors open to every person or body who raised an important issue of social justice through a PIL and thus adhered to a citizen-first policy. This led the Supreme Court to be christened as the People's Court, an epithet that was not only most deserving but reflected its concern to declare and interpret the law, and simultaneously impart justice to millions.

Governance and corruption

Issues of socio-economic justice and environmental justice started a domino effect, and soon citizens raised questions of governance and corruption. The Jain Hawala case (also called the Jain Diaries case) was a watershed in this regard. Investigative agencies alleged that large amounts were being siphoned out of the country through hawala channels and these transactions involved some prominent politicians. That this case did not lead to any conviction is another matter altogether. What is of significance is that the Supreme Court laid down two cardinal principles. The first related to the independence of the investigating agency. The apprehension of the court was that due to the alleged involvement of some prominent politicians, the investigating agency might be compromised and the investigations derailed. The court therefore took it upon itself to monitor the investigations, limited to ensuring that the investigations did not proceed in a direction that would not serve the cause of justice.[6]

The second important principle laid down by the Supreme Court was that of a 'continuing mandamus', which is to say that in matters involving public interest, the court will keep the litigation alive until the public interest is served. This may necessitate several orders being passed from time to time, as had happened in the M.C. Mehta series of cases and later in the Godavarman series of orders and directions relating to deforestation.

In the governance sphere, the rights of women against sexual harassment at the workplace were recognized by the Supreme Court in the case of *Vishaka versus State of Rajasthan*. Even though India is a signatory to the CEDAW[7] and has ratified the convention, no steps were taken[8] for several years to protect women from sexual harassment at the workplace. Notwithstanding the doctrine of separation of powers, the Supreme Court did not falter when it was called upon to be decisive, and it issued directions incorporating a code for the benefit of women who might be victims of sexual harassment at the workplace.

While this might be called a classic case of judicial overreach (an expression frequently recalled in recent times), there was studied silence from the political Executive. The People's Court theory received a massive boost with the Supreme Court telling us that it is there to render complete justice as and when the occasion arises, even if the political Executive fails to act.

These varied but significant developments over the years distinguish public interest litigation from representative suits and are India's contribution to global jurisprudential thought and action. Yet, in answering the question often asked: 'Where should I go to get justice?' the Supreme Court was on a collision course with the political Executive.

Free legal aid and advice

Parallel with the evolution of PILs, another legal revolution was taking place in the form of free legal aid and advice. The indigent and impoverished not only have collective problems, but personal problems as well.[9] Motor accident claims concerning the death of the breadwinner run into hundreds of thousands, even today. How do the poor protect not only their rights but also their interests, particularly when they do not have the resources to pay court fees and engage a lawyer? The solution to this vexed problem emerged in the 1980s when as a step towards providing socio-economic justice to the teeming millions, the idea of free legal aid, advice and services was given bones, flesh and blood. The thought process had begun in 1976 when our Constitution was amended and Article 39A inserted.[10] The State was required to ensure that, as a directive principle of state policy, opportunities for securing justice are not denied to any citizen by reason of economic or other disabilities. Even then, it took more than a decade for the Legal Services Authorities Act[11] to be enacted in 1987 and even longer to be accepted by states, which did so only by the 1990s.

Faithfully implemented through the National Legal Services Authority (NALSA) and the state legal services authorities, the law can bring about an enormous social change, but it has not been so. It is not as if the legal services authorities have not done anything worthwhile but they have not lived up to their potential, which can bring about the necessary transformation for the poor, disadvantaged and indigent.[12]

The Annual Report published by NALSA provides impressive figures of cases settled through lok adalats and legal services provided to women, prisoners and unspecified others. However, the benefits that have actually accrued to them are absent. A social audit report may perhaps reveal an accurate picture, as it did for the Supreme Court Legal Services Committee. That social audit report of 2018 highlighted that applications for filing an appeal had shockingly not been attended to in the cases of a few hundred convicts. In many cases, the convict had served the sentence and yet an appeal against conviction had not been filed.[13] Given this, I believe that a compulsory social audit of all legal aid institutions established under the Legal Services Authorities Act must be urgently conducted in a time-bound manner.

Lok adalats

An area where these authorities have apparently succeeded to a large extent is in holding lok adalats—another significant contribution of our country to jurisprudential thought and action. Lok adalats are literally people's courts as distinguished from the Supreme Court being the People's Court. Petty disputes that should not, but do, clog the justice delivery system are often referred to lok adalats for resolution, and often, a large number are taken up for settlement or expeditious decision. Unfortunately, the percentage of cases disposed of is not particularly encouraging, largely because of a poor selection of cases and equally poor case management.[14] There has also been occasional criticism to the effect that litigants are sometimes 'pressured' into accepting a decision not entirely to their liking only because the alternative of court hearings, delays, expenses and appeals is not a real or viable alternative, or to boost the disposal rate. But the fact is that, notwithstanding all this, millions of disputes and cases have been resolved through the lok adalat process and provided relief to an equal number of citizens.

The resurgence of the Supreme Court positively impacted the last two decades of the twentieth century, instilled hope and generated optimism among citizens that God is in His heaven—all is right with our justice system. The system was, by and large, functioning well and the courts continued to remain a bastion of hope for all citizens including those socially or economically disadvantaged. True, there were hiccups along the way, but that can only be expected. Overall, if a justice canvas had been painted for India, it would have been in colours of bright sunshine with perhaps an occasional dark cloud.

The new millennium

A sprinter does not stop running on reaching the finish line but continues for a short distance. Public confidence, trust and goodwill generated by the Supreme Court over the last fifty years continued, like the sprinter, into the present century. But unfortunately, judicial creativity declined, and the economic boom caused by the reforms initiated in the 1990s slowly began to shift focus from a citizen-oriented judiciary to matters of economic activity. Both the State and the corporate sector were responsible for the shift in trajectory. For example, we witnessed the loathsome exploitation of natural resources for economic gain,[15] and the Supreme Court had to repeatedly step in to lay down or implement fair regulatory norms. Some of the most notable interventions made by the Supreme Court include a decision relating to the cancellation of telecom licences for the 2G spectrum in the case of *Centre for Public Interest Litigation versus Union of India*, which generated considerable controversy due to the cancellation of a large number of licences. We also witnessed retrospective taxation introduced by Parliament to overturn a decision of the Supreme Court in *Vodafone International Holdings versus Union of India*. Arbitrary allotment of coal mines came up for consideration before the Supreme Court in what is known as the Coal Blocks Allotment Scam case.

These and other decisions shifted the focus of the judiciary from the common citizen to the corporate sector. These decisions were, therefore, and in one sense, at the cost of judicial neglect of the concerns of the common citizen, amidst the sound and fury of grave concerns for the economy and the corporate sector. The consequence of a heady cocktail of money, power and political interests placed the Supreme Court on a collision course with the political Executive with renewed imputations of judicial overreach and transgression of the separation of powers.

But it must be said that in the meanwhile, an effort was made in 2015 to address pending public interest issues concerning the disadvantaged when a bench was constituted in the Supreme Court for this purpose. I had the privilege of presiding over this bench, which came to be known as the Social Justice Bench of the Supreme Court. I believe it addressed several vital issues, but unfortunately came to be disbanded in early 2019. The disadvantaged and marginalized are now not accorded any special priority in hearing and are subject to the same procedures of access to justice as any other litigant, virtually destroying the ethos of public interest litigation.

Appointment of judges

The first salvo in the 'collision course' was fired through an amendment to the Constitution, introducing the National Judicial Appointments Commission (NJAC) in August 2014. The commission was constituted to take over the appointment of judges of the constitutional courts from the collegium system.

The Supreme Court had earlier mandated a collegium system of appointment of judges to the high courts and the Supreme Court.[16] The collegium consists of at least three senior-most judges of the Supreme Court with the Chief Justice of India having primacy in the appointment of judges to the constitutional courts. The intention was to insulate the appointment process from the political Executive, which, it was felt, was exerting or could exert influence in the appointment process by pushing its 'candidates'. The NJAC would have displaced the collegium system and placed the appointment process back in the hands of the political Executive. The Supreme Court Advocates on Record Association (SCAORA) felt that the amendment would adversely impact the independence of the judiciary and filed a petition challenging the amendment as violating the basic structure of the Constitution. The Supreme Court held that the amendment indeed violated the basic structure since it directly impinged on the judiciary's independence. The NJAC was held unconstitutional with the result that the collegium system of appointments was sustained. This set the stage for a continuing slugfest between the political Executive and the judiciary that has today reached a crescendo.

While the collegium system initially functioned fairly well, subsequent opacity in the appointment process led to questions being asked of the collegium with calls for transparency. It is true that the collegium system is not perfect; indeed, no system for appointment of judges can ever be perfect. It certainly requires improvements and a greater degree of transparency. The Supreme Court often quotes Louis Brandeis, 'Sunlight is said to be the best of disinfectants; electric light the most efficient policeman'. Unfortunately, the collegium system worked in darkness with Masonic secrecy. I had suggested more than twenty changes in the functioning of the collegium system to the then Chief Justice of India, but only some were implemented. Their implementation status today is not known, but it must be acknowledged that there is now much greater transparency in the appointment process, at least as far as the judiciary is concerned, though that cannot be said of the political Executive, which is, surprisingly, objecting to transparency.

The crux of the problem is not only *how* appointments are made to constitutional courts but also *who* is appointed, and who is disappointed. This raises several questions, including why some persons, apparently deserving of appointment, are overlooked. Is merit the sole criterion or do extraneous considerations, such as regionalism, or a nudge from the political Executive, have an impact greater than one would expect?

Diversity concerns have been raised in judicial appointments. This has several facets, other than matters of caste.[17] Back in the 1980s, it was believed by the government of the day that the Chief Justice of a high court would usually recommend a candidate from his community for appointment as a judge.[18] This nepotistic strain resulted in a policy of appointment of an 'outside' Chief Justice to break the chain. But now, with the collegium system of appointments, this policy has lost relevance. However, the 'outsider' Chief Justice policy continues.

Religion is another aspect for consideration and there have been several occasions when the Supreme Court did not have a Muslim judge, even though Justice Fazl Ali was appointed to the Supreme Court way back in 1950 and we have even had Muslim Chief Justices of India.

Appointment of women judges is the third facet. Anna Chandy became the first female judge of a high court in 1959 followed almost twenty years later by Leila Seth in 1978. Justice Seth became the first Chief Justice of a high court in 1991. Five years after her appointment to the high court in 1978, Fathima Beevi became the first Muslim female judge of a high court in 1983. Later, in 1989, she also became the first female judge to be appointed to the Supreme Court, bypassing Justice Leila Seth, who had a claim on the appointment by virtue of her seniority.[19]

Another facet of diversity relates to sexual orientation. This has gained traction after the decriminalization of gay relationships and with the Delhi High Court recommending a gay lawyer, Saurabh Kirpal, for appointment as a high court judge. The political Executive does not appear to have decided if this falls foul of the diversity criterion. The answer lies in the womb of time.

With the political Executive generally sitting tight (on many occasions for over a year) on recommendations for appointment of judges to the constitutional courts made by the Supreme Court collegium, it appears to an outsider that the *who* question is being answered through the 'same page' theory, which is creeping into the appointment process with merit and diversity taking a back seat.

The appointment process has had serious and often tragic repercussions for millions of litigants. The Department of Justice website had recently indicated that vacancies in the high courts are at about 40 per cent, up from 16 per cent in 2007 indicated on the Supreme Court website.[20] Vacancies in the district courts have remained steady at about 20 per cent since 2006 as per the Supreme

Court website. Vacancies make justice the casualty. The National Judicial Data Grid of the eCommittee of the Supreme Court reveals that over 49 million cases are pending in high courts and district courts across the country.[21] Of these, more than 7,00,000 cases have been pending for twenty years or more.

Keeping court delays in mind, a former Chief Justice of India remarked that a suitor must give a list of his legal representatives along with the plaint or petition so they can be brought on record after his/her death! It is true that court procedures are an impediment to expeditious justice and contribute to the feeling that procedures and processes serve as a punishment even in civil cases. In criminal litigation, the situation is even worse with delays and prisons being hopelessly overcrowded to the extent, nationally, of about 115 per cent and in some district jails even up to 300 per cent. Trial delays are the main cause of this sorry state of prison administration resulting in now over 70 per cent under-trial prisoners.[22] For them, Article 21 of the Constitution dealing with life and personal liberty has no real meaning.

Adequacy of judge strength

The large number of vacancies in the complement of judges has spawned several ineffective theories on the number of judges we actually need. In its 120th Report (1987), the Law Commission of India advocated a judge-population ratio, which is to say that the required number of judges would depend on the population. It recommended a ratio of fifty judges per million population, against the existing ratio of 10.5. This was accepted by the Supreme Court in its 2002 decision in *All India Judges Association versus Union of India* without actually giving thought to an increase in the support staff and the method of recruitment of such large numbers. We are nowhere near this figure and perhaps never will be with the judge-population ratio being in the region of about 15 per cent today in view of the vacancies.

In its 245th Report (2014), the Law Commission of India introduced the Rate of Disposal Method to calculate the required number of judges in the country.[23] This intended to address the problem of the existing backlog of cases, as well as institution of new cases. The figures on the basis of which necessary calculations were made then are today irrelevant, and as in the past, financial and infrastructure issues were glossed over. The Economic Survey 2018–19 provided a third set of calculations and introduced the concept of Annual Disposal Rate (per judge) and the Case Clearance Rate. On this basis, it was calculated that 2279 judges were required in addition to the working strength of 17,891 judges out of a sanctioned strength of 22,750 judges. In other words, there is no need to appoint any more judges. However, to clear the existing backlog over the next five years, it was calculated in the Economic Survey that only 8152 judges were required.

These theories remain theories and academic exercises, far removed from ground realities and incapable of implementation with the problem of numbers persisting.

The rising number of pending cases has been aggravated by the COVID-19 pandemic due to lower disposal of cases during the pandemic. Perhaps, the situation is out of control and will necessarily have an impact on the independence of the judiciary in times to come.

Impact of the same page theory

With the judiciary being crushed under the sheer weight of cases, the same page theory and its spin-offs confound reformers. For example, judges who have delivered judgments perceived inconvenient to the State are taken out of the roster by the Chief Justice or transferred to another high court. On the other hand, judges felt to be 'convenient' are rewarded by the State post their retirement. This is not something of recent origin, but it has been highlighted in public discourse through an overall feeling of the judiciary being 'executivized'.

Even in years gone by, high court judges have been transferred out of their parent high court. But the political Executive's recent control over the appointment of judges and their transfer is rather disconcerting. A case in point is the recent overlooking of Justice Akil Kureshi, an outstanding judge, for appointment to the Supreme Court.[24] Another is the almost midnight transfer of Justice Muralidhar hearing the case of victims of the Delhi riots of 2020. A 'press conference' of judges of the Supreme Court (I was one of the participants) was suggestive of a belief of bench-fixing by the Chief Justice of India, in which 'sensitive' cases were marked to a bench presided over by one particular judge.

Cases of post-retirement benefits to judges are several and again, not of recent origin. Several decades ago, an eminent Chief Justice of a high court was given important ambassadorial assignments and later inducted into the cabinet. At least two former judges of different high courts were appointed, at different times, governor of a state on retirement. A former judge of the Supreme Court was appointed governor of a state. These appointments did not raise a stink, perhaps (and it is only a surmise) because the independence of the judiciary had not come under strain.

It is different now, with a former Chief Justice of India being appointed a governor of a state and another nominated to the Rajya Sabha within a few months of his retirement, overlooking an (unsubstantiated) allegation of sexual harassment of female staff. These appointments were controversial and resulted in a public debate which, to some extent, dented the respect that many in the legal fraternity had for the Supreme Court.

While public perceptions regarding some judgments may be imaginary (and I believe they are), there is nevertheless an impression of a compromised judiciary rewarded for being on the same page as the government of the day. This impression has become acute since, in the recent past, constitutional cases of seminal importance have been kept in cold storage by the Supreme Court for no apparent reason.[25] Consequently, the Supreme Court has lost the People's Court tag, and is now tagged, to an extent, as an Executivized Court. Is this symptomatic of the falling standards of judicial independence and integrity?

Ethical concerns

The questions that naturally pose themselves are—Why is the judiciary facing criticism (both from the political Executive and some sections of society), and is it warranted? Does it have anything to do with ethical issues or has the calibre of judges declined over the years making them prone to being categorized as 'convenient' or 'inconvenient' judges? Do post-retirement assignments justify allegations of an 'executivized' judiciary? I do not have an answer. It will suffice to say that a judge's greatest strength is public confidence and trust, and every judge should therefore pass that test.

Because the judiciary has been deeply aware of such ethical concerns, the Supreme Court unanimously adopted the Restatement of Values of Judicial Life in 1997, which, among other things, focused on institutionalizing transparency and accountability. However, issues of self-discipline remain unaddressed. One of the lesser-known consequences of the Restatement, followed by the enactment of the Right to Information Act, was a demand that judges must disclose their assets and liabilities and place them in the public domain. Many judges did make such a disclosure, but over time, this lost its importance. We have also witnessed unabashed praise of political leaders by judges of the Supreme Court.[26] Who should discipline judges or make them accountable without compromising on their independence? While reimagining the future of our judiciary, we need to objectively discuss and arrive at some solution on this issue of seminal importance.

The judiciary's role amidst an unprecedented social crisis

The COVID-19 pandemic threw up an entirely different set of challenges for the judiciary. For example, like the political Executive, it was totally unprepared to deal with the 2020 migrants' crisis. Millions of labourers trudged home for several hundred miles, on foot, on cycles, in lorries and in whichever way was possible. Many died on the way, including some who were tragically run over by a train while asleep. Yet, the judiciary did not utilize the PIL channel or the substantial justice route to address their suffering, and Article 21 of the Constitution was inexplicably ignored.

Around the same time, dissenters and protesters were jailed by the government of the day for the flimsiest of reasons and the writ of habeas corpus (literally, produce the body) was not issued. Several persons and political leaders were preventively detained under draconian laws, without a trial or formal charges, for several months. This was extraordinary considering that habeas corpus petitions have always been accorded the highest priority of hearing. In the Hamlyn Lecture 'Freedom under the Law', Lord Denning said: 'Whenever one of the King's judges takes his seat, there is one application which by long tradition has priority over all others. The counsel has but to say, "My Lord, I have an application which concerns the liberty of the subject", and forthwith the judge will put all other matters aside and hear it . . . ' Our courts have not gone so far, but have been quite close in the past.

Equally worrying, journalists and the youth have borne the brunt of draconian laws such as sedition. Even the average citizen is not spared by the political Executive and in many cases, detention is ordered not only for sedition but also for alleged terrorist activities and other activities that are said to be a threat to the sovereignty and integrity of India that warrant preventive detention. With the political Executive occasionally riding roughshod over the fundamental rights of citizens including the right to speech, expression, dissent and protest, it is hoped that the judiciary will stand up to the arbitrariness of the State.

Reimagining the judiciary: structural, procedural and substantive reforms

To reimagine a vibrant judiciary, the concerns discussed in this essay will need to be addressed on a mission mode so that public confidence in the judiciary's impartiality and integrity is fully restored, while the rights of the State and the citizen are appropriately balanced. In this spirit, we need to start at the very beginning.

Overhauling judicial education: Educating judges, both before and during their tenure in office, is of paramount importance. Latent biases are present in everyone, including judges. Recently, the Attorney General for India submitted before the Supreme Court that judges need gender sensitization. This remark was provoked by an unpalatable conclusion arrived at by a high court in a sexual assault case. This is really the tip of the iceberg, for there are instances of judges hinting at a compromise between a rapist and a rape survivor. Can such views be countenanced with any degree of seriousness? Judicial academies need to educate judges not only on issues of law, but also on issues of conduct and case management. The role and responsibilities of our judicial academies must be understood as making good judges better judges. There is a crying need to overhaul judicial education and make it more socially contextual.

Paralegal volunteers: NALSA[27] has trained thousands of paralegal volunteers.[28] They give basic legal assistance to persons usually resident in rural areas and provide a working knowledge of their rights and duties. Sometimes, they take up the cause of such persons when it is difficult for that person to visit the district headquarters or some other government office for redressal of a grievance. They are an extremely useful resource who can contribute to transforming legal literacy and awareness at the grassroots level. As of March 2020, more than 64,000 paralegal volunteers have been trained, but unfortunately, only about 22,000 have been deployed for reasons that are difficult to ascertain. Combined with *gram nyayalayas*, an increase in the deployment of paralegal volunteers can go a long way in reducing the caseload by 50 per cent in the courts.

Court managers: The Thirteenth Finance Commission introduced a significant innovation in court administration by presenting the concept of court managers. They were intended to be persons of ability with a master's in business administration. For reasons unknown, the induction of 'outside' professionals was met with resistance from the existing staff in court registries. Although some high courts did take the initiative in recruiting court managers, the necessary support from judges, officers in the registry and state governments was lacking. This resulted in the idea dying a slow death, the immediate casualty being a better managed judicial administration.

It would be wonderful if the proposal is revived with officers from the registry of the courts deputed to undertake an appropriate course for the benefit of the justice delivery system.

Better support for judges: It is acknowledged that judges across the country are overburdened, primarily due to a massive caseload. Some of it can be distributed among law researchers and interns who are fresh graduates. Having personally benefited from the acumen of several such researchers and interns, it can safely be said that they can make a huge difference. They can brief judges in important constitutional cases and assist them in research for the purposes of judgment writing. Importantly, it gives them a flavour of the justice system from close quarters and assists in building a resource for the future, both academic and practical.

Revamping judicial infrastructure: A study of 665 court complexes has revealed the sorry state of their infrastructure.[29] For example, 100 court complexes had no washrooms for women. Of those that did exist, only 40 per cent were fully functional with running water. The facilities for litigants are much worse. Many courtrooms lack basic facilities such as chairs for litigants, adequate lighting, provision for temperature control and so on. A poor ambience affects productivity and adds to the stress that judges have to tackle. While not all courts are infrastructure deficient, revamping court infrastructure urgently needs a collaborative and concerted effort—a *swachh nyayalaya* approach.

Need to enhance budgetary support for judiciary: In noting the infrastructure budget for the state courts, the Supreme Court noted that Tripura incurred the maximum expenditure at 0.73 per cent of the total state expenditure, while Telangana allocated the lowest (0.30 per cent of the total state expenditure).[30] The India Justice Report 2020[31] concluded that the average national spending of the judiciary between 2011–12 and 2015–16 was 0.08 per cent of the GDP. The consequence of such tight-fistedness and the absence of a conducive work environment leads to a drop in efficiency of judges and the staff, particularly in the district courts, and this in turn has a fairly serious impact on the economy. In 2016 alone, judicial delays cost India around 0.5 per cent of its GDP annually, that is, about Rs 50,000 crore.[32] Overall, it appears to be a case of being penny wise and pound foolish.

Information and communication technology: The eCourts Project is intended to introduce technology in all courts across the country, particularly in district courts. This is to streamline judges' workloads and the court staff so that their output increases, if not their efficiency. Phase II of the project more or less achieved the supply of hardware to all the district courts and prisons across India. It also made significant contributions to developing user-friendly software on free and open source. Among its more remarkable achievements was establishing a National Judicial Data Grid, which gives the essential details of every case pending in the country (other than in the Supreme Court). This was lauded by the World Bank in its Ease of Doing Business report of 2018 wherein it was stated that the grid made it possible to generate case management reports in local courts.

A report by the National Council for Applied Economic Research, provided at the request of the eCommittee of the Supreme Court sometime in 2017 (for internal use), pointed out two 'remedial' steps that needed to be taken. First, the eCourts Project needed to concentrate on training staff and second, greater involvement of lawyers in the crossover process. These shortcomings were brought out quite starkly during the pandemic when many district courts were unable to function despite having the hardware and software only because of inadequate training.

The advantages of technology have not been utilized to their optimum. Today, there cannot be a better and quicker method for the courts to reach the citizen or for the citizen to access the courts and justice. The potential is enormous, and with the availability of video-conferencing facilities, online filing of cases, live streaming of court proceedings, eSewa Kendras and so on, access to justice and indeed, justice delivery, can be revolutionized—as I believe it must be.

Need for expertise in case management: For some inexplicable reason, our justice system does not seem favourably inclined to accept the introduction of managerial expertise in the form of case management and court administration. Reports have been prepared by management institutions of considerable repute that can bring about a sea change in the functioning of our courts, including the Supreme Court, but there appears to be a risk-averse mindset, which places a barrier on moving forward. Notwithstanding this, an attempt was made a couple of years ago to monitor the progress of cases, generically, in the district courts and a 'War Room' was established in the Supreme Court for this purpose. Unfortunately, the outcome of the exercise is not available in the public domain.

Process re-engineering: Most procedural rules relating to the functioning of the courts and their registry were framed several decades ago, and many are now outdated. The progression of cases through the system needs re-engineering, keeping in mind today's realities. How grave the situation is can be gauged from the case of Vishnu Tiwari in the Allahabad High Court, which noted that an appeal filed by him was lying unattended over filing defects for about sixteen years during which period he remained in jail. A filing defect is a minor technical defect rectifiable in a couple of minutes or an hour at most. Ultimately, when his appeal was taken up for consideration due to the efforts of a conscientious lawyer, the high court found him not guilty. These faults lie not in our stars but in our outdated processes. It is worth recalling Lord Devlin: 'If our business methods were as antiquated as our legal system, we would have become a bankrupt nation long back.'

Substantive laws: The preamble to the Gram Nyayalayas Act institutes gram nyayalayas 'at the grassroots level for the purposes of providing access to justice to the citizens at their doorsteps . . .' The law loosely incorporates the idea of mobile courts wherein justice is delivered at the doorstep of the litigant. This would be of enormous benefit to litigants in rural areas, many of whom have small disputes not worth taking to district courts. It is a bold and progressive step in ensuring social justice but has not percolated down to the grassroots. The expectation of the Government of India was that the caseload in the courts would be reduced by about 50 per cent—undoubtedly a significant number.[33] This law needs to be rigorously enforced if doorstep justice is to become a reality.

Institutionalizing mediation and plea bargains: We have some progressive procedural laws in our civil procedure code that provide for an amicable settlement of disputes through mediation and the process of judicial settlement. Several programmes have been held by the Mediation and Conciliation Committee of the Supreme Court to encourage mediation. The Thirteenth Finance Commission also provided Rs 1 crore per district for setting up a mediation centre. Many such centres were indeed established. Yet, mediation has not caught the fancy of the legal fraternity or litigants.[34] It needs aggressive promotion.

Criminal justice reform would be incomplete without implementing the chapter on plea bargaining in our criminal procedure code. Through a plea bargain, an accused person pleads guilty (if she/he has in fact committed a crime) and thereby bargains for a lesser sentence in lieu of a trial. This process has been rather successful in the United States, and very few cases actually go to trial. A pilot project was launched in Delhi to encourage plea bargaining in the district courts, and it was a partial success, but it soon died a quiet death. It has been suggested, anecdotally, that delays in a criminal trial work to the advantage of the accused with witnesses turning hostile and crucial evidence getting 'lost', and therefore they decline to plea bargain.

The only solution to counter delays, I believe, is to lay down strict timelines and adhere to them on pain of imposition of costs. That is perhaps the simplest method of providing speedy justice.

A hard rethink on child rights: Children's rights (who constitute more than 35 per cent of our population) are extremely neglected. There is hardly any reform contemplated with respect to cases pertaining to offences allegedly committed by children and offences against children, including sexual offences. Stakeholder institutions need an overhaul—a revamp is not enough.[35] Every case does not have to go through the court process. For example, the Juvenile Justice (Care and Protection of Children) Act, 2015 recognizes the principle of diversion as a measure 'for dealing with children in conflict with law without resorting to judicial proceedings shall be promoted unless it is in the best interest of the child or the society as a whole.' Adopting this principle can have a salutary effect on justice delivery for children and a positive impact on their life, as they could grow up to become responsible citizens of the country.

Many, many more ideas come to mind, but their articulation will not yield results unless there is a strong will and a stronger commitment to reimagine, reform and transform our justice system.

Conclusion

No doubt, our justice delivery system needs revolutionary systemic, substantive and procedural changes, not merely transformative. These changes must also have philosophical and ethical underpinnings. The Bangalore Principles of Judicial Conduct can be the starting point. They have the approval of almost all judiciaries across the globe. There are six core principles—independence, impartiality, integrity, propriety, equality, and competence and diligence.[36] Measures for their effective implementation have been adopted by the Judicial Integrity Group after intensive and extensive research.[37] We have only to adhere to these principles and faithfully implement them.

Our aim must be to provide justice and access to justice to all in accordance with our Constitution—social, economic and political. Justice for all should not be a slogan, but a reality. The goal is achievable—we have only to rise and stand on the shoulders of giants who came before us and learn our lessons well. The time starts NOW.

The Partisan Role of
Governors in New India

Margaret Alva

Introduction: How the office of the governor emerged

I

Governors have been an integral part of India's administrative system. For centuries, Indian emperors used trusted representatives to control and govern their vast territories. Akbar was the first emperor who systematized provincial administration, dividing his empire into twelve divisions (*subas*) each headed by a provincial governor (*subehdar*), who was expected to maintain peace and order and was hence vested with executive, defence and judicial functions. Realizing that subehdars could become potential opponents, Akbar started appointing two governors in each suba in the thirty-first year of his rule. He also frequently transferred them to ensure greater control over them.

By the charter of 1601, Queen Elizabeth I further institutionalized this system by appointing a governor, who was granted legislative powers to make ordinances and laws as required for the governance of the East India Company. However, after a series of adjustments (namely the Regulating Act of 1773, the transfer of power from the East India Company to the Crown, etc.), the post of governor-general (later styled as the viceroy) was created to administer all the provinces. A direct appointee of the Crown, the governor-general was to oversee all the provincial functionaries except the governors, who were also directly appointed by the Crown. It is important to note that Britain granted exercise of sovereignty to the governor-general and governors. That is why the British government retained tight control over the appointment of governors, not appointing an Indian until 1946,[1] a year before India gained independence. Clearly then, absolute fealty to the overall goals of the British government was paramount. Even when they did risk the appointment of an Indian, the colonial government appointed an Indian in Assam, plus chose someone who was not a career civil servant but rather was the son of the former prime minister of Hyderabad state.

The office of governor under the Indian Constitution is starkly different from that of the provincial governors of the Mughal or British empires. It serves as a crucial link between the Union government and the states and plays a vital role in the 'checks and balances' that the Constitution has provided for the stability of our democracy. However, it is to be remembered that the appointment of governors is a political act. Although they are appointed by the President of India, governors are identified and placed by prime ministers (after due consultations with coalition partners, cabinet colleagues, the party leadership and political advisers). For a long time, governors were appointed because of their suitability to function as the primary custodians of India's constitutional values. Consequently, only such people were selected who could function impartially, and above partisan politics.

To a large extent, adherence to this unstated principle is contingent on the commitment of the prime minister and the ruling dispensation to India's Constitution. If the Union government is driven by partisan considerations, the governors they select could be tasked to monitor and interfere in an elected government's functioning. Alternatively, union governments also appoint senior party members as governors either as a reward for their years of service or to circumscribe their political ambitions/possibility of dissent.

II

After the Government of India Act, 1935, came into force, the Congress Party won elections in six provincial legislatures in 1937. Yet, it decided to assume office only if the governors appointed by the colonial government did not interfere in the functioning of elected assemblies. Nonetheless, there was inevitably some friction, and that experience substantively shaped the thinking of India's founders on what a governor should be and more importantly, should not be. The role of governors was consequently extensively debated by the Constituent Assembly and by the Committee on Provincial Constitution under the chairmanship of Sardar Vallabhbhai Patel.[2] Stalwarts such as Dr P.S. Deshmukh, T.T. Krishnamachari, H.V. Kamath, Pandit H.N. Kunzru, Alladi Krishnaswamy Ayyar, Rohini Kumar Chaudhary, Shibban Lal Saxena, K.M. Munshi and Dr B.R. Ambedkar debated the roles, functions and limitations of governors in great detail. Their understanding was that the proposed Constitution was creating 'responsible governments' in the states as much as at the Centre—that is, responsible to the respective legislatures alone. As Dr Ambedkar posited, 'I have no doubt in my mind that discretionary power is in no sense a negation of responsible government'.[3] He would go on to argue that 'it (draft Article 143) is not a general clause giving the governor the power to disregard the advice of his ministers in any matter in which he finds he ought to disregard'.[4] Likewise, Krishna Chandra Sharma would argue that 'it is an impossible proposition that a Minister could ever be responsible to the Governor as distinguished from his responsibility to the people through the majority in the legislature'.[5] Clearly, in this understanding, states were sovereign within their own domain and discretionary power beyond the specific situations mentioned in the Constitution did not authorize a governor to override state governments.

Seized with balancing the twin imperatives of disseminating constitutional morality throughout India and integrating the states into a functional union, Prime Minister Jawaharlal Nehru would go on to posit that a governor should be 'acceptable to the government of the province and that he/she must not be known to be a part of the party machine of the province'.[6] For this reason, he opposed elections to the position of the governor, since that would entail the governor being from a political party. He argued that even though the appointment of the governor by the President 'would add a close link between the Centre and the provinces, the Governor is primarily the head of the state and not an agent of the Central Government'.[7] This mirrored Mahatma Gandhi's stance who had argued much earlier that 'whilst I would resent much power of interference to be given to Governors, I do not think that they should be mere figureheads. They should have enough power enabling them to influence ministerial policy for the better. In their detached position they would be able to see things in their proper perspective and thus prevent mistakes by their Cabinets. *Theirs must be an all-pervasive moral influence in their provinces*'[8] (emphasis added). To summarize, in the minds of India's founding fathers and mothers, governors were primarily supposed to safeguard the Indian Republic's core values, as enshrined in the Constitution. This is most accurately captured by C. Rajagopalachari's exhortation to governors when he urged them to 'develop your influence for good and . . . find means for achieving it without friction and without prejudice to the march of democracy'.[9]

These debates shaped the roles, functions and responsibilities of governors very significantly. Two overriding factors that India's founders were constantly considering were Partition and the secessionist demands. They were seized of integrating India into one whole and staving off the possible Balkanization of the nation. The office of governor was to play a crucial role in keeping centrifugal forces at bay and nudging states to integrate more deeply with the Union of India.

That is why governors of states are appointed by the President of India, who they are accountable to, and hold their office during the 'pleasure of the President'.[10] However, in actuality, the governor is the Union government's appointee, and in so far as she/he acts at their discretion, is answerable to the Union government. She/he is to function as a communication channel between Union and states, drive states to imbibe and follow constitutional values (which post-Independence, were still not widely accepted) and keep the Union government informed about what is happening in the states.

Despite these functions, India's founders ensured that a governor is neither an employee of the Union government, nor an agent of the ruling dispensation. In their wisdom, they especially ensured that the governor was not required to subscribe to the dictates of political parties. Frankly, given the Indian National Congress (Congress Party) commanded brute majorities in the Centre and many states, this decision (to not make a governor's office subordinate or subservient to the Government of India) in the national interest was remarkably sagacious and visionary.

Accordingly, the Constitution of India also assigns a dual role to a governor. It envisages that the governor shall serve as the head of a state and vests executive power in the position. Like India's President, a governor therefore enjoys certain specific powers to preserve, protect and defend the Constitution and the law (as stipulated under Article 159). These include:

1. Legislative: affiliated with ordinance-making and state legislatures
2. Executive: affiliated with administrative appointments and discharges

3. Judicial: affiliated with power to grant pardons and respites
4. Financial: authority over the state budget and money bills
5. Discretionary: to be exercised at the discretion of the governor

At the same time, the Constitution also provides that a council of ministers headed by the chief minister shall 'aid and advise the governor'. Article 163 says that the governor must act as per the advice of the council of ministers, but 'except in so far as he is by or under this Constitution required to exercise his functions or any of them in his discretion'. As the constitutional head of the state, the governor thus has 'a right to be consulted, to warn and encourage' but his role is overwhelmingly that of 'a friend, philosopher and guide' to the council of ministers.[11]

These dual responsibilities provide us with a clear picture of the role of the governor. He is expected to function as per the advice of the council of ministers and yet, use his discretion judiciously. This latter function is most applicable in the appointment of the chief minister. Article 164 (1) of India's Constitution empowers the governor to appoint the chief minister. However, like the discretion of the President in the appointment of the prime minister, the governor's discretion in the appointment of the chief minister is conditioned by the essentials of a parliamentary form of government, which makes the council of ministers collectively responsible to the state's legislative assembly. It is the leader of the largest party who is eligible for appointment as chief minister, and the governor is duty-bound to request him/her to form the government. If there is no party commanding a clear majority in the legislative assembly, the governor may exercise his/her discretion in the appointment of the chief minister according to their personal assessment of the situation at that time. Needlessly to say, she/he must act according to established democratic norms and protocols. As the Sarkaria Commission[12] succinctly put it, the governor's task 'is to see that a government is formed and not to try to form a government', the latter of which many governors are doing to this day.

The moral collapse of the office of the governor

Unfortunately, there has been a steady decline in the public perception of governors over the last few decades, the reasons for which need to be analysed. The office and many decisions of governors across the country, rooted in the unconstitutional, have attracted controversy and judicial interventions. Today, India is rife with avoidable controversies around how governors have selected chief ministers; about how they have determined the timing for proving legislative majority; or how they have demanded information about day-to-day administration, and even delayed giving assent to bills or reserved bills for the President's assent; on how they have commented adversely on specific policies of the state government and exercised their powers as chancellors of state universities. There is a yawning gap between how governors ought to conduct themselves in theory, and what they are actually doing today. Raj Bhawans have unfortunately been reduced to partisan offices. Sadly, some governors no longer conduct themselves in a manner befitting the constitutional head of a state.

For example, it is no secret that the governor and the chief minister of West Bengal are at loggerheads. The governor frequently behaves like a politician rather than a constitutional head of the state. Constantly attacking the state government, issuing partisan statements to the media and making unverified claims does not behove the office of a governor. It is not for the governor, any governor, to behave like a party spokesperson. Such conduct is both unconstitutional and unethical.

India has also been witness to the Union government repeatedly misusing governors to interfere in the functioning of state governments and dismiss elected governments to install governments of their choice. Some of the more prominent instances where the power of the governor was misused include the 2016 Arunachal Pradesh episode,[13] when the governor brought forward the session of the assembly so that the motion brought by eleven Bharatiya Janata Party (BJP) legislators for the removal of the Speaker and subsequently, removal of the ruling Congress government, could be taken up. The unprecedented session was conducted in a hotel room and a majority Congress government was dismissed. The Supreme Court, however, restored the Congress government and in its verdict[14] clearly said that while it is only the governor who may summon the legislative assembly, it is only on the advice of the council of ministers and not suo moto. It labelled the governor's move in Arunachal Pradesh as 'grossly unconstitutional' and rebuked the governor for the excesses in the use of discretion. In doing so, the governor flouted an earlier Supreme Court order, which said that 'if the Governor is found to have exercised the power himself without being advised by the Government or if the Governor transgresses the jurisdiction in exercising the same . . . [then] the Governor has passed the order on some extraneous consideration'.[15]

In the same year, the then chief minister of Uttarakhand moved the Supreme Court after the Union government dismissed the then Congress government and imposed President's rule after nine Congress legislators sided with the BJP on a bill. The Supreme Court subsequently quashed the arbitrarily imposed President's rule.[16]

Similarly, in 2017, the assembly elections to Goa saw the Congress and Nationalist Congress Party (NCP) winning eighteen of the forty seats to emerge as the single largest alliance, needing only three more for a majority. The BJP had thirteen (well short of a majority) with the remaining ten seats in the forty-member assembly going to other parties and independents. Yet, the governor first called and eventually appointed a BJP-led coalition with the Maharashtrawadi Gomantak Party (MGP), which had three seats, the Goa Forward Party with three seats and three other independents. The then governor shockingly admitted in an interview that she took the advice of a senior Union minister in this matter.[17] This is constitutional impropriety of the highest degree.

When this was challenged in the Supreme Court, the then Chief Justice of India astoundingly advised the Congress Party to hold a dharna before the governor instead of approaching the court.[18] Effectively, the CJI's oral advice was that parties should race to the Raj Bhawan and conduct a dharna in case of an unexpected outcome. Even though the Supreme Court ordered a floor test, the result was ultimately a foregone conclusion, since the court did not choose to act against the original sin, that is of the governor calling a smaller party first, and indirectly enabling that party to secure a majority. That particular oral observation also implies that government formation is on a first-come-first-served basis, which negates the entire principle of an electoral democracy.

Similarly, the Manipur assembly election results in 2017 saw the Congress win twenty-eight seats and the BJP twenty-one seats. Even though the single largest party in the legislature of sixty seats was the Congress, the BJP was given the first invitation by the governor, and it went on to form the government in the state. Constitutionally, it was incumbent on the governors of Goa and Manipur to first ask the single largest party if it was in a position to form the government. Instead, not only did the governors invite a smaller party (the BJP) to form a government (even though it was not in a pre-poll alliance), they also facilitated a situation whereby the BJP could cobble together a coalition by ignoring the claim of the largest coalition. The governors did not conduct themselves as neutral arbitrators, instead, they acted as party agents.

In stark contrast, after the results of the Karnataka assembly elections were announced in 2018, though the alliance of Congress and the Janata Dal (Secular) won a clear majority, the Karnataka governor invited the single largest party (BJP) to form the government and even allowed Yediyurappa to take oath as the chief minister. The Supreme Court ultimately ordered a floor test, which the BJP government lost.

Perhaps the most bizarre and blatant misuse of the governor's office was after the Maharashtra assembly election results in 2019.

The alliance of Shiv Sena-NCP-Congress had a clear majority to form the government. Yet, President's rule was imposed in the state to delay the formation of a government by the Shiv Sena-led alliance. After a few days, the governor violated all rules when he recommended the lifting of President's rule in Maharashtra abruptly and administered the oath of office to the BJP chief ministerial candidate in secret, late at night. Although this bizarre political gymnastics did not come to fruition since the Shiv Sena-led alliance ultimately proved its majority on the floor of the House, this episode diminished the office of the governor. In this case also, it took the intervention of a special bench of the Supreme Court to resolve the issue.

In doing so, the Maharashtra governor flouted another Supreme Court verdict,[19] which explicitly states in paragraph 17 that 'when it is time for installation of a new government after fresh elections, the act of the Governor in recommending dissolution of the assembly should be *only with the sole object of preservation of the Constitution and not promotion of the political interest of one or the other party*' (emphasis added). The governor also violated the directives laid down in the famous *S.R. Bommai vs Union of India* (1994) case, which cautioned against the frequent use of Article 356 (which allows the President, on receipt of a report from the governor of the state, to impose President's rule) to remove state governments run by opposition parties. S.R. Bommai has become a yardstick for all Union and state governments, and it is noteworthy that the imposition of President's rule fell drastically from sixty-three instances between 1971 to 1992, to just twenty-seven between 1991 and 2010. This has deepened India's federal structure to a significant extent.

Likewise, there are many other instances where the Union government has insidiously misused the offices of governors to engineer the collapse/dismissal of elected governments and interfere in the governance of states. Below are listed just a few of them.

Karnataka	May 2017	Governor Vajubhai Vala invited the BJP as the single largest party to form the government, ignoring the claims of the Congress-JD(S) post-poll alliance. The governor also appointed K.G. Bopaiah as the pro tem Speaker for the floor test when the BJP had to prove majority. This was wrong by precedence because the senior-most MLA is supposed to be appointed as the pro tem Speaker, who in this case was from the Congress.	'Karnataka Floor Test: Why Congress and JD(S) Opposed K.G. Bopaiah's Appointment as Pro Tem Speaker', News18, 19 May 2018 (https://www.news18.com/news/politics/why-congress-and-jds-oppose-kg-bopaiahs-appointment-as-pro-tem-speaker-1752719.html; last accessed on 28 November 2021).
Maharashtra	November 2019	Governor B.S. Koshyari invited Devendra Fadnavis of the BJP to form the government even though the majority was with the Shiv Sena-NCP-Congress alliance. Fadnavis was sworn-in in the early hours of 9 November in a secret ceremony. The governor did all this without ordering a floor test, which the Sarkaria Commission recommended and the *S.R. Bommai vs. Union of India* case (1994) reaffirmed. It took the Supreme Court's direction for a floor test to be sanctioned, but before it could be conducted, the BJP resigned since it could not muster a majority in the assembly.[20]	'What is the Governor's role if elections produce fractured verdicts?', K. Venkatramanan, *The Hindu*, 1 December 2019 (https://www.thehindu.com/news/national/what-is-the-governors-role-if-elections-produce-fractured-verdicts/article30124436.ece; last accessed on 28 November 2021).

Jammu and Kashmir	November 2018	Governor Satya Pal Malik dissolved the state assembly, even though the Peoples' Democratic Party–Congress Party–National Conference alliance had the requisite numbers to form a stable government. It is now clear that this was done to enable the abrogation of Article 370, which would have been impeded had J & K had an assembly at the time of abrogation.	'Plan for Grand Coalition in J & K Prompts Governor to Dissolve Assembly', *The Wire*, 22 November 2018 (https://thewire.in/politics/plan-for-grand-coalition-in-jk-prompts-governor-to-dissolve-assembly; last accessed on 28 November 2021).
Jammu and Kashmir	July 2019	Governor Satya Pal Malik insinuated that militants should kill politicians of Kashmir by arguing: 'These boys who have picked up guns are killing their own people, they are killing PSOs [personal security officers] and SPOs [special police officers]. Why are you killing them? Kill those who have looted the wealth of Kashmir. Have you killed any of them?'	'Kill Those Who Looted Kashmir, Not Innocent People: J & K Governor Satya Pal Malik', PTI, 22 July 2019 (https://thewire.in/politics/jk-governor-militants; last accessed on 28 November 2021).
Manipur	March 2017	Governor Najma Heptullah did not follow due procedure by calling the single largest party i.e., Congress, to form the government, but instead the governor appointed a BJP coalition.	'Emergence of mercenary politics in Manipur', the *New Indian Express*, 25 October 2021 (https://www.newindianexpress.com/opinions/2021/oct/25/emergence-of-mercenary-politics-in-manipur-2375273.html; last accessed on 29 November 2021).
Bihar	July 2017	Governor Keshari Nath Tripathi ignored the claims of the single largest party and appointed a Janata Dal (United)–BJP government after chief minister and JD(U) leader Nitish Kumar severed ties with the Lalu Prasad-led Rashtriya Janata Dal (RJD) and the Congress.	'Political tool', Purnima Tripathi, *Frontline* (https://frontline.thehindu.com/cover-story/article24440290.ece; last accessed on 28 November 2021).

West Bengal	July 2019 onwards	Governor Jagdeep Dhankar has engaged in unparliamentary behaviour unbecoming of a governor, accusing the state government of ignoring him and not paying proper respect to rushing to Jadavpur University when BJP leader Babul Supriyo made allegations of an attack on him. He also kept raising a public outcry about the 'deteriorating' law and order situation in West Bengal, just prior to the assembly elections.	'On the loose: On West Bengal Governor Jaideep Dhankar', *The Hindu*, 22 July 2020 (https://www.thehindu.com/opinion/editorial/on-the-loose-on-west-bengal-governor-jaideep-dhankar/article32154141.ece; last accessed on 29 November 2021).
Puducherry	December 2019	The Madras High Court had to intervene asking the Puducherry lieutenant governor (LG), Kiran Bedi, to abstain from interfering in the day-to-day functioning of the elected government. In doing so, the high court also set aside two communications of the Union government, which elevated the powers of the lieutenant governor and actively facilitated interference in the government's functioning. When the LG did not stop, the Puducherry chief minister, V. Narayanaswamy, was driven to write to President Ram Nath Kovind requesting that the 'autocratic' LG be removed.	'Puducherry L-G Kiran Bedi can't interfere in govt's daily affairs, says Madras High Court', ThePrint, 30 April 2019 (https://theprint.in/judiciary/puducherry-l-g-kiran-bedi-cant-interfere-in-govts-daily-affairs-says-madras-high-court/229301/; last accessed on 29 November 2021).

Delhi	Since 2015	Delhi's lieutenant governor and chief minister have been at loggerheads on several issues including the appointment of the chief of the Anti-Corruption Bureau, the appointment of secretaries in various departments and even a CBI raid on the chief minister's office.	'DCW chief appointment new flashpoint in Jung-Kejriwal tussle', *India Today*, 22 July 2015 (https://www.indiatoday.in/india/story/dcw-chief-appointment-new-flashpoint-jung-kejriwal-tussle-284026-2015-07-22; last accessed on 29 November 2021); 'Delhi-Centre tussle: SC delivers split verdict on power to appoint and transfer civil servants', *The Scroll*, 14 February 2019 (https://scroll.in/latest/913211/delhi-centre-tussle-sc-delivers-split-verdict-on-power-to-appoint-and-transfer-civil-servants; last accessed on 29 November 2021); 'CBI raids 14 locations in Delhi, UP including Arvind Kejriwal's office', *Mid-Day*, 15 December 2015 (https://www.mid-day.com/news/india-news/article/cbi-raids-14-locations-in-delhi--up-including-arvind-kejriwals-office-16774176; last accessed on 28 November 2021).
Meghalaya	March 2018	Despite not being the single largest party, Governor Ganga Prasad invited Conrad Sangma of the National People's Party (NPP) to prove his majority. Sangma's NPP eventually formed an alliance with the BJP (and other smaller parties) to form the government in the state.	'Meghalaya: Conrad Sangma says governor invited him to form govt, swearing in on Tuesday', *Hindustan Times*, 5 March 2018 (https://www.hindustantimes.com/india-news/meghalaya-conrad-sangma-says-governor-invited-him-to-form-govt-swearing-in-on-tuesday/story-WcJnxhloQ6EICIHOp1PTiI.html; last accessed on 29 November 2021).

Kerala	January 2020	Governor Arif Mohammad Khan hit out against the Pinarayi Vijayan government after it challenged the controversial Citizenship (Amendment) Act or CAA in the Supreme Court, saying 'common courtesy demanded that prior permission' should have been taken from him.	'Political Tussle Between Kerala Government and Governor Heats Up', *Newsclick*, 18 January 2020 (https://www.newsclick.in/political-tussle-between-kerala-government-governor-heats-Up; last accessed on 28 November 2021).
Rajasthan	July 2020	Governor Kalraj Mishra repeatedly turned down the advice of the council of ministers to convene a session of the Rajasthan Assembly, insisting on a twenty-one-day notice, demanding to know the purpose of calling it, and putting other conditions. This was to prevent the Ashok Gehlot government from proving its majority on the floor of the House.	'Why are questions being raised about the actions of Rajasthan Governor Kalraj Mishra?', *The Hindu*, 2 August 2021 (https://www.thehindu.com/news/national/the-hindu-explains-why-are-questions-being-raised-about-the-actions-of-rajasthan-governor-kalraj-mishra/article32249795.ece; last accessed on 28 November 2021).

It is abundantly clear that in all these instances, the governors of the states were partial towards the original party they came from, namely, the BJP. In case after case, they twisted the people's mandate and adopted contradictory positions that were both unconstitutional and illegal to benefit the BJP. The most obvious reading from this is that the BJP government at the Centre misuses governors to impose BJP governments on states by ignoring the people's will and bulldozing opposition parties. But a deeper reading reveals a deep structural fault line that will have grave implications for the future of India's federalism. The father of India's Constitution had famously warned us that 'however good a Constitution may be, if those who are implementing it are not good, it will prove to be bad'. That is the very real worry we face today. Unlike previously, the people being selected as governors today are selected precisely because they are malleable and unconcerned about constitutional proprieties.

The accelerated politicization of governors

India's Constitution makes no provision for the impeachment of governors, which signifies that they should normally hold office for their full term of five years. This was to ensure stability and freedom from any partisan considerations, so they can steer the ship of the respective states they head in the constitutional direction. As former President A.P.J. Kalam said, '. . . the office of the Governor has been bestowed with the independence to rise above the day-to-day politics and override compulsions either emanating from the central system or the state system'.[21] They may resign for personal reasons or (more often) under pressure from the Union government. Although governors are expected to complete a five-year term 'at the pleasure of the President', this constitutional norm has now been replaced by the current convention of 'at the pleasure of the prime minister'—a practice that is becoming the rule. Making governors unstable breeds insecurity, for they would be that much more malleable to partisan considerations. That in part explains the behaviour of governors, who are crawling when they were asked to walk, simply to please the central leadership in hopes of continuance. This insecurity was deliberately institutionalized by the BJP soon after assuming office in 2014. The Modi government quickly removed governors appointed by the United Progressive Alliance (UPA) government, so that they could appoint governors of 'their own'. Several governors expressed displeasure at their unceremonious removal, citing the Supreme Court's observations that governors cannot be removed whimsically (in the case of *B.P. Singhal vs Union of India*). That judgment is worth quoting at length. The Supreme Court held that 'though no reason need be assigned for discontinuance of the pleasure (of the President) resulting in removal, the power under article 156 (1) cannot be exercised in an arbitrary, capricious or unreasonable manner'. The court further held that 'a Governor cannot be removed on the ground that he/she is out of sync with the policies and ideologies of the Union government or the party in power at the Centre. Nor can he/she be removed on the ground that the Union government has lost confidence in him/her. It follows therefore, that change in government at the Centre is not a ground for removal of Governors holding office, to make way for others favoured by the new government'.

This judgment mirrors the Sarkaria Commission (1988) recommendations that governors must not be removed before completion of their five-year tenure, except in rare and compelling circumstances. Additionally, if such a rare and compelling circumstance did exist, the commission said, the procedure of removal must allow the governors an opportunity to explain their conduct, and the Union government must give fair consideration to such an explanation. This was meant to provide governors with a measure of security of tenure, so they could carry out their constitutional duties without fear or favour.

Similarly, the Venkatachaliah Commission (2002) also recommended that ordinarily, governors should be allowed to complete their five-year term. If they have to be removed before the completion of their term, the Union government should do so only after consultation with the chief minister of the state. In fact, the Punchhi Commission[22] (2010) went so far as to suggest that the phrase 'during the pleasure of the President' should be deleted from the Constitution, because a governor should not be removed at the will of the Union government. Instead, he or she should be removed only by a resolution of the state legislature.

The BJP has ridden roughshod over these numerous commissions and Supreme Court judgments that minutely scrutinized the actions of governors in the 1960s and 1970s. Through trial and error, these commissions and judgments forged a functional consensus on the role of governors and established conventions to be followed. The Administrative Reforms Commission of 1968, the Rajamanar Committee of 1969, the Committee of Governors of 1971, the Bangalore Seminar of Experts of 1983 and most importantly, the Sarkaria Commission of 1988, made extremely valuable recommendations to make the office of the governor the 'linchpin of the Constitutional apparatus of the state'. They all also agreed that the image of governors as mere agents of the Centre sitting in state capitals and seeking an opportunity to run down state governments being run by parties different to the party ruling at the Centre, or trying to engineer a government of the same party as at the Centre, would deform our federalism and destroy democracy. Interestingly, at one point, the BJP along with the Left Front government of West Bengal had also agreed with this assessment. They had jointly recommended that the appointment of governors should be made from a panel prepared by the state legislature and that the actual appointing authority should be the Inter-state Council, and not the Union government.

Yet today, the BJP has ignored the wisdom of India's founders and the experiences of the past seventy years. In doing so, the BJP has effectively undone seventy years of progress and seriously impaired the integrity of the nation. After about a quarter of a century (1990–2014) of relative calm, the governor's role and powers have again become a controversial issue in Indian politics. The governor is now perceived to be an agent of the Centre. This is in stark violation of PM Nehru's exhortation that governors should 'represent before the public someone slightly above the party'.[23] This, of course, coincides with the appearance of a single party with a comfortable majority at the Centre.

The good that governors can do

Looking beyond the unfortunate reality of today, governors can spearhead numerous initiatives that enhance the peoples' welfare and deepen federal principles. Speaking from personal experience, there is tremendous scope for governors to serve their states, by being instruments for creating harmony and goodwill and by serving as an informal link between the government and the people. Appointed by the UPA government in 2009, I continued to be governor even under the BJP government. I served as governor of four Congress- and BJP-run states, with no problems in performing my duties.

Steering clear of partisan politics, I focused on responding to the needs of the people in natural calamities by mobilizing funds, material and medicines and ensuring their quick and fair distribution. I also visited jails and hostels, interacting with inmates to redress their grievances. Similarly, attending local cultural events (often unannounced) helped me understand and appreciate local customs and traditions better.

I also strongly felt that Raj Bhawans needed to shed some vestigial colonial practices like motorcades, salutes and excessive security. Over-staffed and cut off from the reality outside their closed gates, governors and Raj Bhawans need greater openness and accessibility to the citizens. That was why I tried to ensure that my doors were always open to all, and I tried to help anyone I could. We consciously organized various celebrations commemorating

Women's Day, Children's Day, Raksha Bandhan, Holi, Diwali, Eid and Christmas. Apart from reinforcing the constitutional principle that governors are for and with all, irrespective of caste, creed, class and gender, such events (which may seem meaningless to the unconscientious observer) also sensitized my staff and officials to the plight of the poor, vulnerable and historically disadvantaged like street children, orphans, etc. We also hosted a wide range of experts, activists and stakeholders at these events. Having served in many governments, I believe that unless those who administer the law are constantly reminded of the socio-economic realities of India, they begin to operate in a bubble. Governance then becomes divorced from the needs and aspirations of the people. Although it is ultimately the duty of an elected government (and politicians) to be responsive to peoples' concerns, governors can play a subtle role in gently reminding them and guests to the state of Mahatma Gandhi's talisman—'Whenever you are in doubt, or when the self becomes too much with you, apply the following test. Recall the face of the poorest and the weakest man [woman] whom you may have seen, and ask yourself, if the step you contemplate is going to be of any use to him [her]. Will he [she] gain anything by it? Will it restore him [her] to a control over his [her] own life and destiny? In other words, will it lead to swaraj [freedom] for the hungry and spiritually starving millions? Then you will find your doubts and your self melt away'.[24]

Additionally, governors enjoy wide-ranging powers under the Fifth and Sixth Schedules of the Constitution, which most of them fail to exercise either because of ignorance or diffidence. Some state governments are wary of governors exercising these powers vested in them by the Constitution for the protection of tribal populations, frequently for considerations that are not people-centric. Although there has been considerable debate as well as litigation on whether or not the powers conferred upon the governor by the Fifth Schedule can be exercised without explicit sanction from the state government (and whether governors are bound by the advice of the Union government), the courts have held[25] that the governor, while exercising his/her powers under the Fifth Schedule, is not bound by the aid and advice of the council of ministers and must exercise the function independently. This is important since governors have rule-making powers regarding the Tribal Advisory Council's composition and functioning, the powers to restrict the application of any Union or state legislation to Scheduled Areas, and make regulations (including amendment or repeal of any Union/state legislation) for 'peace and good government of Scheduled Areas'. To put it simply, governors can genuinely use their powers to make a meaningful impact in Scheduled Areas and help ensure Adivasis, De-notified Tribes and forest dwellers can achieve fullness of life.

Yet, an official committee[26] found that governors have failed to use their powers and 'remained oblivious about the state of the tribal people. Even the mandatory annual Reports by the Governors to the President regarding the administration of Scheduled Areas under Para 3 of the Fifth Schedule are irregular. They comprise largely a stale narrative of departmental programmes without even an allusion to the crucial issues in administration, the main thrust of the Fifth Schedule'. Consequently, despite their powers to restrict anti-people legislations, governors are oblivious to the abuse of the Forest Conservation Act, 1980, and its attendant Forest Policy Act of 1988 against forest dwellers and Adivasis.

Bucking the trend, as governor of Rajasthan, which has large tracts dominated by Adivasis, I used my powers to infuse new life into development schemes and ensured their proper utilization. I also established a special cell in the Raj Bhawan with its own building and staff, solely for monitoring budget allocations, and stopped diversion/misuse. Consequently, Adivasi hostels, toilets and bicycles, especially for girls, received special attention. I was greatly aided in understanding exactly what Adivasis wanted because of my frequent visits and meetings with local officials and Adivasi leaders. My interventions slowly but surely pushed the government to act.

Based on my experiences, I even presented a special report with suggestions for corrective measures at the bi-annual Conference of Governors. Widely appreciated, a special committee of governors was created to follow up on the points I had raised. Two meetings were held in Rajasthan and Maharashtra, and even a blueprint of action by governors was created. But then, the winds shifted, and the new government decided to go another way. Today, the Union government has established a National Tribal Advisory Council under the chairmanship of the prime minister.[27] This council illegally usurps the powers of the governors, the National Commission for Scheduled Tribes (NCST), the Ministry of Tribal Affairs and Tribal Advisory Councils in the states. This has not only destroyed federal principles, but also led to the accelerated diversion of forest and Adivasi land for myopic commercial projects.

Conclusion

While every nation passes through different stages of growth and decay (social, political and cultural), there are some values that must remain constant. India's constitutional framework has laid down a set of principles and goalposts that every government (Union and state) is morally obligated to follow. Furthermore, they must strictly adhere to the institutional protocols and practices that have evolved over the past seventy years. Unless every government (and by extension, political parties) conforms to these principles and protocols, it will be impossible to neutrally adjudicate between India's vast diversities—religious, linguistic, regional, caste, gender, etc. In fact, it is because India is so heterogeneous that our founding leaders consciously adopted federalism as a sine qua non. It was felt that multiple levels of adjudication must be established to institutionalize the widest possible arena for India's diverse interests to negotiate with each other and evolve a consensus on how to move forward, together. That is why the Union, state and urban local bodies/panchayats enjoy legislative, administrative and financial powers in their respective spheres. All these different governance units must work collaboratively and consensually. They are a conjoined union committed to ushering in a constitutional social revolution (which is why the Preamble's first line says that India is a Union of States).

As constitutional statesmen, governors are key to ensuring an objective adjudication among these different units. The manner in which they exercise their responsibilities has a direct impact on Union–state relations. That is why they must nudge all the governing institutions of the State to adhere to constitutional values and governance practices. They need to do so especially because political parties, naturally driven by partisan considerations, may occasionally tend to be disruptive (especially in the heat of elections). That is why a steady hand is needed, both at the Union and state levels, to always keep the boat steady. The President and governors cannot ever be motivated by political considerations. Their pole star must remain the national interest, which is determined solely by the Constitution. That is precisely why our founding leaders insisted that governors should be 'eminent people, sometimes people who have not taken too great a part in politics'.[28]

Governors are not meant to wield significant powers relating to the governance of states. Despite the powers they hold and the constitutional immunity they enjoy, they must restrain themselves. Governance is the job of the elected government, and the governor should always be available as an adviser. She/he should be a friend, philosopher and guide and ensure that the people are served. Both the Union government and governors must remember that governors simply cannot act against or without the advice of the council of ministers. As head of the Executive in a state, they are duty-bound to work with and on the advice of the elected government. If it is ever difficult for any governor to remember this, they must recall that in our federal polity, governors have to discharge a 'dual responsibility' to the Union and the state,[29] and all governments (Union and state) and political parties have to strictly adhere to this.[30]

Article 163 of India's Constitution does carve out an exception wherein the governor has some discretionary powers. Yet, even in exercising discretionary powers, governors must remember that those powers are granted for exceptional circumstances, such as the rare case of a complete breakdown of a state's constitutional machinery. These powers are to be used judiciously, and not used myopically in the appointment of a chief minister, or in calling for a floor test, or to interfere in the functioning of elected governments, or while considering legislation/policies. Lastly, governors should not seize statutory powers for themselves, nor should the Union government be ready to confer them merely to needle an opposition party in office in a state.

Sadly, today the office of the governor is being openly politicized and misused. In appointing partisan people beholden to the prime minister (and not the Constitution), the Modi government has unleashed havoc, not just on India's states and union territories but also on the nation. As things stand today, governors are not constitutional statesmen but unconstitutional hitmen. They are being insidiously used to undermine India's federalism. It is important to safeguard constitutional institutions and the Constitution, to ensure that future generations inherit a free, democratic, liberal India. I hope and pray that the people of India, their representatives and the courts will speak up and do what is right.

Election Commission: The Bedrock of a Democracy

Ashok Lavasa

Introduction

'*Many forms of Government have been tried, and will be tried in this world of sin and woe. No one pretends that democracy is perfect or all-wise. Indeed it has been said that democracy is the worst form of Government except for all those other forms that have been tried from time to time,*' said Winston Churchill on 11 November 1947, a few days after India gained independence and two years before it 'solemnly resolved to constitute' itself into a 'sovereign, democratic republic' on 26 November 1949. Despite scepticism of its survivability, India is one of the few nations that has persevered as a democracy (contrary to the experience of many nations that gained freedom from colonialism but collapsed into theocracies, autocracies and even failed states). Indubitably, the world has seen India as a beacon of democracy worth emulating and partnering with. In a large measure, India's global stature is predicated on the fact that she has managed to prosper economically while being a stable democracy.

A vital component of a functioning democracy is free and fair elections, which India has by and large adhered to scrupulously.

Elections in India are not periodic political events; they have a cultural and moral dimension because Indians firmly believe that their vote contributes to shaping their own, and the nation's, future. They deliberate, cogitate and even fight before casting their vote. That they are able to freely do so at every level—national, state, district and village—is because of the manner in which elections have been conducted.

The Election Commission of India (ECI or EC) has facilitated the operation of India's constitutional democracy by conducting and supervising elections in India for the past seven decades. The ECI came into being on 25 January 1950, a day before India's Constitution became effective.[1] The framers of India's Constitution realized that the institution to oversee the election of a democratic government must precede the provision for one in the Constitution. While it is true that democracy is much more than the successful conduct of elections, it cannot be denied that a bold EC committed to its constitutional charter of conducting free and fair elections is essential for a democracy to have a stable foundation.

Election Commission of India

The foresight that went into the creation of the ECI, its evolution over the years from a mere constitutional apparatus to an effective watchdog, the many methods evolved by it to regulate the conduct of free and fair elections, the professional manner in which it has conducted 17 Lok Sabha, 386 Vidhan Sabha and numerous other elections, has been applauded by political parties, neutral observers and people alike. And for good reason.

Of late it has been argued by many that an organization hailed as a 'gold standard' has lost a lot of its glitter and guts. Those who have critically studied the growth of the EC argue that this independent and powerful body is like a mechanical clock needing periodic winding in order to perform. With the passage of time and the unchecked rise in political ambition, it was left to conscientious individuals occupying the high office of Chief Election Commissioner (CEC) to 'wind' the organization so it could not only keep pace with powerful politicians out to manipulate the electoral process but also check their vaulting ambition in an amoral pursuit of power. Several strong-willed and committed individuals built the ECI's image and earned the confidence of the people. They were aided by the growing polarization in national politics and close electoral contests, which led political parties to seek comfort in being supervised at the hustings by a neutral umpire.

Electoral reforms

The vicissitude in the effectiveness and the image of the EC notwithstanding, the need for electoral reforms has been at the forefront of every debate on the quality of Indian democracy. India has often been characterized as a 'weak' democracy and was recently downgraded to a 'flawed' one as per the 2022 Democracy Index's global ranking according to the Economist Intelligence Unit (EIU). Out of 167 countries, the Democracy Index classified 23 countries as full democracies, 52 as flawed democracies, 35 as hybrid regimes and 57 as authoritarian regimes. India has been classified as a 'flawed democracy' along with countries such as the US, France, Belgium and Brazil. What has, however, not been emphasized enough is that institutions draw as much power from the letter of the law empowering them as the spirit of the individuals manning those institutions. Such individuals, when motivated by the right cause, draw support from other organs of the State sharing similar commitment to public causes, namely, the judiciary, media and civil society organizations (CSOs). The need for them to support each other arises when the principal player in the game, namely the lawmaker, is recalcitrant, obdurate or inactive. That indeed has been the narrative of electoral reforms in India with the EC, CSOs and courts trying to drive reforms, and ruling parties generally stalling them with little opposition from other political parties. No wonder electoral reforms have seldom been the central part of any political party's election manifesto.

Any analysis of the performance of India's electoral system must look at two sides. One is the conduct of polls. This involves an elaborate system of almost continuous elector registration; setting up a million polling stations at the time of polling and getting the largest electorate in the world to the polling stations; and putting together a machinery of around 12 million for election management. This is done before every election, be it to a state assembly or the Parliament, with the ECI kick-starting the process several months before the elections are due. This is made possible by a powerful EC that has rightly evolved a procedure-based system that lays down all procedures elaborately and in tedious detail. This is strengthened by repeated training and an avowed general commitment on the part of public servants involved in the process to put their best foot forward when involved in election management. These are the strengths demonstrated repeatedly in the hundreds of elections conducted by the EC since independence because of which it is justifiably referred to as a 'gold standard'. This is one side of the story.

The other side of the story is cash, crime and conduct. While cash and crime are part of the 'resources' employed by the players (political parties), conduct refers to the way political parties and candidates behave during elections, driven by their desire to win at all costs. The EC has shown persistent concern over this growing perversion and has tried to find ways to deal with these three factors. However, the EC often finds itself constrained by the limits to its authority as well as lack of commitment on the part of other stakeholders.

The relationship between the EC and political parties is generally referred to as one between players and a referee. In a conventional game, no player, whatever be their proficiency or talent, plays to dare the referee. A player generally plays by the rules, sometimes crossing the line in the heat of the game. The referee, being a neutral person, is meant to call out any transgression without assessing the intent of the player. Generally, players do not try to hoodwink the referee (Maradona's 'hand of god' notwithstanding) even though they all play to win. Unfortunately, that doesn't hold good when one looks at the conduct of those contesting elections. It is often a 'catch me if you can' approach with the EC stretching itself in trying to maintain discipline and adhere to its principle of providing a 'level playing field' to all candidates and political parties. Preventing the misuse of cash, curbing the spate of candidates with criminal antecedents and regulating conduct has been the most taxing and talked-about function of the EC. Most of its efforts to clean up the electoral process are around cash, crime and conduct, and so is most of the criticism that the EC has attracted.

Cash, crime and conduct

The principle of providing a level playing field is the keystone of the EC's neutrality because of the disproportionate manner in which political parties and candidates are endowed. A criminal background and use of unaccounted cash give them clout, muscle power and resources by which they attempt to vitiate free and fair voting. The EC has prescribed expenditure limits on candidate spending during the poll period and stipulated the timely filing of returns. It also has an elaborate apparatus for monitoring expenditure and scrutinizing expenditure accounts.

However, it is no secret that the limit has served a limited purpose. Everyone talks of the limitless amount of money spent during elections even though the official accounts submitted by candidates show that only a handful of candidates declare that they have spent as much as the limit allows. The expenditure accounts of the majority of candidates show that they spent just about half of the permissible limit. Despite this, the EC surprisingly agreed to raise the limit before the Bihar elections in 2020. If the statistics on election expenditure brought out by the

Association of Democratic Reforms (ADR)[2] are to be believed, so ineffective seems to be the EC's ability to enforce it that some argue the expenditure limit should be removed altogether, but filing of correct accounts must be strictly enforced. Clearly, and correctly so, the EC has not shown an inclination to do away with the limits, although it continues to grapple with the problem of enforcement. The record of conviction for breaching the expenditure limit is dismal and most of the so-called illicit cash 'seized' during the campaign period is invariably released subsequently. The EC doesn't have adequate staff to thoroughly scrutinize candidate accounts in a time-bound manner nor does it have any authority over the cases of seizure, which are investigated and pursued by the respective regulatory agencies of the government. And thereby hangs a tale!

It is on account of this that offences registered during elections, whether under electoral laws or other criminal laws, languish without being seriously pursued. Proceedings initiated under income tax laws during elections, and cash and goods seized during the enforcement of the Model Code of Conduct (MCC) have a pathetic record of prosecution, not to talk of conviction. The EC has no means, nor has it set up any effective mechanism, to regularly monitor the progress of those cases. This restricts the EC to a body that shows its teeth for a limited period and thereafter exposes its cavities. The least that it could do is to have the Bureau of Police Research and Development classify electoral offences separately and report the same periodically to the EC so their progress can be systematically monitored. Ultimately, the system has to depend on the law enforcement agencies of the State, whether during election time or otherwise. The EC cannot, and should not, take over the role of investigation or prosecution. That is a State function, and the State has to demonstrate its commitment to pursuing alleged electoral offences. Meanwhile, the EC could strengthen its oversight and place these figures in the public domain.

Surrogate publicity

Compounding the problem of excessive expenditure by candidates is the issue of expenditure incurred by persons 'not authorized' by candidates, surrogate publicity, paid news and the money spent by the ruling party from public accounts. The EC has remained either unable or unwilling to deal with this even if it were concerned by the spate of schemes under which the government spends money in the run-up to the elections. Apart from large amounts legitimately doled out under government-approved schemes immediately before or during the elections, there is a tendency on the part of the party in power to spend disproportionate amounts on government publicity as elections draw near in the hope of encashing the gains from government publicity for the ruling party. This invariably places the party in power in a position of advantage.

So far, there are no clear provisions to deal with the surrogate publicity that parties or candidates resort to during an election campaign through paid news, feature films, DTH or social media platforms. The phenomenon of surrogate publicity, hitherto well known in the advertising world, is now being used to further the political prospects of candidates during elections. A candidate wielding power could influence anyone with money to produce a film portraying them in good light, have it released during the campaign period and get away with it by pleading that it was not 'authorized'.

The release of films or books on any candidate or living political personalities with a view to benefiting a candidate during elections without their authorization should be proscribed during the period when the MCC is in effect. The only exemption should be if a candidate or a party admits that the so-called work of art, be it a movie or a book or play or song, is funded by them, in which case it would be an authorized expenditure for their publicity and would be booked as such. In the case of a candidate, it would be counted towards the prescribed ceiling of expenditure.

In cases where it is difficult to establish a direct nexus by evidence of a payment reflected in the statement of accounts submitted by the candidate, the EC could apply the principle of implied authorization. In circumstances where the candidate derives direct benefit because of such publicity or repeated 'news' items, an inference of implied consent is inescapable if there is no evidence of the candidate distancing themselves from such repeated propaganda on their behalf even if they contend that it was not at their behest. When a candidate is accountable for maintaining their poll expenses within the prescribed limit, the onus of establishing that beneficial services being rendered to them during the campaign period are not at their behest should rest on the candidate. They must have proof that they distanced themselves from such 'charitable' services or news at the relevant time and not post-facto.

If such publicity can only be determined on the basis of irrefutable documentary evidence, the subterfuge would gain uncontrollable currency and would be a major setback to curbing the practice of monetizing influence that candidates wield due to their status and network in society, thus deriving an unfair advantage over other candidates. Such an 'unholy alliance' can only be uncovered by a thorough impartial inquiry, which the ECI is best placed to conduct. Restricting the scope of inquiry by the ECI in such matters (by not allowing it to go into the 'contents' of such paid news) would be like allowing it to take a pound of flesh without an ounce of blood.[3]

The present laws or instructions governing the ECI do not provide for categorizing such expenditure in the candidate's account. However, in most cases, candidates accept the expenditure and have it included in their accounts. In an odd case, the inclusion of such expenditure has led to the disqualification of a candidate once the expenditure on paid news was accounted for and breached the expenditure limit. While expenditure incurred by the candidate's so-called well-wishers on tangible things might be possible to catch, that incurred on giving publicity to the candidate in the garb of freedom of expression is the jellyfish that escapes the net.

Such 'invisible' support takes the form of so-called opinion polls, doctored panel discussions on television channels, pushing political propaganda on entertainment channels or producing films for or against a candidate and timing their release with the poll campaign period. This could be curbed by making effective provisions in the MCC or any other instructions of the ECI even if its extraordinary powers under Article 324 are to be invoked for the sake of protecting the principle of a level playing field. For example, the ECI did halt the release of a few feature films in 2019 that were timed to be released during the campaign period. It is time that this is codified even if it means that the ECI has to withstand criticism of curbing the freedom of expression.

There is already a precedent for reasonable curbs on freedom of expression, at least politically, in the form of a stipulation that all political advertisements on electronic media be pre-certified to abide by some acceptable norms. Films/serials made on candidates or the clandestine use of electronic media for political publicity during the MCC period needs to be similarly regulated. The content itself may not be tailored (unless they blatantly violate constitutional norms) but the timing of their release and exhibition can, and should be, regulated by the ECI. This in no way impinges on the right of political parties to transparently finance the production of films for political mileage. As there is no limit on a political party's electoral expenditure, this cannot be questioned although this is intricately linked to the issue of political funding.

Political funding and electoral bonds

This brings us to the provisions governing political funding, which now seem opaque due to the law regarding disclosure (or non-disclosure) of funding received via electoral bonds.[4] The introduction of the bond as an instrument of funding per se cannot be questioned but not making the information public has been challenged as being antithetical to the principle of transparency and the Right to Information (RTI) Act. That political parties have steadfastly resisted being brought under the ambit of the RTI Act despite feeble attempts by statutory bodies speaks volumes about their motivation. The State seems to be colluding with political parties in this obfuscation by granting income tax exemptions to all forms of political funding.

The ECI had consistently argued against electoral bonds in its communications to the government and its submissions before the Supreme Court. It is understood that the ECI recently changed its stance and supported the continuance of electoral bonds.[5]

The Supreme Court had raised some inconvenient questions while hearing the matter and appeared to be seeing the point made by the petitioners who questioned the merit and intent of introducing an opaque instrument for political funding. It even asked the political parties to disclose details of the bonds in sealed envelopes, which were never opened. Eventually, the Supreme Court refrained from either granting a stay on the issuance of bonds or delegitimizing them. It left the petitioners wondering if yet another opportunity to pronounce on a matter of 'great pith and moment' was lost in the absence of 'the native hue of resolution' that left Hamlet debating endlessly,

> 'Whether 'tis nobler in the mind to suffer
> The slings and arrows of outrageous fortune,
> Or to take arms against a sea of troubles,
> And, by opposing, end them?'

There is merit in the argument that the electoral bond is an authorized instrument that serves as an alternative to cash, but the logic of secrecy is not backed by any evidence to show that such a demand was made by potential donors. More baffling is the fact that the State should reward such secret transactions with tax relief, both for the donor and the beneficiary.

The general principle of granting a tax exemption to any organization that receives donations is that the funds received are utilized for the purpose for which they are meant. For example, if the organization claims that it has been set up to assist the orthopaedically challenged, it would have to show that donated funds were used to fulfil the objectives for which the organization was established. Similarly, if a political party receives contributions that are tax exempt, both for the donor and the donee, it should not be allowed to retain that amount indefinitely. It must be obliged to spend that amount substantially in a given period or lose the benefit of exemption. This would curb the tendency of political parties becoming recipients of tax-exempt funds without utilizing them.

This imperative becomes even more pressing as donations received via electoral bonds are from undisclosed sources, even if they are through banking channels. Additionally, it is generally apprehended that some donations to parties are invariably tied to concessions or expectations of favours from the winning party. Redressing this would require a specific provision to be created in the relevant laws by which party accounts are subject to periodic proprietary audit and parties stand to incur tax liability for unutilized funds. This would align the provisions pertaining to political donations with those that apply to tax-exempt donations for other purposes.

Such a reform in tax laws would have to be accompanied by another stipulation specifying limits to expenditure incurred by a political party during an election. There have been suggestions in the past relating to this, including the EC proposing a limit. For example, if the limit on candidate expenditure for a parliament election is say Rs 70 lakh, the political party that has fielded the candidate may be allowed to spend no more than, say, 50 per cent of the expenditure reflected by the candidate in the accounts submitted to the EC. This would automatically limit party expenditure during elections. Thus, if a party were to field a hundred candidates during Lok Sabha elections, it would be able to legitimately spend no more than Rs 35 crore for campaigning from party funds assuming that all the candidates sponsored by that party utilize the entire expenditure ceiling. If the proposed periodic audit by a firm appointed by the Comptroller and Auditor General of India (CAG) conducted every five years were to show that the party was unable to spend the tax-exempt income it received for the declared purpose, it should be liable to pay income tax on the unutilized portion along with interest. Tax exemption should be treated as a form of state subsidy to political parties and subject to the same principle of utilization of subsidy as are other schemes funded by the exchequer. No tax exemption should be allowed on electoral bonds if the details are not fully disclosed. If the donor and a political party want to have a bond of anonymous munificence, such contributions and incomes must be fully taxed. The purpose of all income tax laws and enforcement is honest disclosure, but the electoral bond is a device that incentivizes secrecy.

This secret 'bond' also begs a counterintuitive question. Why is it that in India people prefer to contribute to the cause of democracy in secret? There are countries where people proudly and openly claim to provide donations to political parties (like the Political Action Committees[6] in the United States of America), which are vital instruments of a democratic system. After all, democracy is as worthy a cause as climate change, environmental protection or looking after the homeless and infirm, and an honest citizen would be happy to be associated with such a cause. Isn't that the principle behind making such contributions eligible for tax exemption? Why do we as a society wish to conceal contributions to the cause of democracy and why does our political system support this? This calls for introspection.

Model Code of Conduct

The relationship between political parties and the EC is like the relationship between players and a referee in which neither is superior to the other; rather, they have different roles. No player, howsoever talented, popular or valuable, can grudge the referee their role in conducting a game as per the rules. It is this recognition of the EC's responsibility that prompts political parties and their leaders to submit themselves to the discipline of the code and let the EC pronounce on their conduct even though the MCC is strictly not a law. The MCC, a unique consensual arrangement evolved over long years, becomes a topic for discussion and comes under stress as soon as it comes into force with the announcement of an election. It puts to the test political parties, their leaders, the election candidates, the enforcement machinery in the field, the reporting system put in place by the EC, and the principal referee, the EC itself. All this under the piercing gaze of the media and the critical oversight of the judiciary.

The origin of the MCC can be traced back to 1960 when during the tenure of CEC K.V.K. Sundaram, it started as a small set of dos and don'ts for the assembly election in Kerala, covering holding election meetings/processions, speeches, slogans, posters and placards. In 1968, when S.P. Sen Verma was the CEC, the EC held meetings with political parties at the state level and circulated the Code of Conduct to observe a minimum standard of behaviour to ensure free and fair elections. The code was circulated to political parties again in the 1971–72 general election to the state and national legislatures, and in the 1977 general election (when T. Swaminathan was the CEC). In 1979, during the tenure of CEC S.L. Shakhdar, the EC in consultation with political parties amplified the code by placing restrictions on the 'party in power' so as to prevent the abuse of power for deriving undue advantage over other parties and candidates. In 1991, the code was consolidated and reissued in its present form when T.N. Seshan was the CEC.

The main objective of the MCC is to ensure free and fair elections by providing a level playing field to all political parties and candidates, and to maintain a certain degree of decorum and discipline in public discourse during electioneering. The MCC draws its strength and sanctity as much from the strict, prompt and non-discriminatory enforcement by the EC as from the cooperation of political parties and candidates.

Even though the MCC in its present form has served a useful purpose, the context in which it was originally drafted has changed, and so has the character of political campaigning. The political environment in the country is more charged and campaigning during elections more intense. Elections are hard fought in comparison to the past and more means are now employed by parties and candidates. While the EC has tried to regulate the conduct of candidates and parties during elections, innovative ways are being found to remain in the shadow zone that lies between the letter and the spirit of the MCC. This might not be deliberate in all cases. However, what is certain is that newer areas of influence have emerged that lie outside the ken of the MCC in its present form. Muscle has replaced money. Technology has provided a cover to stakeholders. Use of imagination to dodge the MCC is valued more than the inclination to adhere to it.

The changed circumstances manifest themselves in election after election where instances of violation of the MCC seem to be increasing. Numerous cases are noticed by the field machinery and the general public. These are rapidly disseminated by the electronic media aided by the furious pace of social media. This coupled with applications like cVigil, which have empowered citizens, have raised the expectations of the people and brought enforcement and deterrent action by the EC into sharp focus, sometimes attracting stringent public criticism.

Clearly, there is a need to review the framework of the MCC and modify it with a view to strengthening it and making it more effective. At the same time, some feel that the stringency of the MCC should not rob elections of their festive spirit by imparting to them a funeral sobriety. It is also argued that the MCC cannot be used to curb the freedom of speech, which is a fundamental right. However, it is generally accepted that it is legal and proper to impose reasonable restrictions in a non-discriminatory way to maintain public order and decency when circumstances so warrant.

A significant gap in the present framework is that the MCC does not clearly spell out the consequences of violations or defaults. As a result, it does not have the preventive effect that it ought to have. It is therefore necessary to specify the punitive measures in a manner that is fair, transparent and predictable, especially with respect to violations that are serious and in the category of hate speeches, invoking communal and caste feelings to secure votes, offering inducements to garner votes, using foul, filthy and abusive language against a political opponent, indulging in political propaganda by invoking, praising, questioning or criticizing the Indian armed forces, the recovery of large sums of unaccounted cash from a candidate or their election agent, etc.

The aforesaid violations should attract severe consequences that can be graded and made known publicly. For example, the first case of any such violation could attract a ban on campaigning for a specified period, the second offence could entail a ban for a longer period and the third offence would debar the concerned candidate or political functionary for the entire period that the MCC is in force. Such a ban would entail a prohibition on all public appearances and interaction on all forms of media. The MCC should provide that a person found to be in repeated violation would not be eligible to be categorized as a star campaigner in subsequent elections for a certain length of time. Similarly, the MCC could spell out punitive action against a political party if some of its important functionaries or star campaigners (other than the candidates in that area) are involved in proven cases of MCC violation. This action could take the form of imposing a predetermined fine and action under the Election Symbols (Reservation and Allotment) Order after a specified number of offences.

The procedure for identifying and dealing with cases of reported violations of the MCC should be streamlined such that punitive action is taken within seventy-two hours of the occurrence and a standard procedure is laid down so as to follow a uniform approach in dealing with these cases. A list of all such cases should be compiled and a statement of their disposal/pendency be regularly placed before the EC. The EC should maintain a database of all MCC violations and make the information public during the period of the MCC. During the election period, the EC takes action against many officials who either violate the MCC or whose conduct is found to be questionable. A list of all such officials against whom action is taken by the EC, including transfers, should be maintained state-wise and department-wise for the EC's reference.

There are certain violations of the MCC that are directly connected with specific provisions of extant law under various acts. It is the responsibility of the law enforcement machinery to initiate legal action in all such offences as per the provision of the relevant law without the matter being referred to the EC. If a complaint is received regarding a particular violation being a violation of the MCC as well, then action is taken by the EC, such as issuing a warning or imposing restrictions on campaigning, etc., after following due procedure of inquiry. It should be mandatory in such cases of violation of the MCC that legal action by the law enforcement machinery, as provided in law, should follow immediately. There should be no need for the EC to issue any specific direction in such cases, and an action-taken report should be sent by the law enforcement agency to the EC within twenty-four hours of the action taken.

The EC should set up a high-level monitoring team that regularly monitors the prosecution of all cases of electoral offences registered during the period the MCC is in force. The team would keep track of all cases where FIRs are filed for election-related offences and ensure time-bound investigation, filing of charge sheets, tendering of prosecution evidence and other activities necessary for their expeditious disposal by competent courts and place such information in the public domain.

The above would not only deter potential violators and instil an element of self-regulation in the conduct of political parties, it would also limit the discretion exercised at the time of decision-making, thereby sparing the EC allegations of bias or discrimination. The uniform procedure to be adopted in dealing with these cases, coupled with the predictable consequences of violations or defaults, would make the MCC more robust, transparent and effective. The ECI, as the enforcement agency of the MCC, would also bind itself publicly to proceed against cases of transgression in a time-bound and credible manner, which in turn will inspire greater public confidence in its commitment to conducting free and fair elections.

Reactive or proactive

Another criticism that the EC is often subjected to is that it is turning more reactive than proactive, thus diluting the dignity of its constitutional eminence. During the 2019 general elections, when several complaints of MCC violations against top political leaders remained undecided for a few days, the Supreme Court observed that it appeared that the EC had gone to sleep and needed to be reminded of its powers in dealing with complaints of MCC violation. In its interim order of 15 April 2019, the court recorded that the EC counsel pleaded that it has little power beyond issuing advisories against hate speeches. The media reported that the Supreme Court had termed the EC 'toothless'. It expressed its displeasure at the EC not exercising the extraordinary powers vested in it by the Constitution. It was only when the EC took action against some violators that the court observed that the EC was now awake.

Similarly, when the Calcutta High Court observed on 22 April 2021 that 'circulars are not merely advisories to be wrapped up by the political parties or those involved in the political propaganda or even the public at large', it was underscoring the EC's duty of issuing instructions and its capability and inclination to rigorously enforce those instructions. That the EC is accused of not doing so by the highest courts in the country dents its image. The court rather sharply observed:

'Issuance of circulars and holding of meetings by themselves do not discharge the onerous responsibility of the ECI and officers under its command in due performance of not only the statutory power and authority under the Representation of People Act, 1950 and the Representation of People Act, 1951 but the confidence that the Indian polity would have on it to carry forward the mechanism of upholding the Democracy.'

Similarly, the judgment of the Kerala High Court dated 12 April 2021 pertaining to holding Rajya Sabha elections raised issues concerning the electoral process as enshrined in law and the manner in which those provisions are interpreted and applied. It also brought into focus the EC's interface with other public institutions, namely the government and courts. It seemed unusual that the Secretary of a legislative assembly (a constitutional body) filed a petition in the court (another constitutional organ) against the ECI, which is also a constitutional institution. The sequence of events, as explained in the court order, was that the EC announced its intention to hold elections to three Rajya Sabha seats only after it had announced the schedule for the legislative assembly elections. When it sent the draft notification to the President for being notified, it received a communication from the Union Ministry of Law and Justice raising objections with regard to the right of outgoing legislators to exercise their right to vote for electing members to the Rajya Sabha. The communiqué argued that voters would have already cast their vote to elect new legislators, so outgoing legislators may not represent the will of the people if they were allowed to vote at this point. The EC therefore agreed to have the matter legally examined and ordered the schedule to be held in abeyance. The motive behind the government's concern regarding the rights of legislators and the EC's willingness to review its earlier decision are difficult to fathom. In its judgment, the court observed as follows:

'As pointed out by the learned ASGI, it cannot be said that the Government of India wanted to influence the Commission . . . ECI which is conferred with wide powers and entrusted with onerous duties enjoined under Article 324 is not expected to be influenced on the basis of a reference. Commission which itself had announced and notified the election to the legislative assembly was very aware of the situation when it issued the press release with the schedule of election to the Council of States proposing completion by 16.04.2021 . . . It is seen that at least after it arrived at the decision that it is its duty to see that the vacancies are filled up at the earliest, the Commission is yet to take any steps for the same. When the Commission itself has admitted that it is duty bound to conduct the election and complete the process at the earliest, it is only appropriate that it takes expeditious steps without further delay to complete the election before another electorate comes into existence on 02.05.2021.'

While the court refrained from imputing any motive to the EC's actions, it did remind the EC of its duty and pointed out the glaring gap between its avowed assertions and action.

The observation made by the Madras High Court in April 2021 regarding the EC being 'responsible' for facilitating the spread of the coronavirus infection while conducting the general elections to five state assemblies raised an unseemly controversy, which was prolonged by the petition challenging the oral observations of the high court. The final order of the Supreme Court did not refurbish the EC's image.

Conclusion

A democratic set-up depends on each constitutional authority discharging its duty in keeping with its statutory obligation, irrespective of the pressure brought upon it by another. That pressure may not be due to any vested interest, as is often alleged. This power play between authorities is not alien to realpolitik but it is precisely in times of such tensions that constitutional bodies are expected to stand firm against extraneous considerations. The foundations of a functional democracy rest on its public institutions working as per their constitutional/statutory mandates, and asserting themselves when the need arises, especially if there is a perceived attempt to trample its authority. That is how institutions such as the Supreme Court and the Election Commission have established and maintained their credibility, even while working in politically charged situations.

It is only if public institutions function as they are meant to, conscientiously and sincerely, that citizens will have faith in them (and ultimately, the democratic process itself). In this light, the government, besides the EC itself, must consistently take steps to strengthen this compact. However, the impression that governments don't act on its repeated recommendations undermines the EC. Similarly, if political leaders persist in challenging the EC's authority through provocative utterances, they diminish the EC's effectiveness.

The EC has consistently and assiduously championed electoral reforms, and a long list of recommendations have been submitted to the government, which it pursues regularly. These, inter alia, include the following: (i) In the matter of the appointment of election commissioners through a collegium instead of the current system of appointment, a Bill has since been introduced following the directions of the Supreme Court. The Bill, titled the Chief Election Commissioner and other Election Commissioners (Appointment, Conditions of Service and Term of Office) Bill,

2023, proposes to exclude the Chief Justice of India from the panel to select the CEC and ECs. This has led to questions being raised regarding the neutrality of the proposed process. The debate brings to mind Dr B.R. Ambedkar's warning from 1949, 'There is no provision in the Constitution to prevent the appointing of . . . a person who is likely to be under the thumb of the executive.'[7] The challenge for the lawmakers clearly is to establish a process that is seen to be credible. But then, the credibility of any process is only as good as the credibility of the people involved in the process. (ii) amending the relevant sections of the law to impose more stringent punishment for electoral offences and bringing more offences under the ambit of disqualification from contesting elections; and (iii) making the EC budget a charged expenditure. However, it has met with limited success. In numerous electoral reform–related petitions, the EC has highlighted this before the Supreme Court. Yet, the courts have rarely stepped out of their crease to enter the legislative domain and have left it to the 'wisdom' of the Parliament to take a call. Meanwhile, civil society organizations studiously pursue the agenda of electoral reforms through their petitions. The question is not *what* needs to be done but *who* will do it.

While nobody denies the need for urgent electoral reforms, especially pertaining to the issues of cash, crime and conduct, few favour granting more powers to the EC. This perhaps stems from what a former Secretary General of the Lok Sabha sagaciously argued:[8]

'There is no doubt that the ECI, through the conduct of free and fair elections in an extremely complex country, has restored the purity of the legislative bodies. However, no constitutional body is vested with unguided and absolute powers. Neither citizens nor the ECI is permitted to assume that the ECI has unlimited and arbitrary powers. It would be useful to remember the insightful words of Justice S.M. Fazalali, in A.C. Jose vs Sivan Pillai (1984): "if the [Election]

Commission is armed with such unlimited and arbitrary powers and if it ever happens that the persons manning the commission shares or is wedded to a particular ideology, he could by giving odd directions cause a political havoc or bring about a constitutional crisis, setting at naught the integrity and independence of the electoral process so important and indispensable to the democratic system.'''

Many believe that the ECI is sufficiently empowered and that it will have to keep 'winding' the clock to deal with the dynamics of deteriorating political behaviour. The political environment is changing fast; technological tools, tact and sophisticated tricks are being employed to win elections. In the absence of self-restraint and organizational ethos, it seems every election is becoming a game of guile. The referee will have to be ahead of the game. Winning this game will need both defenders and dribblers, those that can defend the goal post of impartiality, neutrality and fair play and those that can dribble courageously and move forward to keep the game and its spirit alive. In this spirit, let us be reminded that when the Constituent Assembly of India met on 26 November 1949, the then Chairperson (and later India's first President) Dr Rajendra Prasad said:

'Whatever the Constitution may or may not provide, the welfare of the country will depend upon the way in which the country is administered. That will depend upon the men who administer it . . . If the people who are elected are capable and men of character and integrity, they would be able to make the best even of a defective Constitution. If they are lacking in these, the Constitution cannot help the country. After all, a Constitution like a machine is a lifeless thing. It acquires life because of the men who control it and operate it, and India needs today nothing more than a set of honest men who will have the interest of the country before them.'

India's Fading Federal Institutions

Dr T.M. Thomas Isaac

Introduction

The concept of unity in diversity, an important ideal of the national movement, was given life through a federal India. This was because India's founders understood that the governance of a country as vast and diverse as India could never be unitary and must necessarily be a multilevel process. It is therefore crucial that the world's largest elected democracy be truly representative. This can only be realized by ensuring governance of, by and for the people at all levels. The Constitution of India envisages such a federal and democratic polity. It defines India as a 'Union of States', which has substantially deepened after the 73rd and 74th constitutional amendments. India is now a Union of States with self-governing institutions even at the local levels.

Yet, over the last seventy-five years, we have witnessed two contradictory trends in inter-governmental relationships. On the one hand, there has been some movement for greater devolution of powers to local governments whose institutional structures and procedures have been enshrined within the Constitution itself. Yet, local government structures continue to be weak, without adequate funds, functions and functionaries. The constitutional provisions are only enabling clauses with the choice left to the states, which are often handicapped by a lack of adequate resources. It is now becoming increasingly clear that there cannot be effective decentralization to the local level without restructuring Centre-state relations.

On the other hand, when it comes to Centre-state relations, the tendency has been towards greater centralization of powers. This is partly because of how India's federalism was originally conceived. Due to the surcharged atmosphere of Partition, and because of the socio-economic and political situation India was in after centuries of colonialism, the Constitution tilted greater powers towards the Centre. For example, the division of powers between the Union and states also included a concurrent list in which the Centre had overriding powers. Furthermore, the Union could enter into international agreements and treaties even on subjects within the domain of the states without consultations with the latter. There has been a steady encroachment into the legislative domain of the states throughout the post-independence period. In fact, it has been the common denominator of most of the recent central legislations.

The Union continues to have wide-ranging powers to intervene in the administration of the states including issuing of directions and dismissal of state governments on the grounds of 'constitutional breakdown' in a state. The governor, the formal head of the state government who is a nominee of the Union, has acted on partisan considerations on many occasions. Additionally, there is a growing trend to intervene in the administration of the states through the agencies of the all-India Services. Likewise, the Union government has also attempted to bypass state governments by directly connecting with local governments or autonomous implementation agencies.

Similarly, the share of the states in the combined government expenditure is 60 per cent while their share in the combined government revenue is only 40 per cent.[1] This imbalance has been sought to be rectified through constitutional amendments as well as other mechanisms that devolve finances to the states. However, the vertical imbalance in public finance has only worsened over time. The capacity of states to mobilize resources and their fiscal autonomy have been methodically whittled down through public finance rules and tax 'reforms'.

The growing contradictions and tensions in India's Centre-state relations have been the subject of serious political debate and protest from powerful regional parties, particularly during the 1965–80 period. In this context, the Sarkaria Commission (Government of India 1987) and the Punchhi Commission (Government of India 2010) reports on Centre-state relations have been important landmarks in that they posed redressals to structural faultiness. Yet, it is equally true that after the 1990 neoliberal reforms, resistance from regional parties has weakened significantly. The regional bourgeoise classes have also adopted a neoliberal ideology and champion the need for an unfettered pan-India market. Given that regional parties and state governments have stopped being assertive, the recommendations of these commissions have not been properly implemented, and the systemic disempowerment of state governments continues unabated.

It is in this context that it is critical that we examine the experiences of key federal institutions during the last seventy-five years, namely 1) the Union Finance Commission; 2) the Planning Commission and the National Development Council; 3) the Inter-State Council; and 4) the Goods and Service Tax (GST) Council. While discussing these institutions, we shall also explore the devolution of resources, India's fiscal regulatory framework, planning process and tax reforms. Unfortunately, there has been a growing imbalance in Indian federalism, marked by a steady erosion or eclipse of our federal institutions. It is important for the future of the nation that we critically reimagine these federal institutions.

Union Finance Commission

The most important federal institution enshrined in the Constitution is the Union Finance Commission (hereafter FC), which is appointed every quinquennium by the President of India under Article 280. Given the distribution of functional responsibilities and revenue-raising powers between the Union and the states, it was rightfully understood that there would be a serious mismatch between their revenues and expenditure.

Accordingly, as defined in Article 280 (3) of India's Constitution,[2] the core function of the FC is to make recommendations regarding the vertical devolution of funds from the Centre to the states and horizontal distribution among the states. Roughly 85 to 90 per cent of the total award from the FC consists of tax devolution. The remaining constitutes special grants to states facing revenue deficits even after tax devolution, or states facing special problems.[3] Two clauses[4] were added to devolve funds to local governments as per the 73rd and 74th constitutional amendments. Additionally, through Article 280 (4), the Constitution has empowered the FC to 'determine their procedures' for deliberation and decision.

Overall, the FCs have functioned autonomously and proved to be important mechanisms contributing to India's fiscal federalism. However, there have been strong countervailing currents that have seriously undermined fiscal federalism, which has had far-reaching implications for India's federal structure as a whole.

Declining share of FC award

India's Constitution has not envisaged any other route for the devolution of funds to state governments other than through the FC. But through an Executive Order in 1951, the Planning Commission was formed and soon became an important route for fund flow to state plans. Eventually, the FC was limited to making recommendations only on the non-plan revenue component of state budgets. This was further compounded by Centrally Sponsored Schemes (CSS), which were implemented by states but whose criteria were fixed by the Centre and emerged as yet another conduit for the transfer of funds. These alternative channels for the transfer of funds to states have been criticized[5].

In addition, the Centre also gave discretionary grants to states with special needs. These grants were disbursed invoking provisions of Article 282 of the Constitution, which is classified under 'Miscellaneous Financial Provisions', meant to be used sparingly under special circumstances. But this constitutional provision has become the basis for routine disbursal of grants by the Centre to the states. Consequently, the contribution of FC awards as a proportion of the total resource transfer to the states gradually came down to less than 60 per cent, until the fourteenth FC increased the share of taxes.[6]

Back-door measures to reduce the divisible tax pool

State governments have always demanded a larger pool of shareable taxes inclusive of all central taxes. After extensive deliberations by successive FCs, the tenth FC agreed to this demand. Accordingly, the 80th constitutional amendment was passed in 2000 to institute Article 270 by which proceeds of all central taxes, except surcharges and cess, were to constitute the divisible pool. Subsequently, the eleventh FC (2000–05) recommended the ratio of 29.5 per cent as the tax share of states. The twelfth FC (2005–10) increased it to 30.5 per cent while the thirteenth FC (2010–15), further increased it to 32 per cent. The fourteenth FC (2015–20) did away with the practice of recommending specific grants but sharply increased the states' share to 42 per cent. However, these efforts by the FCs have been largely undone by the Centre's manipulation.

For example, the expansion of cess and surcharges has been used to reduce the share of the divisible pool of revenues and increase the non-divisible part that is retained by the Union government. As a proportion of gross tax revenues of the

Centre, surcharges and cesses have jumped from 6.47 per cent (in 2011–12) to 19.9 per cent (in 2020–21). In fact, a substantial part of the enhanced devolution by the fourteenth FC was offset by enhanced cess and surcharges, by raising the state share in CSS, and by reducing non-FC grants.[7]

Just to cite three examples to further illustrate this point, in the 2017–18 budget, the rate of income tax (up to Rs 5 lakh) was reduced from 10 per cent to 5 per cent and the loss of revenue was sought to be compensated by imposing a surcharge on taxes on incomes above Rs 50 lakh. Had this been done by raising the slab rates, the divisible pool would not have become smaller. Similarly, in the 2018–19 budget, the excise duty on petroleum products (which is shareable with the states) was reduced by Rs 9 per litre but road cess, which is not shareable with the states, was increased by an equivalent amount. In 2021–22 it was the excise duty that was reduced rather than road cess to give relief to consumers from the petroleum price escalation.

These attempts to truncate the divisible pool of taxes that are shareable with the states defeats the constitutional scheme that is specifically designed to ameliorate vertical imbalances. Consequently, the financial loss to the states between 2015–16 and 2018–19 due to the shrinking of the divisible pool amounted to a shocking Rs 5,26,747 crore. This translates to an average of about 3 per cent of the gross domestic product (GDP) at current prices.[8]

As a result, the post-devolution resource gap of the states has risen to record levels in recent years. Widening from 1.95 per cent of the GDP in 1950–51, it steadily increased to 6.39 per cent in 1986–87 and has since tended to fluctuate but spiked to a peak of 7.85 per cent in 2014–15.[9]

Conditional transfers

The FCs were supposed to act as neutral arbitrators to equitably allocate resources from the Union to states, and to fairly distribute these transferred resources across states. However, in recent years, the FCs have morphed into instruments to impose the macro-economic policies of the Central government on the states. For instance, the terms of reference (ToRs) of the eleventh FC included the mandate to 'draw a monitorable fiscal reforms programme aimed at reduction of revenue deficit of the States and recommend the manner in which grants to States . . . may be linked to progress in implementing this programme'. This is in direct contravention of India's federal principles, for under Article 275 of the Constitution, the FCs have no powers to impose conditionalities on resource transfers to states in the form of statutory grants assessed on the basis of needs of each state. Yet, despite criticism from several quarters (including the dissent note[10] to the eleventh FC's report by one of its own members, namely, the late Amaresh Bagchi), the FC exceeded its constitutional brief in proposing conditionalities on central transfers.

Similarly, the twelfth FC recommended a fiscal restructuring plan in its report,[11] which would eliminate the revenue deficit and bring down the fiscal deficit to 3 per cent in a time-bound manner. Each state had to enact a fiscal responsibility legislation to this effect. The debt relief and a loan write-off scheme were linked to the absolute amount of reduction of revenue deficit of the state in each successive year as well as the containment of the fiscal deficit. Further, the benefits of both these schemes were to be made available to only those states that passed fiscal responsibility and budget management (FRBM) legislations. In this again, the FC exceeded its brief.

Likewise, the thirteenth FC set a combined target of 68 per cent debt to GDP for the Centre and states. The commission also extended the benefit of debt consolidation and relief facility (DCRF) to Sikkim and West Bengal on the condition that they adopt a fiscal responsibility legislation. The fourteenth FC allowed a borrowing flexibility of an additional 0.50 per cent provided the states met revenue deficit targets.

Despite the Union government unilaterally imposing fiscal targets (in violation of federal principles) on states, by and large, the states have complied with nearly all conditions imposed by the FCs. For example, all states other than West Bengal and Sikkim passed FRBM Acts within the stipulated time frame.[12] Furthermore, states have scrupulously complied with the FRBM targets of reducing revenue and fiscal deficits, often much more effectively than the Union government. In fact, most states had exited from the revenue deficit status and had reduced fiscal deficits to 3 per cent or below before the COVID-19 pandemic hit. In stark contrast, the Central government has always remained in revenue deficit and has a much higher fiscal deficit. Yet, this asymmetric impact of FRBM on the Union and states has sadly become a feature of Indian public finance.

Unilateral terms of reference

The Constitution includes a provision under which the President can refer to the Finance Commission any other matter in the interests of 'sound finance'. The definition or scope of the term 'sound finance' is not elaborated in the Constitution. But the ToRs of the FCs since the 1990s have continuously stretched this provision and imposed restrictions and conditionalities on the functioning of the FCs.

The ToR of the fifteenth FC[13] explicitly included items that weaken India's federal architecture.[14] For instance, the ToR explicitly mandated the Commission to review the 'substantial enhancement' of tax devolution recommended by the fourteenth FC. Until the fourteenth FC, the FC was concerned with the non-plan account of the central budget. But with the abolition of the Planning Commission already on the cards, the fourteenth FC considered the entire revenue account and not only the non-plan revenue account in determining the tax devolution. Therefore, the devolution ratio of the fourteenth FC is not comparable to its predecessors.

Yet another idea that is repugnant to federalism in this ToR is the fact that it requires the fifteenth FC to take account of the Central government's commitments to selected programmes, that too, in subjects that fall within the domain of the state governments. This is against the principle of federalism since it is the duty of the FC to consider the expenditure commitments of the Centre, the states and local governments holistically as all of them are equal stakeholders working collaboratively to further India's constitutional promise.

The fifteenth FC's ToR also mandated the commission 'to examine whether revenue deficit grants be provided at all', ignoring Article 275 of India's Constitution, which expressly provides for such special grants. This was and remains a crucial source of flexible funds as part of the central resource transfer and is an important means for augmenting the Consolidated Fund of the states.

Furthermore, the ToR mandated determining conditions that the Government of India (GoI) may impose on states while providing consent under Article 293 (3) of the Constitution (for market borrowings). This is unnecessary given that FRBM Acts have been passed by state legislatures and limits for borrowings have been specified therein. Why should further conditions be imposed? It is obviously a move to further restrain the borrowings and constrain the fiscal space of state governments. The chairperson of the fifteenth FC, while heading the FRBM Review Committee, had recommended a debt-GDP limit of 60 per cent (40 for the Centre and 20 for the states). To achieve this objective, public borrowing had to be curtailed. The Centre's FD to GDP ratio is to be lowered from 3 per cent to 2.5 per cent by 2022–23 and that of states from 3 per cent to 1.7 per cent by 2022–23. This is uncalled for as there are already legislative restraints on borrowing. If further restrictive conditionalities are put, the fiscal space for capital expenditure of the states would be severely constrained, with adverse consequences on economic growth and development.

Similarly, the same ToR sought to incentivize or penalize states based on how effectively they implemented the Union government's flagship schemes, while state welfare schemes were sought to be circumscribed by caricaturing them as 'populist'. This was not only anti-federal but undemocratic. The FC was effectively being given carte blanche to restrain democratically elected governments from implementing their promises to the people contained in their election manifestoes. Any measure related to welfare pensions, food subsidy and the public distribution system can be selected for control under the FC's ToR. This strikes at the root of democratic politics and imposes a neoliberal, anti-people agenda on states. It also provides the FC with wide latitude to stride into the domain of electorally mandated democratic practice and policymaking by state assemblies. This is an unacceptable incursion into the rights of elected state governments.

These fears did not materialize because the commission chose to assert its constitutional right to 'determine their (own) procedure' after the ToR of the fifteenth FC drew strong protests from several state governments who organized a series of national seminars and consultations. Additionally, the outbreak of the COVID-19 pandemic and the economic recession was obviously not an appropriate environment for fiscal conservatism. So, further tightening of FRBM parameters did not materialize and the revenue deficit grants continued. Yet the dangers and threats to India's federalism remain.

Planning Commission

Unlike the FC, the Planning Commission (PC) was not a constitutional institution but was established with the advent of five-year plans. It played a key role in formulating development strategies and drawing up national plans and approving state plans. Consequently, it also became a conduit for transferring plan assistance to the states based on an objective criterion known as the Gadgil formula (population 55 per cent, per capita income 25 per cent, fiscal management 5 per cent and special problems 15 per cent).

The PC proved to be an important federal institution with its own procedures for consultation with the states for approving state plans. There has been criticism that the planning process was centralized and bureaucratic. However, on the matter of determining the borrowings of the state governments, an important source of plan finance, the PC was an important check on the Union finance ministry.

The planning process also brought into existence an apex body, called the National Development Council (NDC), which strove to evolve a consensus regarding the plan budgets and development policies. It was headed by the prime minister and included all the Union ministers, chief ministers and representatives of the PC.

The NDC was an active deliberative body and held fifty-seven meetings between 1952 when it was formed and 2012 when it was decided to freeze its activities. This reflected the growing feeling of the irrelevance of planning itself, with the shift of economic policy from import substitution and public sector promotion to neoliberal policies of deregulation and privatization.

In 2014, the PC was abolished and NITI Aayog was constituted. It has a governing council with a similar composition to that of the NDC. But it is neither a constitutional nor a statutory body, and is only an advisory think tank. The observation made by Patnaik[15] in 2014 cited below aptly summarizes the implications of the abolition of the PC:

'It signifies the completion of a transition from a "Nehruvian state", even a residual Nehruvian State that willy-nilly pursues neo-liberal policies rather than anything remotely resembling a Nehru-Mahalanobis strategy, to a full-fledged neo-liberal state . . . Such a full-fledged neo-liberal state is characterised not just by a set of policies that fall under the rubric of neo-liberalism. It has a set of specific institutional features as well. These include: the "autonomy" of the central bank; the

elevation of the Ministry of Finance to the status of a super
ministry dominating all others; . . .'

Through the abolition of the PC, the states lost the gross budgetary
support (GBS) for state plans from the Centre. In this manner, the
Union government has neutralized the additional resources made
available to the states by the fourteenth FC when it increased the
share of taxes to be devolved from 32 per cent to 42 per cent. The
resource allocations of the erstwhile plan budget, which accounted
for all new projects and schemes, are now announced unilaterally by
the Union finance minister without any consultation with the states.

Yet, the CSS is a legacy of the plan era that continues to
flourish. As part of the central plan, schemes were formulated in
the functional domains of the state governments. The schemes
were to be implemented by the states but under the Centre's
guidelines. The uniform central guidelines often proved to be too
rigid to accommodate the regional diversities of India and curtailed
the fiscal space of the states since they had to share a part of the
cost of the schemes. This was exacerbated since the share of states
in the CSS was gradually revised upwards. While it was around 20
per cent in the past, currently it is around 40 per cent, imposing an
additional fiscal burden on the states.

A recent example is the National Health Protection Programme,
Ayushman Bharat, which replaced the Rashtriya Swasthya Bima
Yojana (RSBY) health insurance programme. The new scheme
is basically a public-funded health insurance programme for poor
households. Such insurance programmes are inappropriate for a
state like Kerala, which has a well-functioning universal public
health system. Moreover, the coverage of the national programme
is only 10 crore beneficiaries in Kerala, determined by the socio-
economic census. This is too narrow a coverage, and the number of
beneficiaries would have to be at least double if all the beneficiaries
of the existing RSBY were to be covered by the new scheme.
Besides, the state government is also running a health assurance

programme providing Rs 2 lakh for all families in the state outside the Ayushman Bharat Limited public insurance net.

Second, the Union government is to pay only the central share of the premium, subject to a ceiling. As a result, for instance in the case of Kerala, the Union government's contribution to the overall expenditure of the health insurance scheme amounts to less than 20 per cent.

Third, since private hospitals are also accredited and included in the programme, state governments are being forced to subsidize the private sector massively. For Kerala, which has one of the best public health systems in India, this is counterproductive.

In short, the scheme runs counter to the basic tenets of cooperative federalism and distorts the health expenditure priorities of the state. Improvising on existing state-level schemes with central assistance, taking into consideration region-specific requirements, would have been more desirable.

Inter-State Council

Article 263 of India's Constitution provides that an Inter-State Council (ISC) may be established 'if at any time it appears to the President that the public interests would be served by the establishment of a Council'. The clause was operationalized in 1990 on the recommendation of the Sarkaria Commission as a permanent statutory body. The composition of the ISC includes the prime minister as the chairperson, chief ministers, six Union cabinet ministers, governors of states under President's rule and administrators of union territories not having legislative assemblies. It also has a standing committee with the Union home minister as chairperson. The objectives of the ISC are to deliberate on central-state relations, subjects of common interests and disputes among states.

Since its inception in 1990, twelve meetings have been held as of 2017 though the council was expected to meet thrice a year. The last time the council met was in November 2017. Though there have been occasional meetings of the five zonal councils, by and large, the ISC has become dormant and moribund. Consequently, anti-federal laws are being ramrodded without consulting states. A case in point is the Union cooperatives ministry. Even though cooperatives is a state subject, and there are successful and strong cooperatives across many states, the Union government is trying to create a parallel structure that will be under the Union government's control.[16] It is clear that this move is politically motivated and does nothing to promote the people's welfare. This is just one problem that highlights how the Centre has unilaterally imposed undemocratic policies motivated by partisan considerations. That is why the proper functioning of the ISC is crucial. States must have an institutionalized forum to discuss issues and negotiate with the Centre and with each other. The ISC's disuse does grave disservice to India's federalism since a critical instrument of dispute resolution and dialogue has been allowed to atrophy.

Goods and Services Tax (GST) Council

The GST Council is the youngest of India's federal institutions and is the most active of all of them. It is a constitutional body formed under Article 279A with the Union finance minister as the chairperson and state finance/tax ministers or any other minister nominated by the state governments, and the Union minister of state in charge of revenue or finance as members. The council is empowered to determine the rates of tax for different commodities and services, the threshold limit of turnover for the purpose of taxation, exempted goods, special rates for special purposes such as natural calamities for a specified period, tax administration and any other matter related to GST. The decisions of the GST Council are binding for both the Union and state governments. The GST Council in turn is bound by Article 279A, which stipulates that it shall be guided by the need to create a harmonized GST structure and a harmonized national market for goods and services.

The GST Council was preceded by an Empowered Committee of Finance Ministers to implement a harmonized system of value added tax (VAT) in the states. The VAT system was expected to reduce the complexity and cascading effects of the indirect tax structure that was prevalent in the states. VAT was introduced on 1 April 2005. The standardization of rates was done through consensual decisions of the Empowered Committee of State Finance Ministers. GST in a sense was extending the VAT system across state borders and integrating the central indirect taxes (other than customs duties) with state VAT into one single tax system for the entire country. The discussions for GST started in the Empowered Committee and it took nearly a decade before a near national consensus emerged and constitutional amendments were passed.

The new tax system has not stabilized even after five years, and there has been a general disillusionment because of low buoyancy of GST. Furthermore, hardly any state has been able to mobilize sufficient GST revenues to go beyond the guaranteed increase of 14 per cent growth of revenues through a compensatory mechanism. Though both the Centre and states surrendered their taxation powers with respect to indirect taxes subsumed in GST, there is a serious asymmetry in the loss. While the Union government still enjoys buoyant direct taxes and customs duties, state governments have lost control of their most important source of tax revenue. GST has in effect worsened the vertical fiscal imbalance.

The situation has been worsened because the GST Council has stopped working consensually (as it was during the deliberations of the Empowered Committee and in the early stages of the council itself). There has been a severe erosion of trust between the Centre and opposition states and increasing partisanship in the deliberations recently. The major cause of confrontation has been regarding the payment of compensation.

The compensation mechanism involved a cess on tobacco and a few luxury goods, the proceeds of which would constitute a Compensation Fund from which any shortfall of state revenues from the guaranteed 14 per cent increase would be compensated. During the discussion of the GST Council regarding the draft GST law, states were assured by the then Union finance minister that if for some reason the Compensation Fund was exhausted, money could be temporarily borrowed, and repayments done by extending the cess for a year or two or until the money could be fully recuperated. But during the pandemic, the Union government unilaterally changed its earlier stance by demarcating normal shortfall in GST revenue from COVID shortfall, which was described as an act of God. Though a consensus was eventually worked out, the acrimonious debate soured relationships in the council. The controversies brought to the forefront the unequal power balance between states and the Union in the GST Council.

Similarly, the GST Council's meetings mandate a quorum of one-half of the total number of its members. Every decision of the council was to be taken at a meeting by a majority of not less than three-fourths of the weighted votes of the members present and voting. The vote of the central government is to have a weightage of one-third of the total votes cast, and the votes of all the state governments taken together are to have a weightage of two-thirds of the total votes cast, in a particular meeting. Hence, even if all states come together about a proposal at the council, no decision can be taken without the consent of the Centre.[17]

The great expectations of the GST Council, which hailed as the best example of cooperative federalism during the first anniversary celebrations of the GST, have not been realized. COVID has been a major blow to the stabilization of the new tax system. Hasty reductions in the rates with an eye on elections have created inverted duty structures and rendered the rates non-revenue neutral. The IT backbone of the GST, which is not yet complete, has also affected revenue buoyancy. Therefore, all states have demanded that the compensation mechanism be extended for a few more years. The Centre has been myopically stonewalling this demand even though it has no implication for Union finances because the additional resource mobilization is through a proposed special cess. All these have rendered the GST Council a terrain of contestation.

Conclusion: way forward

The experience of the institutional framework of India's federal system is disappointing. This has severe implications for the functioning of the federation. As things stand today, the overall trend has been towards greater centralization and weakening of the states. The atrophying of key inter-state institutions, the problems of sharing tax revenues/GST compensation, the manner in which the Union government has bypassed states through legislations/policies, etc., are collectively exacerbating the structural issues plaguing India's federalism. These need to be urgently redressed in the national and people's interests.

Firstly, the Finance Commission must firmly anchor itself within its constitutional moorings. Additionally, the wide laxity currently abrogated to the interpretation of 'sound finance' in the FC's ToR must be restricted. This is an issue that has come up in the context of the fifteenth FC, and the national debate on it should be taken forward to its logical conclusion.

Secondly, that the Union government misuses the loophole in the Constitution to subvert tax devolution by taking recourse to cess and surcharge has been exposed. This needs to be redressed urgently. The cess and surcharges must be included in the divisible pool and devolution redefined as a ratio of gross central tax rather than the present practice of net tax collection.

Thirdly, the great threat that hangs over every state like a Damocles sword is the FRBM Review Committee Report, the acceptance of which would severely restrict their fiscal space.

Implementation of the report would drastically bring down the fiscal deficit ceiling of the states from the present 3 per cent to 1.7 per cent of GSDP and consequently the capital receipts of the states would dwindle.

Fourthly, the Planning Commission should not be resurrected as it used to exist given the transformation of national policies from the 1990s. However, the abolition of the PC has converted the Union finance ministry into a super ministry with unparalleled resources and decision-making powers at its disposal. We need to therefore reimagine the PC, different from the past with no pretensions to comprehensive planning but with the objective of setting the priorities for new projects of the Union government and dovetailing them with those of the states, and providing an antidote to widening inequalities as well as protection, however limited, to the domestic economy in the globalizing world.

Fifthly, planning is discussed mostly in the context of local governments. Kerala is the only state that still has a State Planning Board and plan budget. Ever since the People's Plan in 1996–97, the local governments in Kerala have been preparing comprehensive local plans with the direct participation of local communities. People's participation can be ensured in farming, small-scale production, services, etc., through gram sabhas, seminars, action committees, etc. In fact, it is because of the people's active participation in hospital development committees of primary healthcare centres that Kerala did very well in managing the COVID-19 pandemic.[18] This is a sustainable model that needs to be replicated across the nation.

Sixthly, without an active Inter-State Council there is no federal forum for discussion between the Centre and states on the one hand, or between states on the other. Numerous policy changes are being made such as electricity acts, the labour code, the three controversial agricultural laws, and even privatization of the public sector (including but not limited to the myopic National Monetisation Pipeline), which all have adverse implications for the states and the nation as a whole. These perforce need to be thoroughly discussed threadbare, which can only happen at the Inter-State Council. The scope of discussion at the GST Council is limited to GST. Furthermore, only state finance ministers have representation on the council.

Seventhly, there is widespread awareness that GST will have to be revamped and the rates rejigged. This can only be done if the GST functions consensually and democratically. If the trust deficit between the Centre and the states is bridged (the onus of which lies largely on the Centre), the GST Council can be leveraged to move towards a tax system with greater federal flexibility such as a narrow band of rates for intra-state trade. The style of transactions during the early years of the GST Council can provide useful lessons for cooperative federal functioning.

Finally, can we reimagine India's federal system on the principle of subsidiarity? All that can be best undertaken and implemented at the local level should be devolved to the local levels. Only residual powers, whether financial, political or operational, should be taken to the higher level. This will not only make governance more inclusive and people-centric, but also make scheme implementation more effective, accountable and transparent. Ultimately, this is the only way to expedite development and ensure it truly addresses the needs and aspirations of the people.

However, this inversion of the present power pyramid, though desirable for many reasons, has little chance of being realized in today's political climate. Sadly, the political climate in the country has degenerated to such an extent that diversity is rejected and national homogeneity is idealized. Today, all platforms for dialogue and negotiation between the Union and India's constituent units (including the states) are being deliberately undermined and destroyed. This high-handedness is premised on the flawed notion that differences of opinion and approaches are anti-national. However, this 'my way or the highway' approach is not conducive to governing a nation as vast and diverse as India, and it is imperative that the Union government take everyone along in the national interest.

Given this, in this undemocratic and frankly untenable situation, devolving greater powers and autonomy to the lower levels would be anathema to the new nationalist ideal. Nevertheless, such an imagining would be a powerful tool in resisting further centralization. It would also help in recapturing whatever is left of India's lost federal space and act as an effective check against future authoritarian tendencies.

Re-Empowering the People: Strengthening India's Information Commissions

Wajahat Habibullah

'The great democratising power of information has given us all the chance to effect change and alleviate poverty in ways we cannot even imagine today. Our task, your task . . . is to make that change real for those in need, wherever they may be. With information on our side, with knowledge of a potential for all, the path to poverty can be reversed'

—United Nations Secretary-General Kofi Annan

Introduction: Lifting the shroud of secrecy

As India's Right to Information (RTI) Act, 2005, passes its sixteenth year, there has been much concern on the course that democratic function, exacerbated by the onset of a pandemic, has taken in our country. 'Scams' centring on government initiatives leading in the opening years of the present decade, and the subsequent clamour for an effective ombudsman, a 'lokpal', can be said to have been among the causes for the discomfiture in the national elections of 2014 of the very government that piloted the act. But the government that has succeeded it, although avowedly retaining the credo of transparency and accountability with prime ministerial candidate Narendra Modi promising in his 2014 campaign 'maximum of governance with minimum government', coupled with increased participation of the people in governance with his slogan of '*sabka saath, sabka vikas*' (together with all, development for all), appears instead to have subverted the very foundations of democratic function.

It is universally accepted that the essence of government in a democracy must be transparency, with every organ of government—the Executive, the judiciary and the legislature—being answerable to the citizen. Mahatma Gandhi, the father of the nation, described it best when he outlined his vision of self-government for India, saying: 'Real Swaraj will come not by the acquisition of authority by a few but by the acquisition of capacity by all to resist authority when abused.' Seen in this light, accountability in governance is predicated on response-ability.

India's RTI Act therefore declares that vital to democracy is an informed citizenry, which can come only from transparency of, and ready access to, information. This alone can contain corruption and hold governments and their instrumentalities accountable to the governed. Seen in this light, the RTI was designed as an instrument to help strengthen, not weaken, governance. Introducing the bill in the Lok Sabha, then Prime Minister Dr Manmohan Singh rightly declared on 11 May 2005:[1]

'I believe that the passage of this Bill will see the dawn of a new era in our processes of governance, an era of performance and efficiency, an era which will ensure that benefits of growth flow to all sections of our people, an era which will eliminate the scourge of corruption, an era which will bring the common man's concern to the heart of all processes of governance, an era which will truly fulfil the hopes of the founding fathers of our Republic.'

By and large, Indians have taken to the RTI with enthusiasm, demanding accountability from officials at every level of government. Over six million RTI queries are filed annually,[2] inquiring about delays or stoppages in government schemes, quality or availability of essential goods and services or to expose rent-seeking/diversion of funds in government contracts and programmes. The RTI has thus empowered ordinary citizens tremendously, by giving them the right to demand information at par with members of Parliament and members of Legislative Assemblies (who can ask questions of the Executive to hold them accountable). It has gone a long way in lifting the web of secrecy shrouding governance in India.

Contradictions in governance

Now, more than fifteen years later, we the people need to ask ourselves whether governance is achieving the end that Prime Minister Singh spoke of in May 2005. Despite the clamour for better governance, the answer today will unfortunately be resoundingly in the negative. Inevitably, change in the form and content of government has been marked from the time of Independence. From a means to perpetuate imperial rule, governance in India developed into a means of seeking and furthering equitable economic growth. Yet, the bureaucratic infrastructure has remained relatively constant and firmly grounded in mistrust. The reason for this mistrust can be found in the legacy that the government in India built on— stemming directly at the district level from the Mughal[3] zila, headed then by an *amal guzar,* predecessor to the British titled collector (meaning the collector of land revenue, the government's principal resource base at the time). The government adapted and bound itself in an archaic secretariat system or steel frame of the colonial structure modelled on the permanent civil service of Whitehall, which was originally designed to maximize extraction from India and transport it to Britain. The elitist nature of both systems sadly continues to subsist. The welfare state strongly influenced by the wartime licensing legacy for distributing shortages ushered India into independence. India's economy therefore remained rooted in the concept of shortage.

That elite bureaucratic structure did indeed call for replacement. But whereas change has admittedly been constant, the question today is whether instruments of democracy are actually strengthening democracy. Is there even a political consensus on what these instruments need to do to achieve this? Institutions intended to secure means of public participation in governance are now increasingly expected to act as 'lions under the throne'.

To be true to democracy, governance must be distinct from the exercise of power. Even security of life and property, both of which are predicated on the security of the nation, must be as perceived not by the security forces or the bureaucracy, but by the people of India. If this is understood, it is easier to see why perceived needs have not been met by the existing system, even though widely understood. At the same time, we can also see that today we face new challenges in India's democratic functioning.

India's founders, our first political leaders after we won our freedom, were Westernized in their education, and therefore if not in demeanour, certainly in their approach to management of governance. Government was hence paternalist. The civil services were an object of respect. Such service, even though not legally so, was in practice close to being hereditary. It was this civil service that oversaw the running of a 'socialist' economy; with the State omnipresent. The welfare State was seen as a necessity. However, its achievements, although many, were hardly commensurate with investment. The inevitable advent of liberalization at the close of the twentieth century together with the increasing indigenization of government practices has seen the State finding itself in transition across the board: social, economic, political.

Politicization of the civil services, once the mainstay of government, is an inexorable offshoot of democratic rule, which commenced in the late 1960s, and picked up pace in the early

1970s. The civil service had been trained not to question political decision-making. With the maturing of the political element in governance, the civil service also realized its strengths. The demands of management therefore (and perhaps inevitably) led these two basic elements of governance to synergize their understanding of functions and demands, and even to constructive collaboration. Despite the transformation, however, this convergence has to this day remained largely elusive and now appears to be drifting into outright confrontation.

An unfortunate ramification of these changes has been the rise of corruption and the dilution of established ethical norms. This has been compounded, not mitigated, by economic change. That change is what is described as liberalization. For the State this meant giving up control of the means of production and shifting towards regulating different sectors of the economy. Access to decision-making for those working within government has become more restricted. With the rise of the assertiveness of business houses, entrenched means of access to ill-gotten gains by the state hierarchy is increasingly limited, hence supplanting traditional corruption channels with, instead of coordination, collusion, which is now marked between those earlier considered outsiders including politicians and business houses—termed 'cronies'—and bureaucrats. There is gossip of bureaucrats being on sale.

Legislation for transparency was intended to arrest this slide. Instead, with unprecedented growth in GDP terms, liberalization and globalization, which increased the disposable income in the hands of the middle class, have deepened the disparity between the richest 10 per cent and the poorest 20 per cent of society. It is understood that good governance must be participatory, transparent and accountable.[4] However, the present system in India, thanks to perceptions enshrined in the Official Secrets Act, 1923 (which is still not abrogated), remains firmly grounded in mistrust. The basic question that needs to be asked therefore is, for whom are the benefits of governance intended?

To answer this query, one might examine as an example the guarantee of public health for every citizen, a primary objective of any democratic government. Consider the case of healthcare in India. Despite the endeavour of successive governments, a network of primary health centres down to the level of every panchayat, and the multiplicity of schemes for the welfare of the poorest— leading up to the present prime minister's Ayushman Bharat scheme that seeks to enhance accessibility to healthcare—ready and easy access to quality health facilities still evades too many. We have among the world's best doctors in our midst and hospitals to which patients gravitate from across the world to seek affordable and quality treatment, and India is the world leader in producing prophylactics. The primary aim of the National Health Policy, 2017, is to inform, clarify, strengthen and prioritize the role of the government in shaping health systems in all its dimensions.[5] This would enable India to develop high quality and better institutionalize medical pluralism, which should give millions of Indians the choice of holistic medical systems (which have ensured widespread healthcare to our people for centuries, at a time when Europe was still struggling with primitive instrumentation) apart from the allopathic. Yet, the bitter reality is that investment by governments in health forms a negligible proportion of India's budgetary provisions. Consequently, our healthcare infrastructure is atrophying, and our healthcare personnel are migrating outwards looking for and finding better opportunities elsewhere. There could have been no more dramatic demonstration of government and governance failure than the buckling of the country's health administration in the face of the onset of the COVID-19 pandemic in 2020–21.

Notwithstanding the pace of development activity, because of the demands of national security, the exercise of individual freedom and social security, which are the heart of a democracy that respects the sovereignty of individual liberty (secured with the pronouncement of the apex court clearly defining the right to privacy), has remained ephemeral at best. A tragic example is the recent passing of Father Stan Swamy, an accused in the Elgar Parishad case of Maharashtra of whom former Union minister Jairam Ramesh tweeted[6] on 5 July 2021, 'Who in the apparatus of the Indian state will be held responsible for this tragedy? Make no mistake—it is the Indian state that killed Fr Stan Swamy, who was such a passionate crusader for social justice.' Although there are, and will be, disgruntled elements in any society and there will even be incendiaries and extremists who would love to undermine the country, this is what governance must be designed to overcome, by giving each citizen a sense that they are a participant in governance through being able to hold not only the political leadership, but every section of government from the lowest to the highest, accountable to them. Surely then security becomes the concern not of a few but of all.

Similarly, what is known as the Maoist movement today has convulsed poverty-stricken tribal areas down the east coast from Odisha to Telangana, with tremors across the tribal belt in Jharkhand, Madhya Pradesh and Rajasthan. Herein the tribals have seen minor forest produce, which is theirs by right, being expropriated by multinational corporations (MNCs) for their profit, with little or no benefit to themselves. Worse still, despite progressive legislation embodied in the Forest Rights Act, 2006, areas that were forests and home to the tribals through millennia have been mined and rendered uninhabitable, with the local people benefiting at best through paltry incomes from labour. The reason Maoists found easy purchase initially was because of these glaring inequalities and inequities in the development process. A lack of inclusive development foments the rise of militant and extremist groups. To address this, we had passed the Panchayats (Extension to Scheduled Areas) Act, 1996 (PESA)[7] to return governance to the tribals. But have we even begun to reverse the path to poverty? Recent trends show a backslide. And has there been greater participation of our citizenry in their own security?

The point being made is that governance in India has been, and sadly continues to be, top-down. Continuing the colonial tradition of viewing governance as an elite and paternalistic activity, the underlying assumption is that those in charge of policymaking and implementation know best for the people and the nation. This trend has exacerbated under the Bharatiya Janata Party (BJP) government, with extreme centralization in the Prime Minister's Office,[8] which had already grown from being an office to service the prime minister's official needs into a political leviathan eclipsing even the Cabinet Secretariat. Consequently, there is little involvement of citizens in governance, and information of bureaucratic processes and procedures is treated as a State secret. Citizens are at best seen as passive recipients of government aid. The chaos of democratic functioning, of consultative and inclusive governance, is viewed as a hindrance to the functioning of the government.

Understanding a citizen's right to information

In this context, it is important to reflect on the definition of 'information' in the Right to Information Act. Armed with information on government functioning, the citizen's ability to form informed opinions and raise their voices is meaningfully enhanced, thereby deepening democracy substantially. Such information can be gleaned from any material in any form including records, documents, memos, e-mails, opinions, advices, press releases, circulars, orders, logbooks, contracts, reports, papers, samples, models, data material held in any electronic form and 'information relating to any private body which can be accessed by a public authority under any other law for the time being in force'[9]. Opening the doors for such information to be accessed by any citizen was nothing short of a 'governance revolution'. It was predicated on the belief that people are the penultimate ends of development and democracy, and that governments are just a means to furthering their well-being. As PM Manmohan Singh boldly declared in his address to the Annual

Convention of Information Commissions in 2013, this was purposely intended so as 'to bring under the Act almost the entire scope of the economic firmament, which thanks to the heritage of our "welfare state" is answerable to government in a wide host of sectors'.

Some of the key concepts under the right to information include the following:

- transparency and accountability in the working of every public authority;
- the right of any citizen of India to request access to information and the corresponding duty of every government to meet the request, except exempted information; and
- the duty of every government to proactively make key information available to all.

In making every citizen a participant in governance, the RTI Act places a responsibility not only on Central and state administrations, but also on all sections of the national fabric—the citizenry, non-governmental organizations (NGOs) and the media. To ensure this, governments must cleave to the statutory obligation so clearly enunciated in Section 4 (1) of the Act, which states:

'Every public authority *shall* [emphasis added] – (a) maintain all its records duly catalogued and indexed in a manner and form which facilitates the right to information under this Act and ensure that all records that are appropriate to be computerized are, within a reasonable time and subject to availability of resources, computerized and connected through a network all over the country on different systems so that access to such records is facilitated.'

This then was the only law to capitalize on one of India's greatest assets—our revolution in information technology. And the National Informatics Centre, an arm of the Government of India, has moved on designing systems to apply, appeal and get decisions on the Internet with great alacrity. The government has followed through with a vigorous programme towards digitization. The right to information includes the right to inspect works, documents, records; take notes, extracts or certified copies of documents or records; take certified samples of material; obtain information in the form of printouts, diskettes, floppies, tapes, video cassettes or in any other electronic mode or through printouts. It does not extend to information not held in material form.

Yet the law has been undermined in recent years by the simple expedient of refusing information on grounds of security or, worse, if the information concerns the dirty secrets of an influential personality, privacy. The latter has been pleaded even in cases of degrees issued by public institutions of education. This is a clear violation of the RTI Act, which only exempts the following information from disclosure (under Section 8 of the Act):

- Information, the disclosure of which would prejudicially affect the sovereignty and integrity of India, the security, strategic, scientific or economic interests of the State, relations with a foreign State or lead to incitement of an offence.
- Information that has been expressly forbidden to be published by any court of law or tribunal or the disclosure of which may constitute contempt of court.
- Information, the disclosure of which would cause a breach of privilege of Parliament or the state legislature.
- Information including commercial confidence, trade secrets or intellectual property, the disclosure of which would harm the competitive position of a third party, unless the competent authority is satisfied that larger public interest warrants the disclosure of such information.
- Information available to a person in his fiduciary relationship, unless the competent authority is satisfied that the larger public interest warrants the disclosure of such information.

- Information received in confidence from a foreign government.
- Information that would impede the process of investigation or apprehension or prosecution of offenders.
- Cabinet papers including records of deliberations of the council of ministers, secretaries and other officers.
- Information that relates to personal information the disclosure of which has no relationship to any public activity or interest, or which would cause unwarranted invasion of the privacy of the individual; infringes copyright, except of the State.
- Where practicable, part of a record can be released.
- Intelligence and security agencies are exempt—except in cases of corruption and human rights violations.
- Third party information to be released after giving notice to the third party.

Yet, on several occasions, requests for information under the RTI Act have been rejected, even when such requests don't fall under the earlier-mentioned exemptions. For example, RTI requests on demonetization were repeatedly denied by the Government of India,[10] as were RTIs seeking the list of wilful loan defaulters listed by the Reserve Bank of India,[11] on the Prime Minister-CARES fund,[12] on the cabinet note on the constitutional amendment introducing reservations for the economically weaker sections of society,[13] on electoral bonds[14] and a host of issues that the people have an inalienable right to know. All these issues have a profound impact on India's society, economy and politics, and yet an iron wall of secrecy has descended over these.

This is deeply saddening because, under the proviso contained in Section 8(2) of the RTI Act, notwithstanding any of these exemptions or indeed even India's Official Secrets Act (a colonial construct of 1923), a public authority may still allow access to information if *public interest in disclosure is deemed to outweigh the harm to the protected interests*. And most exempt information is at any rate to be released after twenty years, with some exceptions, although also provided that the information, which cannot be denied to Parliament or a state legislature, shall not be denied to any person. Yet, there has been little endeavour by any government—Union or state—despite repeated pronouncements of the Central and State Information Commissions, to make such information readily accessible after the appointed time, thus obviating the government's responsibility in storing information that needs to be withheld in the public interest as secret and placing in the public domain that which doesn't. This absurdity can be seen in the extenuated debate in 2015 over the release of documents concerning the circumstances of the death of that icon of India's freedom movement Subhash Chandra Bose, 'Netaji' to Indians. Documents that should have ideally been in the public domain in any case under the law, were found, with the onset of the present government, to have concealed nothing in the first place.

While conceding that the responsibility for the successful implementation of the Act is shared with citizens, NGOs and the media, this cannot exempt governments from their primary responsibility of ensuring transparency and accountability. In fact, the RTI Act places a host of responsibilities on all public authorities, at all levels. Authorities were made primarily responsible for raising awareness, educating and training not only officials but also members of the public. For this, every department was expected to develop and organize educational programmes to advance the understanding of the public, particularly the disadvantaged, to exercise their right to information. Several gram panchayats, notably in the state of Rajasthan, have in fact taken the lead in painting necessary information on to Panchayat walls to guide the public. Not having done so, other governments can hardly blame the public for misuse.[15] In addressing the Annual Convention of Information Commissions in 2012,[16] Prime Minister Manmohan Singh had declared that government must monitor trends of RTI applications so as to identify the shortcomings in the functioning of each of its organs. This never happened, and Prime Minister

Modi's flagship *Mann ki Baat* programme, ostensibly a step towards more transparency, has been used only as a means for the PM to talk down to the citizenry, with no inbuilt mechanism to answer questions.

But the law itself has helped generate the wider use of modern technologies across villages. The use of cellular phones is widespread, and information has begun to be disseminated through this instrument.

The pluralist society

In their Report of the People's Assessment, 2008,[17] two eminent NGOs, Right to Information Assessment and Analysis Group (RaaG) together with the National Campaign for the Right to Information (NCPRI), have, based on an exhaustive analysis of feedback from eleven states under the guidance of eminent RTI activist Dr Shekhar Singh, found that awareness levels by that year, compared to equivalent awareness of any other law in its infancy, were high. Thus, over 40 per cent of urban respondents knew about the RTI Act, although the figure was fewer than 20 per cent for rural respondents. The sources of awareness in rural India were newspapers (35 per cent), followed by television and radio, friends and relatives (10 per cent each), and NGOs (5 per cent). In urban areas, on the other hand, the sources were newspapers (30 per cent), NGOs (20 per cent), TV (20 per cent) and friends and relatives (10 per cent).

On the negative side was the finding that administrative problems continued to dog the filing of applications. This has been exacerbated by the fact that there are 114 different sets of RTI rules to implement the Act in India and no one place where they are all available. Some states insist on correspondence in the local language despite Section 4(4) of the RTI Act that requires that information be disseminated in the 'most effective method of communication in that local area', which in a multi-linguistic nation like India, can become a deterrent to migrants. This has been worsened by poor signage, multiple windows, multiple visits to offices and even a multiplicity of public information officers (PIOs).

What will be of great interest to those in government, however, is the assessment of these findings on the impact of the RTI Act on public authorities. The report found that over 20 per cent of the rural and 45 per cent of the urban PIOs claimed that changes had been made in the functioning of their offices because of the Act. Over 60 per cent of these changes pertained to improving record maintenance, which has been a grossly neglected area in government—a fact that I, as Chief Information Commissioner, can attest to based on hearing cases from a cross-section of some of our most efficient offices. Interestingly, in 10 per cent of the rural offices and as much as 25 per cent of the urban public authorities, what had resulted were adaptations in procedures of functioning and decision-making to bring them in line with the RTI Act. This figure would have grown considerably since, in at least as much as the Government of India is concerned. Thus, there is empirical evidence that when implemented effectively, the RTI Act helps transform governance for the better. It may result in uncomfortable disclosures about rent-seeking, misuse of power and violation of rules/protocols in the short run, but surely these are issues that need to be weeded out permanently. Why would any government want to hide or help cover up sins of commission and omission (unless it was part of the problem)?

The descent of the iron wall of secrecy

Transparency and accountability are principles that have been promised by every government. Despite this, by and large, the State is wary of 'opening up'. This is partly due to the structural and conceptual problems that free India inherited and chose to continue from the colonial government. In the past few years, however, this hesitance has assumed gargantuan proportions. This may be due to the fact that political parties tend to behave differently when in opposition than when they assume office. This is perhaps best illustrated by considering the examples of many leading lights of the BJP such as Arun Jaitley[18] (later finance minister) and former foreign minister Jaswant Singh who made extensive use of the RTI. Similarly, the BJP's RTI cell reportedly managed to unearth files with a noting on spectrum allocation in September 2011, and again got information on the Commonwealth Games. It used both issues devastatingly, and successfully managed to put the then United Progressive Alliance government on the back foot.

Yet, once the BJP assumed office, it made a volte-face. For example, it introduced an amendment to the RTI Act in 2019, which has compromised the Act's neutrality. With this, information commissioners, who originally had statutory five-year tenures and salaries on par with those of the Election Commission of India, will have 'terms as may be prescribed by the central government'. Their tenures and salaries shockingly now lie at the discretion of the Union government, the very institution that the information commissions are supposed to hold accountable.

The government has also declined to disclose information previously accessible under the RTI Act. In 2016–17, the home and finance ministries rejected close to 15 per cent of the applications they received while the RBI and public sector banks rejected 33 per cent.[19]

This was exacerbated by the BJP government not appointing a chief information commissioner for a year after the incumbent retired in August 2014, and not filling vacant information commissioner posts in the Central Information Commission (CIC) between 2016 and 2018, a year when, consequently, only seven commissioners out of the sanctioned strength of eleven were in place. Only with the intervention of the Supreme Court were some appointments made in January 2019, but four posts remained vacant. Yet, despite the court's intervention, there continues to be a mismatch between the sanctioned and actual strength of information commissions (both at the national and state levels, even though the central government has assumed greater authority in appointments). Nine out of twenty-nine information commissions (31 per cent) in the country are without a chief information commissioner, which going by a strict reading of the law, puts into question the judicial validity of their decisions.

Consequently, there is a massive backlog of 35,880 cases[20] in just the CIC. Instead of clearing this backlog sincerely, the CIC has disingenuously amended the RTI rules to minimize this statistic by refusing applications as invalid on specious grounds at the very stage of admission, which the law sought to make automatic. Additionally, the CIC used to initially hold the hands of central PIOs so as to sensitize them and ease their dealings with the RTI Act, which at the time was an unprecedented administrative procedure. Sadly, today, what was once an informal nudging-to-perform better has descended into colluding-to-conceal. Furthermore, most information commissioners are overwhelmingly retired government officials, whilst the Act had been designed to include eminent citizens with a wide range of experiences. Retired officials tend to lean towards maintaining secrecy on most issues, rather than wanting to open the doors to public scrutiny. Thanks to these evolutions working in tandem, the CIC, which is to be the penultimate authority to guarantee transparency and accountability in governance, has become the biggest weapon against transparency and accountability in governance.

Similarly, there is also a massive backlog in all information commissions. According to an SNS-CES study,[21] as of 31 July 2020, a total of 2,21,568 cases were pending with twenty information commissions. This has been exacerbated by the fact that between 1 April 2019 and 31 July 2020, a total of 15,738 show-cause notices were issued to PIOs under the penalty clause of the Act.[22] Yet, information commissioners have been frugal in imposing penalties. And the high courts, in responding to public interest litigations (PILs) have ruled against decisions of the information commission, although supportive of the RTI Act, have been less than forthcoming in ruling on penalties, partly because they are unconvinced in the face of poorly argued matters by information commissioners.

Finally, public-spirited citizens who have become full-time RTI activists have been routinely targeted and attacked. In the last few years, eighty-six RTI activists have been murdered, 170 have been physically assaulted and 183 cases of threats or harassment have been registered.[23] The Whistle Blowers Protection Act, 2011,[24] which sought to address persistent threats to whistle-blowers, was passed by Parliament but never enforced. Even more worryingly, according to a proposed bill amending the Whistle Blower Protection Act, whistle-blowers may be prosecuted for possessing documents on which a complaint has been made. If this bill is ever passed, it would serve as a deterrent to whistle-blowers, who would be discouraged from proactively reporting any wrongdoing.

Thomas Paine once argued that 'a body of men holding themselves accountable to nobody ought not to be trusted by anybody'. This can be held true of all governments. If any government is truly representative of the people, has nothing to hide and is only guided by the national interest, it will inevitably be transparent about its conduct. Yet, the BJP government has so far conducted itself otherwise, choosing instead to clamp down on all mechanisms to promote transparency in governance.

Unexpected blows to transparency

Yet, set against all its unequivocal pronouncements for transparency and accountability in governance, the Supreme Court has been strikingly inconsistent. In the recent *Chief Information Commissioner vs High Court of Gujarat,*[25] the court overturned the principle that no reasons are required to be given for requesting information under the RTI Act. This is despite Section 6 (2) of the RTI Act being explicit that, 'an application making request for information *shall not be required to give any reason for requesting the information* or any other personal details' (emphasis added) allowing only for such details 'as may be necessary for contacting him.' Besides, the law is clear that if the RTI is inconsistent with any other law, the provisions of the RTI Act would override that law, including the draconian Official Secrets Act, 1923 (Ref. Section 22). Such unthinking judgments establish a dangerous precedent that can be misused by governments to evade answerability but are in keeping with the argument of a former chief[26] in governance, myopically implying that it was impeding decision-making, an observation without basis in fact.

On average, PIOs received forty-two queries annually in 2012–13, which gradually increased to sixty-eight by 2018–19.[27] In effect, one PIO services just about six RTI requests per month. On the other hand, if the former chief justice of India (CJI) meant that the RTI Act scared institutions of the State to take decisions that could be perceived to be detrimental to the public interest, then that is a very welcome consequence of the Act. Nobody can seriously dispute that public servants must at all times be conscious of the consequences of their every action on their fellow citizens and on the nation.

Similarly, in a November 2019 judgment,[28] while the Supreme Court brought the CJI's office under the ambit of the RTI Act in finally disposing of a PIL on the Central Information Commission's decision of 24 November 2009,[29] it also severely restricted the scope of the Act by adding to the list of exceptions under Section 8 of the Act. However, it went further, and paragraph 59 of the judgment suggests that the list of exemptions is only 'indicative'. This effectively opened the door for any public servant to deny any information citing this judgment. There is evidence to show that state governments did subsequently leverage this very paragraph to direct PIOs to be cautious in disclosing information, as was the case with a Haryana government circular.[30]

Ironically, this goes against the Supreme Court's own observation, which earlier upheld the right to information as a fundamental right flowing from Article 19 of India's Constitution, which guarantees every citizen the right to free speech and expression.

Decentralization—Panchayat

The RTI Act is therefore not simply an Act to contain corruption or indeed to hold government accountable for its actions. It is no less than a declaration of the objective that we have set ourselves as a democracy. As discussed, this means that the Act applies to all elements of governance in the widest sense of that term, which in a democracy must include the people themselves. When India attained freedom, Mahatma Gandhi hoped that, 'Independence must begin at the bottom. Thus, every village will be a republic or Panchayat having full powers. It follows therefore, that every village has to be self-sustained and capable of managing its affairs even to the extent of defending itself against the whole world'.[31] In stark contrast, Dr Ambedkar in introducing India's draft Constitution for a second reading was condemnatory of village self-government: 'What is the village but a sink of localism, a den of ignorance, narrow mindedness and communalism? I am glad that the Draft Constitution has discarded the village and adopted the individual as its unit . . . '.

Section 243 (d) of the Constitution of India reads: 'Panchayat' means an *institution (by whatever name called) of self-government* [emphasis added] constituted under article 243B, for the rural areas.' The objective of Prime Minister Rajiv Gandhi in bringing this 73rd amendment (which was subsequently passed by the successor Narasimha Rao government) was to give voice to those without voice in the governance of their own neighbourhoods. In a sense, it was the precursor to the RTI Act, since it sought to empower citizens at the grassroots and give them a say in decisions affecting their lives. Since every resident of a village was a member of the gram sabha, everyone had a voice and say in decision-making. Key to the effective inclusion of even the most far-flung and isolated communities in governance is the institution of the gram panchayat (the village council), which is the repository for scheme information, citizen surveys, fiscal information, etc., and of which the gram sabha is the legislature.

India has for decades been the world's largest investor, in terms of its GDP, in poverty eradication. Panchayati raj institutions (PRIs), more than any other instrument of the State, were specially designed to induct citizens in rural areas into areas of governance. Gram sabhas, designed to be the font of the country's legislative framework, make every citizen a legislator. Empowering them, and ensuring that they act to ensure the basic necessity of better health and nutrition in the villages, is vital for public participation in governance. Government initiatives such as monthly village health and nutrition days (VHNDs) have, where effective, already done much to improve access to and delivery of essential health and nutrition services. It only remained to ensure that these government initiatives were integrated with the panchayat plans of village development. While helping educate the public on benefits provided by government, gram panchayats can educate government on the aspirations of residents of the villages. But this requires the devolution of functions, funds and functionaries by state administrations. Already far from comprehensive, such devolution has now been reversed, with teams from district headquarters now being assigned village visits to teach fellow citizens residing in villages how to manage themselves. Consequently, panchayats have been reduced from institutions of 'self-government' (as envisioned by Article 243 of the Constitution) to mere organs of the state administration. The effects of the COVID-19 pandemic were compounded in rural areas, partly because of this state-sponsored undermining of decentralization.

Conclusion

Today, the right to information is a reality in our country and represents a major leap in evolving towards a fuller democracy. The passage of the Right to Information Act was described by one Magsaysay Award winner as 'the fall of the Bastille', since it promised to make us not only the world's largest, but also among the world's foremost democracies. Thus our social relations down to the village level that had become a hotbed of social vices as observed by Dr Ambedkar, an exploitative economic system with emerging public-private partnerships, a corrupted majoritarianism tilted towards exacerbating differences, a vitiated system of public distribution cornering resources for cronies, an educational system increasingly universal but not credited with any innovation, all stand to gain from the building of mutual trust that is in essence the fountainhead of transparency. While governments such as those in the United Kingdom struggle with the ramifications of the implementation of their Freedom of Information Act—the former prime minister of the UK Tony Blair described himself as a 'nincompoop' for having brought such a law—the people of India have firmly established their ownership of this law. With the institution of social audit, so successfully employed in several states, can we thus make this the thread for an ever more responsive democracy?

The RTI has now become an intrinsic part of what we perceive as good governance and indeed is a test of that, enabling benchmarks for any voter at the time of election. It is a silver bullet to combat the impression that government is unaccountable and inaccessible, a suspicion that in some part spawned a violent insurrection by the Maoists. If we need to progress and prosper together, we need to acknowledge that economic progress in India, spectacular as it has been, giving us all reason to be proud, has been anything but uniform. There are wide disparities—state-wise, region-wise within states, or even within social and professional categories of citizens. With the bottom falling out of the economy with the onset of COVID-19, government policy towards those who have felt deprived has served to exacerbate the vulnerabilities they face by further denying them the fruits of prosperity, which they see snatched from their own neighbourhoods by distant business entities in which they have no share, except at best as humble labourers. These citizens feel increasingly alienated from the prosperity they see before them. The only way to redress this is that people *feel* they are and actually *are* equal partners in India's story. That means ensuring governance is sensitive to the needs and aspirations of the people. A vital part of this is that people have to be able to use the RTI to hold government accountable and assert their voices. In this spirit, Justice Mathew's words, oft quoted in judicial circles, come to mind:

> 'In a government of responsibility like ours, where all agents of the public must be responsible for their conduct, there can be but few secrets. The people of this country have a right to know every public act, everything that is done in a public way, by their public functionaries . . . to cover with veil of secrecy the common routine business, is not in the interest of public.'

[*State of Uttar Pradesh v Raj Narain* (1975) 4 SCC 428.]

This mirrors the words of Justice Brandeis, that great American apostle of democracy, whom President Barack Hussain Obama cited in his pledge on taking office as the President of the United States of America. Justice Brandeis observed that 'sunlight is the best disinfectant'. It is only when sunlight can shine into every crevice of governance that we can finally declare our RTI Act has been a success. There are miles to go, but until that day, we must persevere in our quest to make governance participative and inclusive, which is the essence of democratic governance, and of which the information commissions must be vital instruments.

Patronage and Professionalism in the Indian Bureaucracy

Dr Naresh Chandra Saxena

Introduction—India's flailing state syndrome

Despite impressive economic growth in the last three decades, India has failed to make substantive strides on the United Nations Sustainable Development Goals particularly in hunger, health, nutrition, gender and sanitation. Today, India fares poorly on most human development indicators. In the 2021 Global Gender Gap Report,[1] India fell 28 spots to the 140th rank, much behind Bangladesh's rank of 65. Similarly, India ranked[2] 94 among 107 countries in the Global Hunger Index 2020 and continues to be in the serious hunger category. Likewise, India ranked[3] 131 out of 189 countries in the 2020 Human Development rankings, much below Sri Lanka (72), China (85) and Vietnam (117). Despite its strength, why does India continue to fare so poorly?

This dichotomy in India, of fast growth coupled with exclusionary development, effectively debunks the argument that growth by itself will take care of the poor and underprivileged (popularly known as the trickle-down theory). Despite this, Indian governments have not sufficiently invested in improving human development indicators or in combating inequalities. Instead, India has done exceedingly well on infrastructure projects (such as road transport and power supply), partly because such projects involve contractors. On all other programmes that require the active involvement of grassroots bureaucracy without contractors—whether it is the quality of education, immunization, healthcare, reducing malnutrition through *anganwadi* centres, correct identification of below poverty line families, maintenance of land records, etc., the system fails to deliver.[4] This is not only because of the politician–contractor nexus, but also because the contractors exert pressure on the bureaucracy to expedite release of funds. Ironically, despite its legitimate obsession with weeding out corruption, India's middle class valorizes accelerated infrastructure projects—*the* hotbed of corruption—as a measure of *vikas* (development).

Despite their individual competence, IAS officers,[5] who occupy almost all senior administrative positions in the states and the Centre, have not been able to improve development outcomes. This is despite the fact that those at the top are comparable to the best administrators in the world. This is largely due to the fact that India's political culture, especially in the states (and increasingly so at the Centre) is patronage-based, wherein politicians leverage the civil service to augment private gains and pursue personal political goals. Political pressures (both from within and without) to distribute patronage are so intense that there is no time or inclination for ministers and bureaucrats to engage in conceptual/strategic thinking, design good programmes, weed out/streamline those who are not functioning well, monitor programmes to improve the effectiveness of delivery, or undertake systemic reforms.

Consequently, the system consistently fails to ensure that teachers and doctors are present at their designated postings and providing quality services, or in ensuring timely pensions to widows and the disabled. Other areas of chronic failures include programme evaluation and monitoring, ensuring accuracy of land records and their updating without rent-seeking, ensuring harassment-free livelihoods for street vendors and rickshaw pullers, and assuring honest measurement and reporting of outcomes.[6]

This phenomenon has derisively been referred to as the 'flailing state syndrome', 'a nation-state in which the head, that is elite institutions at the national (and in some states) level, remains sound and functional but that this head is no longer reliably connected via nerves and sinews to its own limbs. Thus, field-level agents of the state, from health workers to teachers and engineers, are increasingly beyond the control of the government, at the state and national level. In police, tax collection, education, health, water supply—in nearly every routine service—there is rampant absenteeism, indifference, incompetence, and corruption'.[7]

This mismatch between capabilities, capacity and commitment between senior bureaucracy in the central ministries and implementation staff at the district and block levels is one of the reasons that despite the best of intentions and policies, often, things don't seem to change on the ground. It is the latter that requires greater capacity-building, transparency and accountability. Yet, attracted to the corridors of power, the media invariably (if at all) focuses on political/bureaucratic lethargy and failures of elite institutions. Except in isolated cases, they do not adequately understand or give coverage to where the real problem lies—at the sub-state (district, municipal/panchayat and block) level. To understand why India's system fails to deliver on accelerated outcomes, we must first objectively analyse some systemic issues in the political and bureaucratic system. For the purposes of brevity, we'll limit this to six structural issues.

Political expediency over public welfare

In a well-functioning democracy, political pressure can be healthy if it results in greater demands on administration for efficiency and better services to the people. This is, however, not happening in India.

It is an open secret that India's political and bureaucratic elite insidiously misuse public office for personal benefits.[8] State resources are the most valued prize for both politicians and their constituencies, which lead to the establishment of a client–patron relationship between the holders of state power and those seeking favours. It is little understood that the political system in most states is accountable not to the people, but to those interests who drive/support individual elected members of legislative assemblies (MLAs). These are often contractors, mafia, corrupt bureaucrats, media barons and manipulators who have enriched themselves through the political system, and are therefore deeply invested in the continuation of governance chaos and a patronage-based administration. That some politicians are either criminals or have strong criminal links further compounds the problem.

Though some reformist chief ministers have been invested in improving governance, unfortunately only a few have been able to concretize this. This is partly because one of the chief minister's key interests lies in keeping the MLAs and ministers of their government united and satisfied. This is especially difficult in a coalition regime, or if the ruling dispensation is constrained by a thin margin in the assembly, or if the principal coalition party is divided into factions. A reformist chief minister is inevitably stymied by their own party members, who hate getting sidelined in the process of establishing rule-based policy procedures. Sadly, a good chief minister is someone who has successfully *managed* corruption within the system. Nothing more. Conversely, in other states, chief ministers are averse to professionalizing administration since the benefits from those policies do not yield any immediate socio-political or economic benefits.

Experience teaches that patronage is controlled by individuals, not established institutions (that are duty-bound to follow set procedures). Where power is highly personalized and weakly institutionalized, the decision-making process is unavoidably riddled with arbitrary and behind-the-scenes transactions. In such an environment, power is misused to fudge rules, dependence upon corrupt civil servants increases, the public treasury is plundered, and there is decay in governance. When the fence starts eating the field, there is little chance of *vikas* reaching the poor. India's own Second Administrative Reforms Commission admitted that the 'criminalisation of politics continues unchecked, with money and muscle power playing a large role in elections. In general there is a high degree of volatility in society on account of unfulfilled expectations and poor delivery. Abuse of authority at all levels in all organs of state has become the bane of our democracy'.[9]

That is why the almost universal belief is that the bureaucracy is wooden, disinterested and corrupt. Bright men and women join the IAS, but an adverse work environment, constant political interference, frequent and often meaningless transfers, and corruption below and above them all lead to the death of idealism and encourage them to misuse their authority. Over the years, whatever virtues the IAS (once lauded as the steel frame of India) possessed—integrity, political neutrality, courage and high morale—are showing signs of decay.

Posted for weeks, collecting weekly bribes

One of the main reasons why systemic reforms have not been affected is the lack of stable tenure for officials. Appointments and transfers are two well-known areas where the evolution of firm criteria is circumvented in the name of administrative efficacy. This game of musical chairs aka transfers is also an arena of massive rent-seeking for corrupt officials and politicians. As tenures shorten, both efficiency and accountability suffer. For example, in Uttar Pradesh, the average tenure of an IAS officer in the last twenty years is reportedly as low as six months. The average tenure for an Indian Police Service officer in Uttar Pradesh is even lower, leading to the wisecrack, 'if we are posted for weeks, all we can do is collect our weekly bribes'.

Transfers have also been systematically used as instruments of reward and punishment to control and tame the bureaucracy. There is no transparency, and short tenures are stigmatized, while victimized officers can hardly defend themselves. This is exacerbated since service conduct rules[10] do not permit external public discussion or defence of one's position.[11] This leaves an honest civil servant at the mercy of superiors, both bureaucratic and political. To avoid succumbing to extra-legal/illegal directives (of rent-seeking, circumvention of rules, etc.), honest officials seek transfers themselves.

Robert Wade (1985)[12] has rightly argued that the Indian State cannot improve its functioning because this corruption-induced transfer mechanism adversely impacts bureaucratic initiative and dampens the urge to learn and master details and reform administration. Under Article 310 of the Indian Constitution, the right to transfer state government officials, including those officers of the three all-India services who are working under the state governments, is clearly vested with the state ministers. The Second Administrative Reforms Commission of 2008 recommended[13] that all senior posts both in Central and state governments should have a specified tenure. The task of fixing tenures for various posts should be assigned to an independent Civil Services Authority. However, none of the state governments have made the tenure of its officers stable, say, for a fixed period of at least two years.

Rapid changes destroy organizations because uncertainty erodes administrative efficiency, destroys institutional memory and compromises pro-people governance. This deep-seated structural problem has been brought to the attention of the highest offices, in vain. It is perhaps impossible for those benefiting from this rotten system to effect any constructive change. For example, while presiding over a meeting of the Planning Commission in 2001, Prime Minister Atal Bihari Vajpayee lamented that the problem with poor states was that they did not have any industry. I cheekily remarked, 'Sir, these states have a flourishing transfer and posting industry', inviting an angry glare. Needless to say, despite multiple exhortations, no discussion or action was taken on the said issue.

Too many cooks spoil the broth

Another structural problem is that the civil service exerts pressure on the system to create a large number of redundant promotional posts in the super-time and superior scales, which have circumscribed the responsibilities attached to every post. For instance, states have several chief secretary ranking-officers doing jobs that were previously done by junior officers. The previous post of health secretary is often split amongst five senior secretaries in charge of health, family planning, medical and medical education respectively, whereas the fifth one as principal secretary or additional chief secretary oversees the work of the other four secretaries! Imagine the logistical and organizational nightmare this can create, especially during national disasters like the COVID-19 pandemic. Officials jostling to protect their own turfs results in delays, while lakhs of citizens suffer.

Similarly, four decades ago, there was only one Inspector General of Police in Punjab, controlling the entire police force. Now there are fourteen director generals! However, the one dealing with crime and law and order enjoys the highest status, and those in home guards or training, though drawing the same salary, consider themselves sidelined. They subsequently hobnob with politicians to secure more important slots,[14] and an officer who retired as cabinet secretary, describes the situation in Bihar as follows:

'Every new Chief Minister would have his favourite as the new Chief Secretary. At one time, there were about 8 to 10 IAS officers drawing the pay of a Chief Secretary only because their juniors were appointed as Chief Secretaries at one time or the other. There were so many ex-Chief Secretaries that it was jokingly said that they could even form an Association of Chief Secretaries. The result of this on the civil service morale in Bihar does not need any elaboration'.

This was originally done to avoid demoralization due to stagnation, but the net result has been just the opposite. First, it leads to cut-throat competition within the service to grab coveted posts, destroying the old camaraderie. Second, this leads to political lobbying and more pliability, which politicians instrumentally exploit. Third, those officials who are in 'marginalized' positions turn against the government and approach tribunals and courts for promotions and postings, a phenomenon that was unheard of two decades ago. Obsession with status and perks plays havoc with integrity and neutrality amongst civil servants.

Too few amongst too many

In most states, about 50 per cent of all government employees are support staff unrelated to public service—drivers, peons and clerks. Key public services—education, healthcare, police and judiciary—are starved of qualified regular employees, whereas many departments are overstaffed with Group C and D support staff that have mostly become irrelevant in view of computerization and changing techniques of information management. For example, India still boasts of a shocking seven doctors per 10,000 population, as opposed to thirty per fifty in European countries.[15] Similarly, India has only 1.7 nurses per 1000 population, 43 per cent less than the World Health Organization norm (3 per 1000).[16] Likewise, sanctioned posts are not filled up in vital organs of delivery—be it teachers, nurses or policemen. A World Bank report[17] has accurately described the situation as follows:

'A given section officer (the lowest working level officer in the secretariat) can have from 5 to 10 assistants, consisting of

upper division clerks, lower division clerks, and peons. Many
are being made redundant through advances in information
technology, yet continue to draw their salaries. Ironically,
this excessive logistical tail often exists alongside significant
shortages of staff with skills in information technology,
financial management, and policy analysis. In many states,
there is also often a dearth of staff in critical front-line
positions such as primary school teachers, police, and rural
health workers—yet differing cadre rules and the tradition of
a "job for life" can make it very difficult to let go of staff or
to transfer them from surplus areas into those where there is
more demand.'

India's bureaucracy also faces an acute shortage of supervisory
staff. For instance, of the total 2.5 million regular employees in the
Union government, 63 per cent and 26 per cent were in Group C
and D posts respectively. About 8 per cent were in Group B posts,
and only 3 per cent were in Group A posts.[18]

Unpaid bureaucracy

It is little known that the salaries of regular government staff in
India are one of the world's highest, as a multiple of per capita
income, as shown below.

**Table 1: Average government wage as multiple of per
capita GDP**

Region	Multiple
Africa	5.7
Asia	3.0
Eastern Europe and Central Asia	1.3
Latin America	2.5
Middle East and North Africa	3.4

Region	Multiple
Organization for Economic Co-operation and Development countries	1.6
India	7.2
Overall	3.0

Source: Campo, Salvatore Schiavo, Giulio de Tommaso, Amitabh Mukherjee, 'In International Statistical Survey of Government Employment and Wages', World Bank, 2003 (https://documents1.worldbank.org/curated/en/300221468739461854/113513322_20041117144534/additional/multi-page.pdf)

Shockingly, pay increases in India are not intended to serve as a reward for increased productivity, but are given instead to gain support from the unions and to eliminate the threat of labour unrest. Moreover, government servants manage election booths, and no political party can afford their collective anger. High salaries have unfortunately not resulted in better outcomes. Transforming this needs political will.

Nevertheless, what's important is that the Government of India (GoI) annually transfers more than Rs 2.5 lakh crore to the states. However, many state governments, especially the poorer ones, are unable to draw their entitled funds from the GoI, or to release these to the districts/villages in time. Consequently, the GoI is often constrained to divert the unclaimed funds to better-performing states. This directly impacts the administration, which are unpaid or paid belatedly. An evaluation of Integrated Child Development Services (ICDS) in Bihar in 2007 by UNICEF showed that less than 10 per cent of grassroots workers received their honorarium regularly, while most received it only biannually, rather than monthly.[19] Another study showed that only 18 per cent of officials in Jharkhand working at the grassroots level are paid their salaries on time.[20] More recently, doctors, nurses and paramedic staff from Kasturba Hospital, Hindu Rao Hospital and Rajan Babu TB Hospital in Delhi went on strikes because they were unpaid for months during the peak of the COVID-19 pandemic.

The GoI's own studies[21] show that even electronic transfer takes months, delaying inordinately payments in the mid-day meals programme to ground staff such as cooks and helpers. Consequently, the Food Corporation of India withholds supply of grain, and mid-day meals are served only for 60 to 70 per cent of working days in some states.[22]

This has lately been exacerbated by inordinate delays in the transfer of monies by the GoI as per the provisions of the Goods and Services Tax Act. Several lakh crores were disbursed belatedly, and this severely impacted the ability of the states to pay their staff and implement their welfare agendas. It is common sense that non-payment of salaries to staff severely impacts their morale and professionalism, and inevitably leads to rent-seeking. Yet, almost no attention is paid to redressing such issues.

Absenteeism and bogus reporting

The bulk of expenditure in education and health typically flows to the salaries of teachers and health workers. Yet, teacher absenteeism is endemic, particularly in India's northern states. Almost two-thirds of government teachers were either absent or not teaching at the time of investigators' unannounced visits (World Bank 2008, 2019). Similarly, the Planning Commission found (2009),[23] on a surprise inspection in Bihar and Rajasthan, that just a quarter of doctors were physically on duty at the community health centres operating at the sub-district or block level.

Governments try to resolve this by using more and more tax revenues to provide (quantifiable) higher salaries for (less quantifiable) high quality services. Ironically, the system exists for the service providers but not for service provision. This hurts the poor and vulnerable, denying them basic goods and services, and defeats the very raison d'être of governments. Just two examples will suffice to illustrate this point.

A few years ago I visited a rural school in district Singhbhum, Jharkhand. I wrote on the blackboard a two-digit subtraction (31 minus 18) and asked the class V students to do it. Then I went round the desks and found that hardly half of the students could do it correctly. The next day when I met the district collector I asked him if he or his team monitored quality of learning. He said, 'Sir, you are the first person to be asking me this question. Government has never asked this, they only want to know if I have spent the allotted budget, built the new classrooms, and recruited the requisite number of teachers. There is no column in my format about the quality of learning.'

In 2008, Sachin Pilot (then just a member of Parliament) visited remote tribal areas to understand how the ICDS functioned. He was surprised to see that the anganwadi worker had to keep eighteen registers while the number of children present at such centres was much less than the number of registers. He also discovered that all the data on the children's weight, vaccinations, health records, etc., was fudged to make the Centre's performance look good![24] Both these small examples reiterate the point that governance seems to prioritize and benefit service providers, but not service provision. Service providers and reports become the yardstick to measure development, and the real beneficiaries of governance— the people—are conveniently forgotten.

As things stand, officials at all levels expend tremendous time and resources in collecting and submitting information. Unfortunately, this is not used to take corrective and remedial action or for analysis but is only forwarded to progressively higher levels, or to answer questions in legislatures. Outcomes and benefits are rarely measured, and the system gets away with inflated reporting. This is partly because the very act of collating information has become an end in itself rather than seeing it as a means to an end—which is to improve governance and service delivery. This is also because there is great pressure on field staff to spend all allotted funds in the prescribed time frame (lest governments be accused of diversion of funds). However, there is no attention given to measuring or achieving longer-term results. Those are never monitored, and financial planning is shockingly divorced from physical planning.

The situation can easily be corrected by greater transparency of district records that should at the very least be put on a public website. This can be complemented by frequent field inspections by an independent team of experts, nutritionists and grassroots workers. The Union ministries can also closely coordinate and monitor state departments to do and be better.

India since 2014—blitzkrieg on India's steel frame

Rather than focusing on systemic reforms to transform India's bureaucracy, since 2014, the Bharatiya Janata Party (BJP) government has aggressively promoted a patronage-based administrative culture. Driven by their obsessive furtherance of their ideology at any cost, the BJP government's actions have systematically hollowed out the steel frame of India. The most visible manifestation of this is that IAS and IPS officers from the Gujarat cadre have been inordinately rewarded—often bypassing equally or more competent officers. They have been consistently allotted plum posts primarily by virtue of their proximity to the prime minister or their willingness to submit to Hindutva—the ideology of the ruling dispensation and its ideological parent. In doing so, the BJP government has not adhered to the time-tested and fairer method of screening and selection (by relying on annual confidential reports as the basis for shortlisting and empanelment). In prioritizing ideological malleability over merit and experience, the BJP government has institutionalized a culture of mediocrity.[25]

For example, it has been pointed out that officers who were rejected for empanelment as secretaries since they were not considered up to the mark were brought in and promoted just because 'the PM or the RSS [Rashtriya Swayamsevak Sangh] so desired'.[26] While all governments are universally motivated by their ideologies (a hallmark of democracy, which is the playground on which different ideologies compete with each other), there *has to be* an impregnable firewall between civil servants and the political class. Breaching that leads to undesirable outcomes—in policy design, programme implementation as well as in the neutrality of public institutions, which do not remain impartial adjudicators between competing interests.[27]

From all accounts, this has already happened in these past few years. For instance, according to the Civil Service (Conduct) Rules, 1968, public servants/bureaucrats ought to be politically neutral and maintain a wall of separation from the media. However, the BJP regime now encourages serving civil servants to publicly take positions on and defend its ideological positions.[28] Recently, and to the great dismay of an overwhelming majority of civil servants, an IPS officer used his social media handle to air brazenly communal opinions. Similarly, a Rajasthan IAS officer has repeatedly used his Twitter handle to express partisan opinions.[29] Even if one disregards the Civil Service Rules (which no upright civil servant working in the national interest would do), officials in any post have a special responsibility to hold themselves to a higher standard. This is because they also serve as role models. It is therefore unconscionable for public officials to be involved in anything that smacks of partisanship, or unconstitutionality.

It is the GoI's duty to set straight any errant officials that flout the Civil Service Rules. But if the government itself engineers partisanship and unconstitutional statements by bureaucrats, it is difficult to implement rules and protocols. This is borne out by how the GoI has conducted itself on two separate instances. In the first instance, at the GoI's request, the Jammu and Kashmir government initiated a departmental inquiry in 2018 against IAS officer Shah Faesal for a tweet expressing his anguish at increasing violence against women. Faesal had tweeted, 'Population + Patriarchy + Illiteracy + Alcohol + Porn + Technology + Anarchy = Rapistan'. While it is unclear how Faesal's tweet violated any guidelines, the BJP government's action against Faesal—a Kashmiri Muslim—is in stark contrast to its silence over the social media posts of a Hindu IAS officer that directly violated Service Rules as these were blatantly communal.[30] The overwhelming perception is that this partisan application of the rule book had to do both with the officials' ideological and political proclivities, as well as where they came from.

Emboldened and in some part influenced by these rabid posts, some serving and recently retired officials have used their social media handles and public platforms to air communal, casteist and anti-people views, presumably to pander to the ruling dispensation. The main guiding force of civil servants must be a steadfast commitment to the Constitution of India rather than to the political party in power.[31]

Modi-fied bureaucracy's bias against Muslims and civil liberties

One especially alarming consequence of this new 'committed bureaucracy' is its willingness to support and endorse attacks on minorities.[32] Even during Congress governments, the police had displayed bias against Muslims during communal riots. But even a perception of bias always elicited outrage and pressures (both within and without) to hold perpetrators to account. Unfortunately, since 2014, this has changed. After coming to power in state after state, the BJP has openly fomented hatred against Muslims, because it feels it is electorally beneficial to suppress them.[33] It has also ignored mob lynchings of Muslims, which has reduced them to second-class citizens, with no security of life, liberty and property.[34] While delivering a judgment on a set of petitions against mob lynchings, the three-member bench of the Supreme Court headed by the Chief Justice observed that 'horrendous acts of mobocracy cannot be permitted to inundate the law of the land',[35] adding that violence cannot become the new normal.

Unlike before 2014, there is a near absence of push-back from within the system (both from the political and bureaucratic class, stuffed with Gujarat cadre officials) to check the tsunami of communal hatred engulfing the nation. Ramachandra Guha's observation on the handling of the Delhi violence in 2019 by the Delhi Police is worth noting in this regard:[36]

'The recent depredations of the Delhi Police, their absolute disregard for truth, justice, and due process, represent something qualitatively different. That, in the country's capital today, a non-violent, peace-loving citizen cannot expect fair treatment from the so-called custodians of the law merely because of her religious or political affiliation is a chilling marker of how degraded our democracy has become.'

This has been coupled with the BJP government placing all kinds of unethical and unconstitutional restrictions on civil liberties. Intellectuals, artists, students and activists have become the government's favourite targets.[37] The electoral verdict of 2019 was taken as an endorsement of such actions, and post 2019, we have witnessed an even further acceleration of attacks on rights and freedoms.[38] The case of Father Stan Swamy, who maintained until the very end that the documents used to incriminate him were planted on his laptop (which seems to be borne out by an independent and credible report[39]) is just the tip of the iceberg. It is almost as if the rise of Hindutva has absolved the rulers of their responsibility to provide a clean, equitable and humane administration. It has been argued that if the current trends continue, India will become a majoritarian and illiberal democracy.[40]

PM's tirade against the IAS

India's prime minister also took a swipe at 'babus' (bureaucrats) in Parliament, expressing frustration with delays in the decision-making process. Questioning the traditional wisdom of vesting power in the hands of the bureaucracy, he asked, 'Babus will do everything? Because they became IAS [officers], they will run fertilizer factories, because they are IAS, they will run chemical factories . . . even fly planes . . . What is this big power we have created?'[41]

The prime minister's emphatic denouncement of the bureaucracy surprised and shocked many because his style of governance has involved heavy reliance on IAS officers, both earlier when he was chief minister of Gujarat and now as prime minister, invariably at the expense of his ministers. In fact, this tirade was especially surprising since between 2014 and 2021, the Union government's functioning has largely been concentrated and run by officers from the Prime Minister's Office (PMO).

Lambasting the slow decision-making process, the prime minister pointed to ten-year delays in land acquisition for implementation of railway and highway projects, expressing concern about cost overruns, the opportunity lost in terms of economic growth, jobs and benefits to the people. Unfortunately, none amongst his coterie of committed bureaucrats had the guts to point out that the blame lay not with individuals, but with the central legislation[42] (as has been the case with many other central policies).[43]

An even more committed bureaucracy

A few years ago, the PMO asked all Union ministries 'to examine if service allocation/cadre allocation to probationers selected on the basis of the civil services examination could or should be made only after Foundation Course'. The PMO also asked them to 'examine the feasibility of giving due weightage to the performance in the Foundation Course and making service allocation as well as cadre allocation to All India Services Officers, based on the combined score obtained in the civil services examination and the Foundation course'.[44]

This seemingly innocuous proposal raised alarm bells, as everyone familiar with the training academies feared that it would unleash an army of sycophantic and self-serving bureaucrats. The rationale of training many services collectively at the foundational course is to develop inter-service and intra-batch camaraderie and to encourage free, frank and critical discussion on governance issues (which are multi-sectoral, requiring a multi-pronged approach). If the candidates' service or cadre is determined based on the discretion of the faculty (as the proposal suggests), all the government need do is appoint pliant trainers who could then promote only those candidates who are ideologically and politically aligned to the ruling dispensation. This would further weaken the civil service.

Sardar Patel had famously argued that 'the (civil) service must be above party and we should ensure that political considerations, either in its recruitment or in its discipline and control, are reduced to the minimum if not eliminated altogether'.[45] Driven by this exhortation, the Union Public Service Commission (UPSC) has over the decades acquired a reputation for transparency and independence, which has deepened its credibility as India's steel frame. Given this, many retired civil servants and intellectuals rightly expressed concern about the BJP government's proposal to undermine the merit-based system evolved by the UPSC and substitute it with subjective assessment by government-appointed directors of various academies. This proposal was seen as a continuation of the current government's efforts to politicize all independent institutions of high credibility.

Throttling freedom of expression

Distressed at the willingness of serving and recently retired civil servants to pander to the ruling dispensation's ideological sensitivities, numerous conscientious officials (both serving and retired) have been compelled to raise their voices. Bound by constitutional principles and the Civil Service Conduct Rules, they are entirely justified in urging their fellow officials to refrain from making communal, casteist and partisan comments. Yet, at the ruling dispensation's behest, a group of retired officials desirous of post-retirement jobs and favours for their kin have not only attacked their fellow officials, but also taken strident positions that destroy the nation's pluralistic social fabric. This creates politically aligned factions in the bureaucracy, which will ultimately destroy the effectiveness of India's steel frame.

But the ruling dispensation has gone a step further, and through a Central government order of 31 May 2021, has prohibited officials who retired from twenty-five departments they deemed sensitive from publishing anything without prior clearance.[46] While this seems acceptable for departments that work on national security, there is no earthly reason to prohibit officials who worked in organizations such as the Central Bureau of Investigation, the Enforcement Directorate or the Income Tax (Investigation) department. Clearly, the motive is not to protect state secrets, but to protect illegal and partisan orders by the ruling dispensation, which has frequently misused these agencies to harass innocent NGOs, news organizations, human rights activists and political opponents.

What is especially shocking is that the Union government has made the pensions of retired officials contingent on their silence. This is not only unethical, but also an insult to the long and dedicated years of service put in by civil servants in the duty of their nation. Pensions are not some reward that can be given or withheld at the whims and fancies of the ruling dispensation, but an official's right. It is a binding obligation that the State has to fulfil, as has been explicitly laid down by the Supreme Court in *Dr Hira Lal vs State of Bihar* (February 2020).

The Union government has also systematically diluted the right to information (RTI)[47] to stop any failures or lapses from coming to light. RTI requests on demonetization were repeatedly denied by the GoI as were requests to reveal the list of wilful loan defaulters held by the Reserve Bank of India.[48] Any conscientious government would have been transparent about both these issues.

Such patently illegal measures are a sign of a government averse to accountability. How can any democratically elected government be so afraid of the people asking questions? Any government that is honestly working in the peoples' and national interest would have nothing to hide.

A good government would own up to any failures or missteps and collectively work with all stakeholders—the Opposition, civil society, experts/academics, international agencies and organizations, etc.—to find better ways to make policies and systems more robust. It would constructively use the bureaucracy to facilitate this infusion of fresh ideas and out-of-the-box thinking. The governments under India's first prime minister, Jawaharlal Nehru, did so, as did Prime Minister Atal Bihar Vajpayee and more recently, Prime Minister Manmohan Singh. This new trend under Prime Minister Modi, of prioritizing publicity over inclusive governance; of governing with the false assumption that all knowledge/wisdom is limited to the PMO; and of treating all stakeholders in the nation as adversarial is detrimental to the national interest.

Way forward: structural reforms

Self-serving bureaucrats know the advantages of playing their cards right. Consider the cases of a former secretary with oversight over intelligence agencies, a former ambassador, a former police commissioner and other senior bureaucrats, who resigned the service and were immediately accommodated within the BJP, given tickets and allocated important ministerial portfolios. As Sircar has argued:[49]

'The obsessive insistence on only yes-men and their parroting of what PM wants to hear means that professional advice is neither required nor safe to offer. This neurosis has already led to disasters like demonetisation, the premature and faulty introduction of GST, and even the infliction of unprecedented misery on migrant labourers during the Covid pandemic. But bigger disasters await as yes-men take charge of key constitutional watchdogs. The administration of this vast, complex country requires real professional skills and not just agreeability or the carrying out of commands. The problem is that the prime minister insists on the complete subjugation of the bureaucracy.'

The knowledge that such 'help' can be a means of accelerated growth demotivates honest and dedicated bureaucrats who still constitute a sizeable number in the higher bureaucracy. To prevent this, except for very few constitutional posts such as the Comptroller and Auditor General of India, etc., most of the quasi-judicial posts should be offered to civil servants well before their retirement, discouraging service beyond their normal age of superannuation. This step would go a long way in eliminating the practice of sycophancy and manipulating decisions to further the government's ideological/political agendas just to secure a post-retirement job.

There is another inter-connected issue, that of the gradual erosion of faith in public institutions. The current dispensation has made a fetish of misusing enforcement agencies to intimidate, throttle and suppress. It is deeply shameful that many civil servants have pliantly given up. As Sircar argues:[50]

'Though other governments have also displayed meanness and malice at times in the past as well, this sort of an institutionalised vindictiveness with mafia-like ruthless precision has never been witnessed in post-Independence India's governance. More disturbing is the fact that the hitherto-independent constitutional and statutory institutions that served for decades as defensive fortresses of democratic governance have been systematically wrecked or hijacked. Here, we do not mean the Central Bureau of Investigation or the Enforcement Directorate or even the Income Tax department that are part of the executive and have served as cat's paws even earlier. The difference, of course, is that they have now sharpened their claws and fangs and are let loose on whoever stands up to the government—with lightning speed and fury. These organisations are currently packed with loyalists just waiting for orders, and many officers are simply following brutal directions without any choice.'

Apart from misusing public institutions to suppress dissenting voices, the BJP government has also cynically coerced or induced some to favour its corporate cronies[51] simply so it can fill its party coffers. Rules have been bent and even flouted to favour large corporations, often at the cost of the peoples' welfare and the ecology.

It is therefore important to institutionalize mechanisms to insulate the bureaucracy from political pressures. One of the ways to do so is to share political power among different stakeholders, which not only kick-starts competition (thereby increasing bureaucratic efficiency), but also enhances accountability and a check on patronage distribution. This would also mean a guaranteed involvement of credible experts working in the national interest.

Another reform that must be instituted is to mandate a compulsory cooling-off period after retirement, before a civil servant can enter politics or take up any other public post. Ideally, this cooling-off period should be a minimum of two years so as to avoid any impropriety or quid pro quo.

Thirdly, the bogey of a committed bureaucracy has become a systemic policy issue that all future governments (at the Union and state levels) will have to grapple with. Almost no attention has been given to the tactics of infiltration, subversion and conversion that have created an ideologically aligned faction within the civil service. The BJP's ideological parent has trained and methodically inserted ideological apparatchiks into the civil service. Efforts have also been made to convert and coerce sitting bureaucrats to serving an ideology that is unconstitutional and subversive. The very real danger is that should a non-BJP government come to office, its policy and welfare agenda will be continuously stymied by this ideologically committed bureaucracy. Apart from stricter background checks during their induction, perhaps making the State Public Service Commissions more autonomous and mandating that fresh civil servants commit to not being a part of any organization could be solutions to be considered.

Finally, as the second Administrative Reforms Commission recommended, serious consideration should be given to statutorily codifying the status of a civil servant vis-à-vis the government. Checks and balances on the principles of natural justice and constitutional values would have to be institutionalized in such a law. This law could establish an independent agency—the Central Civil Services Authority—to recommend tenure for important posts, institutionalize a performance management system, serve as an appellate body for disciplinary proceedings and ensure strict adherence to the Civil Service Rules (including conforming to a code of ethics).

Conclusion

A good civil service is necessary but not sufficient for good governance, while a bad civil service is sufficient but not necessary for bad governance. A dilapidated civil service has been a key factor in Africa's economic decline. Conversely, a strong civil service is one of many reasons why several East Asian economies, especially Japan, Singapore and South Korea, have prospered. Greater responsiveness and openness can legitimately be demanded of public administrations in many East Asian countries. In this light, radical reforms in the civil services can further unleash India's as yet unrealized potential.

In stark contrast, what India is witnessing is the ideological and political capture of the civil service. Because politics has become majoritarian and authoritarian, a few people at the top put pressure on the entire system so as to achieve their ideological goals. Governance reforms are intractable under such illiberalism that by definition is uninterested in transparency and accountability (or for that matter, good governance). A pliable civil service is actually desirable for the current ruling dispensation since bureaucrats dependent on the political Executive's discretionary largesse can be induced to become the regime's accomplices. Faced with this Hobson's choice, many honest, dedicated and talented officials are opting out of senior postings with the Union government.[52] Then there are also some young and talented officials who feel compelled to leave well before their prime, as was evidenced in the resignations of Kannan Gopinathan and S. Sasikanth Senthil.

Yes, reform is needed; and yes, there are areas in which the civil services can and must do better. But this cannot happen by politicizing the bureaucracy and twisting it in the pursuit of regressive and partisan agendas. It also cannot be treated like some blunt instrument that is outdated and irrelevant. Its strengths and efforts have contributed very significantly to helping India grow from one of the weakest and poorest nations in the world (a legacy of colonialism) to one of the brightest jewels of the world.[53] The Green Revolution, the White Revolution, the IT Revolution, the 1991 economic reforms, India's missions to Mars, the many progressive laws that were part of the rights-based paradigms, etc., were all planned, effected and successfully executed by India's bureaucracy that the prime minister so callously dismissed out of hand.

The civil service's institutional knowledge and ability to deliver must be harnessed well. This requires capable political leadership that is consensual, has faith in the strengths of the Indian people, is not scared of uncomfortable truths and most of all, is driven only by national interest. When we get leadership that is all these, India will thrive and prosper like never before. For the well-being and future prosperity of *all* our peoples, I pray for change—transformational and visionary.

An Agenda for Policy Reform for Civil Society in India

Prof. Ingrid Srinath

M ost of us are familiar with the opening words of Jawaharlal Nehru's speech to the Constituent Assembly marking India's independence from colonial rule in 1947. 'Long years ago,' he said, 'we made a tryst with destiny, and now the time comes when we shall redeem our pledge, not wholly or in full measure, but very substantially.' Many are less conversant with his remarks as he goes on to spell out a mission for the newly free nation: 'The future beckons to us. Whither do we go and what shall be our endeavour? To bring freedom and opportunity to the common man, to the peasants and workers of India; to fight and end poverty and ignorance and disease; to build up a prosperous, democratic and progressive nation, and to create social, economic and political institutions which will ensure justice and fullness of life to every man and woman.' While precise definitions of the term 'civil society' can be elusive, Nehru's words encapsulate its purpose perfectly.

Civil society has been described as the social basis of democracy[1] and likened to society's immune system, defending it against threats to its health and vitality. It isn't easy to sharply define its boundaries, but most agree that it encompasses the space or arena outside the realms of State, market and family where individuals act, usually collectively, towards ends beyond their own particular interests. Private action, in sum, for the public good. The term most commonly used in the policy discourse in India is the 'voluntary sector'. It has been argued that true inclusion of civil society requires the Constitution to recognize its pivotal role, necessitating, among other changes, that civil society institutions (CSIs), like cooperative societies, be a defined term in the Constitution. Further, it has also been argued that the Directive Principles must be made a conjoint responsibility of the State and CSIs, and the State's role in ensuring CSIs' promotion, autonomy, democratic control and professional management, as well as its responsibility to establish mechanisms to consult, fund and collaborate with CSIs must be clearly enunciated.

This essay will consider the spectrum of collective action from grassroots movements and community groups to research organizations, non-profit media, think tanks, philanthropic foundations, development non-governmental organizations (NGOs) as well as those focused on policy analysis, campaigning and advocacy, workers' collectives and social enterprises. Inclusion will be a function of substance, not form, and will ask the qualifying question: Is the entity clearly *not* an arm of government and is the public good, rather than private reward, the *primary purpose* of the entity?

It is this complementarity and contrast with institutions of the State and the market that make civil society an integral component of a vibrant and democratic society. As much as periodic elections, it is the freedom with which civil society operates that is the hallmark, and best defence, of democracy. From protecting society's most vulnerable, to defending democratic rights and freedoms and channelling the voice, creativity and agency of citizens in building inclusive, just, sustainable societies, civil society is neither homogenous nor monolithic. Being part of civil society allows people to express and negotiate their interests, values and identities;

to claim their rights and hold power-holders accountable; to improve their own lives and influence developments in their societies; and to engage with others in a peaceful way. As an eminent political scientist has argued:[2]

'There is more to democracy than elections. Elections are one, albeit, decisive moment in conversations that governments have with citizens, and citizens have with each other. Substantive democracy holds that citizens have the competence to judge their leaders. It is about monitoring governments and holding them responsible. And when citizens hold up a mirror to the government, they become the authors of their collective fate. Elections are an overdramatised moment in democracy. Real democracy is when citizens stand up and struggle for liberation from the very government some of them voted for.'

Though the term is often used interchangeably with NGOs, civil society does in fact encompass a growing diversity of groups, organizations, networks and movements that play myriad roles in strengthening the common good. Some of these roles include:[3]

Watchdog: holding institutions, both public and private, to account, promoting transparency and accountability.

Advocate: raising awareness of societal issues and challenges and advocating for change.

Service provider: delivering services to meet societal needs such as education, health, food and security; implementing disaster management, preparedness and emergency response.

Expert: bringing unique knowledge and experience, especially from communities most directly concerned, to shape policy and strategy, and identifying and building solutions.

Capacity builder: providing education, training and other capacity-building input to individuals and organizations within civil society as well as outside it.

Incubator: developing solutions that may require a long gestation or payback period.

Representative: giving power to the voice of the marginalized or under-represented.

Citizenship champion: encouraging citizen engagement and supporting the rights of citizens.

Solidarity supporter: promoting fundamental and universal values.

Definer of standards: creating norms that shape market and state activity.

Beyond these, however, voluntary associations and other forms of civil society organization demonstrably build a more cohesive social fabric, providing the spaces where diverse groups of citizens find meaning and purpose. These associations also enable citizens to learn and practice tolerance, cooperation, mutual understanding and respect. In a nutshell, they are where we learn the practices of democracy. They are where we agree and disagree on the one hand, and agree to disagree on how we wish to coexist on the other. The structures, processes and legal instruments, and the absence of restrictions that govern those spaces make it possible for citizens to associate, organize and act on issues of interest to them.

These freedoms of association and peaceful assembly are guaranteed to India's citizens, both by our own Constitution under Articles 19 (1) (b) and (c), and by our obligations under international law including Article 20 of the Universal Declaration of Human Rights, which India signed in 1948, and Article 22 of the International Covenant on Civil and Political Rights (ICCPR), which India acceded to in 1979. Beyond legal and treaty obligations, however, forward-looking governments and businesses alike recognize the value of civil society in getting citizens more engaged, involved and responsible for their communities; in improving and delivering better, more responsive public services; in empowering communities to access and defend their rights and freedoms; in upholding the rule of law and holding institutions to account; and in ensuring that the rights of future generations, the species we share our planet with, and the global commons are protected. As the World Economic Forum's report on 'The Future Role of Civil Society'[4] framed it, the changes that civil society is undergoing strongly suggest that it should no longer be viewed as a 'third sector'. Instead, civil society should be the glue that binds public and private activity together in such a way as to strengthen the common good.

It would be nigh impossible, as even authoritarian regimes have found, to ensure a range of services from education and healthcare to relief in times of calamity—so dramatically demonstrated by the COVID-19 pandemic—without the active support of citizen groups, non-profit organizations and philanthropy. It is evident, even to the most strident critics of civil society, that India's progress towards the Sustainable Development Goals (SDGs), hugely dented by the pandemic, would be unattainable without the active collaboration of philanthropy and non-profits. It is when civil society seeks to claim roles beyond the delivery of humanitarian relief and services, such as the advancement of rights and freedoms and to hold to account those charged with their protection, that governments and business often seek to limit its scope and mandate. In recent years, we have witnessed how gross overuse and misuse of provisions such as Section 144 in India's Code of Criminal Procedure,[5] internet shutdowns,[6] for which India holds the global record, the ongoing weakening of workers'[7] rights to organize, and a complex, opaque, arbitrary maze of regulations for non-profits,[8] are eroding those freedoms and making it virtually impossible for legitimate civil society organizations to achieve sustained viability or autonomy.

Regulatory regime: It is widely recognized that many domains of life in India continue to be governed by archaic laws and regulations that are a legacy of the colonial era. Some of these, corporate law in particular, have seen significant reform aimed at simplification, improving transparency and governance, and at making laws fit for contemporary purpose. Indeed, 'ease of doing business', despite controversies, has become a key performance metric for governments. Unfortunately, civil society regulation in India has not seen any similar reform. As a consequence, regulation in the sector resembles fossil layers deposited over time requiring sophisticated archaeological skills to decipher. The statutes that account for the vast majority of non-profit registrations are: the Societies Registration Act (1860), various state societies registration acts, the Indian Trusts Act (1882), the Bombay Public Trusts Act (1950) and Section 8 of the Companies Act (1956/2013). Each entity may choose the statute or statutes under which it wishes to register. The statutes do not differentiate entities by purpose, leaving hospitals, schools, colleges, clubs, private trusts, think tanks, campaigning groups, industry associations and development organizations bundled together with a host of others. The practice of registering multiple entities, including both for-profit and non-profit types, to avail of diverse funding options has gained popularity in recent years. Further, there is huge variation in the administration of these frameworks across states and even across districts within states. A few years ago, the Central Bureau of Investigation responded to a Supreme Court query with a list of 3.1 million registered organizations.[9] This list was compiled by the Ministry of Statistics and Programme Implementation (MOSPI) from the records of district registrars of societies as part of a 2011 exercise to comply with United Nations guidelines. MOSPI further validated the existence of 6,94,000 of these organizations. In 2023, the Income Tax Department listed over 4,65,000 organizations[10] as being tax-exempt under various sections. Following recent mass deletions by the Home Ministry, they now list about 16,000 organizations[11] as eligible to receive foreign funds under the Foreign Contribution Regulation Act (FCRA). The NITI Aayog's NGO Darpan listed over 1,63,000 organizations in 2023.

Any attempt to bring coherence to the sector *must* rationalize and streamline registration, clearly differentiating between types of organizations including clubs, associations, service delivery organizations such as schools, colleges or hospitals, development NGOs, campaigning/advocacy organizations, grant-making organizations, research organizations, think tanks, social enterprises and the like. Membership-based organizations such as trade unions and cooperative societies, among others, need also to be clearly differentiated, as should religious organizations.

Arriving at a relevant typology must be among the first steps of a reform process. How surpluses and profits are to be used, viz., distributed to shareholders or redeployed, and the composition of revenue by fees, grants, membership dues, etc., could provide basic classifications. The organization's purpose and thematic areas of operation would provide further clarity. The United Nations typology[12] would facilitate international comparisons. Equally, the administration of these provisions must be transparent with explanations for refusal or withdrawal of registration and easy access to redress where and when necessary.

Details of such a law are covered by the draft guidelines evolved by the task force for a central law to register voluntary organizations, which are comprehensive and informed by deep expertise and experience. They provide a thorough template for the design and implementation of such a law and for a Commission to oversee the sector.

In a context where many individuals and institutions across government, business, media, even sport, have been discredited by allegations and evidence of corruption, it is perhaps unsurprising that regulations are framed based on mistrust rather than trust. Or does the causality run the other way? The legal frameworks that define and regulate civil society are no exception. Firstly, there are simply too many intersecting frameworks,[13] leading to the fragmentation and incoherence described above.

The many authorities charged with regulating or monitoring civil society include the Home Ministry, the Income Tax Department, the Charities Commissioner, the Registrar of Societies, NITI Aayog, the Registrar of Companies and the Ministry of Corporate Affairs. Ironically, none of these entities is tasked with developing or strengthening the sector or with facilitating the initiation, growth or health of the organizations within it. They are all designed to supervise and regulate. Therefore, it would be expedient to establish an independent, non-ministerial government department accountable to Parliament akin to the Charity Commission of England and Wales[14] or the Australian Not-for-Profit and Charities Commission.[15] These offer potential models, even if they are less than perfect, on ways to redress most of these issues. Such an authority could be responsible for:

- creating and maintaining a register of all eligible organizations established for social impact purposes and coordinating reporting to various authorities;
- taking enforcement action when there is malpractice, misconduct, criminality or violation of constitutional values;
- ensuring social impact organizations meet their legal requirements, including providing information on their activities each year;
- making appropriate information about each registered social impact organization widely available;
- providing services and guidance to help social impact organizations run as effectively as possible and strengthening the sector as a whole.

The benefits of such unifying bodies, at state and national levels, are manifold. Beyond the obvious benefits of accurate, timely, reliable data on the sector, they could permit measurement of the sector's contribution to GDP and employment; enable coherent research on it; facilitate transparency and trust among potential donors, volunteers, employees, etc.; catalyse a range of partnerships and collaboration; as well as ease both, the reporting burden on social impact organizations and the burden of ensuring compliance on statutory authorities. It is critical, of course, given the role civil society plays in holding government bodies to account, that any regulatory body for the sector must be, and is seen to be, independent. Good practice and learning from other sectors—the media, advertising, microfinance—and from other countries, would be worthy of emulation. The 2019 study[16] on Regulatory Frameworks for India's Voluntary Sector: Global and Cross-sectoral Review of Initiatives and Practices by the Centre for Social Impact and Philanthropy at Ashoka University provides a road map.

Civil society capacity building: Such a commission could also host a civil society development fund contributed to by government, philanthropy and civil society. The fund would support research, capacity building, convening within civil society and between civil society and other stakeholders, and investments in civil society infrastructure. The lack of such an ecosystem of support has severe adverse impacts on the sector including a lack of coordination, knowledge sharing, policy voice and solidarity mechanisms. These gaps were particularly evident during the COVID-19 pandemic causing delays, inefficiencies and considerable cost to lives and livelihoods. As is the case in other countries, and as the draft guidelines suggest, such a fund could also be financed via a cess on net investment income from philanthropic endowments.

Participatory governance: Ensuring that the design and implementation of policy includes citizen voices, especially from marginalized communities, improves governance outcomes across the board. Many civil society organizations are effective channels and platforms amplifying the views of these citizen groups. Children, women, farmers, the elderly, people with disabilities, gender and sexual minorities, members of Scheduled Castes and Tribes, followers of minority religions and those following no faith, human rights defenders, unorganized labour, defenders of the environment and of the other species with whom we share our planet are all under-represented in policymaking. Participatory governance mechanisms that permit citizens to contribute to, evaluate and collaborate in processes of policy design and implementation must be institutionalized at all levels of government. A parliamentary caucus focused on amplifying the concerns of civil society at the highest levels of policy debate would be extremely valuable.

Every policy, from annual budgets to international agreements, would benefit from the inclusion of citizen voices. Citizens' councils comprising representatives of civil society across these stakeholder groups, at both state and national levels, charged with ensuring citizen participation in policy design and evaluation, would go a long way towards improving democratic governance and accountability. These councils would also report on the activities of the national and state commissions protecting human rights, women, children, minorities, Scheduled Castes and Scheduled Tribes, the environment and the right to information in addition to the Lokpal/Lokayukta. In addition, facilitating civil society participation in international fora and conferences is necessary to build oversight of, and collaboration with, state and business representation at such gatherings.

Promoting civic engagement: Nurturing citizen participation via volunteerism, civic action, financial support, responsible consumption, environmental consciousness and participation in governance is a key determinant of the health and resilience of democracy. Inculcating awareness of these and providing opportunities for tangible engagement should, therefore, be a vital component of education at all levels from primary school through to university and beyond. Instead, the past decade has witnessed a systematic discrediting, even demonization, of civil society as ineffective, inefficient, potentially corrupt and possibly anti-national. In a country where civil society has been at the heart of democratic and social movements from the freedom movement and the struggle to restore democracy during the 1976 Emergency, to the movements for the rights to information, education, food and work, this is particularly shocking. Indeed, the accomplishments of Indian civil society are far better known and celebrated internationally than they are in India. The Magsaysay Award, which recognizes 'outstanding individuals and organisations whose selfless service has offered their societies, Asia and the world successful solutions to some of the most challenging problems of human development' has been won by Indians in fifty-eight of its sixty-one years.[17] And innovative Indian models for issues ranging from solar energy[18] to child protection[19] have been replicated worldwide. A recent report seeks to remedy this gap providing a snapshot of the contributions of the non-profit sector to the nation since Independence.[20]

Policy action on curriculum design, partnerships between educational institutions and civil society organizations, incentives for volunteerism and for contributions of time, skills and money are all necessary components of building a vibrant civic culture. Likewise, support to educational institutions that nurture talent in the domains of social work, social enterprise, philanthropy, non-profit management and the like would go a long way towards attracting talented Indians to the sector, enhancing the availability of skills and commitment dedicated to these domains.

Democratic freedoms: A quick scan of India's recent ratings on global indices relating to human rights,[21] freedom of expression,[22] religious freedom,[23] civil society space,[24] media freedom[25] and democracy reveals declines across the board. The V-Dem Institute in 2020[26] labelled India an 'electoral autocracy'. Its 2023 report[27] continues to track the decline and, in addition, reports the sharp decline in academic freedom between 2012 and 2022. Activists, journalists, academics, cartoonists, even students have been targeted by law enforcement agencies and trolls—offline and online—resulting in intimidation, silencing, physical attacks, incarceration for years without even having charges filed and, in the most extreme cases, assassination.[28] Media houses, businesspersons and philanthropists too have been subjected to harassment. Publishers, advertisers, film-makers, artists and authors are threatened with boycotts and violence by various groups taking 'offence'. Predictably, this has had a 'chilling effect' on dissent, media freedom and the willingness of funders to support causes that may be deemed 'anti-national' by the government of the day. Seen as a whole, the combination of constraints on civil society resourcing, censorship in all but official name of independent media, and politicization of state agencies and the judiciary,[29] represent an existential threat to democracy itself.

If civil society is to play its core role as a guardian of democracy including:

holding the government of the day to account for its performance against rights, entitlements and service delivery to all citizens;

amplifying under-represented and marginalized voices in policy formulation, developing and incubating innovations in development and governance; and

critically analysing proposed legislation and policies and proposing alternatives

then all policies likely to hamper these—including onerous registration procedures, intrusive monitoring, unreasonable constraints on communication and protest offline and online—need revision. Norms on protection of data, due process, proportionality and right to redress when these rights are violated must be developed with adequate transparency and inclusive participation by civil society. The onus of ensuring that such participation takes place, is inclusive and is seen as effective by citizens, rests on the State. So too does the role of ensuring compliance with these norms and laws by business entities and others. Further, the definitions of terms such as 'activity of a political nature', 'interests of national security', etc., are overly broad and blurred and must be urgently revised in line with international best practices[30] and Supreme Court judgments to ensure core freedoms are not being abridged. Critical to ensuring these freedoms must be the repeal of legislation that muzzles free expression, assembly and association. Our anachronistic, draconian laws—on sedition (IPC 124A), UAPA, AFSPA and the NSA—are all inconsistent with constitutional values and must be repealed. Equally, protections available to these freedoms in the physical world must be available in electronic media and the Internet. Three new bills—the Bhartiya Nyaya Sanhita Bill, 2023, the Bharatiya Nagarik Suraksha Sanhita Bill, 2023 and the Bharatiya Sakshya Bill, 2023—were introduced in Parliament in August 2023 ostensibly to modernize and 'decolonize' the laws that form the backbone of criminal jurisprudence in India. While seemingly repealing the offence of sedition, stayed by the Supreme Court in 2022, the draft adds new provisions on 'subversive activities' dealing with 'Acts endangering sovereignty, unity and integrity of India' and provides for punishment in the form of imprisonment ranging from seven years to life, and, in fact, widens the ambit of the offence by including 'financial transactions' and 'electronic communication'.[31]

Access to resources: Any progressive policy framework for civil society must uphold its right to access resources. Ensuring this right entails incentives promoting domestic and diaspora philanthropy as well as rational policies with regard to international funders. Government actions, over the past decade in particular, have eroded tax incentives to domestic giving and deterred international funding. The philanthropy sector in India, though still relatively small at $13 billion (INR 1.05 lakh crore) in 2022, has shown heartening growth over the past decade. Corporate giving under the corporate social responsibility (CSR) requirement of the Companies Act grew at 13 per cent, for instance, and family philanthropy at 12 per cent over the past five years.[32]

Tax incentives are a proven way to incentivize giving at all levels. They also serve to signal government support for giving. As the Centre for Asian Philanthropy Studies (CAPS) recently reported,[33] the empirical evidence that tax deductions are an effective incentive for unlocking philanthropic capital across income groups is strong. The report also points out that the tax price elasticity of giving is generally greater than 1, which means the deduction of any loss in tax revenue for government is compensated by donations to non-profits delivering charitable services. Further, the report compares India's incentives, now minimal, with other Asian countries', revealing the huge gap between Singapore at one end, where tax incentives touch 250 per cent, to Myanmar where they are at 0 per cent, with eight of the fifteen countries surveyed offering incentives of at least 100 per cent. The ceiling on the percentage of income deductible, currently at 10 per cent, should also be abolished as is the case in the UK, Australia, Ireland, Pakistan, Singapore and Vietnam. It has been deeply disheartening to note that, even as senior government leaders appealed to civil society for support during the COVID-19 pandemic, India failed to offer the modicum of support in the form of increased tax incentives that were provided by even countries such as Russia and China, neither renowned for its championing of civil society.[34]

Beyond incentives for charitable giving, the CAPS report also highlights the fact that tax deductions for estate and inheritance taxes send an important message: Philanthropic giving through an individual's estate is a societal good. These also spur redistribution of wealth by increasing the volume of resources reverting to society over and above those from progressive taxation. Studies have found the estate tax, accompanied by a tax deduction for charitable donations, to be a significant determinant of charitable bequests.

India has also narrowed the tax exemptions available to non-profit organizations on their own income. Together with the requirement to expend 85 per cent of each year's income[35] or face taxation, made even more stringent in 2023,[36] these policies, albeit possibly well-intentioned, have had the effect of making the already precarious subsistence of social impact organizations even less sustainable. A coherent redefinition of 'charitable purpose' to bring it in line with twenty-first-century modes of intervention, coupled with 100 per cent exemption for income for such purposes, is vitally necessary. The inclusion, in Australia for instance,[37] of the promotion of, or opposition to, changes in laws, policies and practices (wherever the change furthers or opposes other charitable goals) as a legitimate charitable purpose, is exemplary in this regard. The 85 per cent expenditure rule too needs urgent review as does the provision in the 2019–20 budget for peremptory withdrawal of 12A exemptions.

Access to international resources—financial and non-financial—is intrinsic to the right to free association as the United Nations Special Rapporteur on Freedom of Association and Assembly categorically stated in his 2016 analysis. As the issues confronting our societies have ever more global causes and become amenable only to global responses, it is critical that civil society in India faces no higher barriers to international resources and solidarity than does the business sector.[38] Recognizing the threats posed by international terrorism and illicit cross-border financial flows, it is imperative that restrictions to access and provisions for reporting or monitoring are shown to be proportionate and amenable to redress. The positioning of all civil society organizations as potential supporters of criminality via the draconian and opaque administration of the FCRA borders on collective guilt and punishment. Especially in light of the relaxation of these provisions with respect to political parties, the FCRA needs to be redrafted from scratch. As the

International Commission of Jurists (ICJ) commented on the 2020 amendments to the law,[39] 'The legislation fails to comply with India's international legal obligations and constitutional provisions to respect and protect the rights to freedom of association, expression, and freedom of assembly.' The ICJ stressed that 'the Bill's provisions would impose arbitrary and extraordinary obstacles on the capacity of human rights defenders and other civil society actors to carry out their important work.' It further warned that, 'this hasty lawmaking that clearly undermines human rights and the work of civil society, is yet another attempt by the government to destabilize the functioning of democratic institutions in India.'

Partners, not vendors: Another area of grave concern is the way that partnerships between government entities and civil society are managed. Based on the author's own experience, the prevalent approach more closely resembles industrial models of procurement aimed at contracting the delivery of citizen entitlements at the lowest cost, often failing to even meet minimum wage, occupational safety and employee welfare laws, rather than equitable partnerships towards shared goals with each party bringing its particular strengths to the relationship. Such modalities foster mistrust, erode the quality of services that citizens are entitled to, and limit the contribution of civil society organizations to that of a contracted 'implementing agency' rather than permitting realization of their full potential as innovators in strategies and models for development and governance.

Public accounting: Missing in the realm of public reporting is authoritative data on the size, composition, growth, impact and contribution of civil society to the national economy. Including measurements of the sector's financial and human resources would significantly shape perceptions within, and about, the sector. Ensuring that national statistics and national accounts adequately cover the sector's activities is an urgent necessity. The merger of public entities focused on collecting and reporting national statistics mooted by the NITI Aayog may provide opportunity for fresh thinking in this domain.

Corporate philanthropy and responsibility: While the strong signalling effect of the CSR provisions in the Companies Act (2013) is positive, as are the requirements for transparent reporting and board-level oversight, the narrow list of suggested philanthropic activities, micro-management of selection filters for civil society partners and an entirely regressive norm of 5 per cent of total mandated spending on what are termed 'administrative overheads' dilute the law's potential impact. Ensuring corporate responsibility for human rights and the environment, compliance with the letter and spirit of all prevalent laws and standards, and preventing undue influence in governance and policymaking, ought to be the focus of state intervention in this domain. To the extent that the law facilitates greenwashing of corporate reputations by delinking responsibilities for protecting human rights and the environment from corporate social responsibility, buying the silence of civil society by raising the non-profit sector's dependence on corporate philanthropy, especially as international funding is increasingly constrained, privatization of public services by stealth through the substitution of private, philanthropically funded services for state-guaranteed entitlements, or purchase of political access and influence by prioritizing contributions to causes, districts and organizations which are supported by key political figures from the PM-CARES Fund, Swachh Bharat, etc., it is anti-democratic and anti-development.[40] Business has key roles to play as a partner in development. Building a just, prosperous nation through responsible investment, generating inclusive, equitable opportunities for dignified employment and sustainable stewardship of natural resources and the environment are some of these. Guaranteeing the freedom of civil society to play the roles of watchdog, critic and partner of business in these areas, and in facilitating the development of just labour laws, rigorous environmental standards, as well as in ensuring the rights of communities affected or threatened by business operations is a core responsibility of the State.

COVID-19: 'Crises', said Lorenzo Fioramonti, 'are revelatory moments. They break the repetitive continuity of ordinary processes and present us with unexpected threats and opportunities. As disruptive events, they force us to rethink conventional wisdom and become imaginative. In the evolution of political institutions, crises have been fundamental turning points opening up new space for governance innovations or, by contrast, reducing the spectrum of available options. They have ushered in phases of progress and prosperity or plummeted our societies into the darkness of parochialism and backwardness.'[41] The COVID-19 pandemic is clearly such a moment. At every stage of its spread through India—from the initial delay in focusing public attention and resources on the crisis; to the deployment of pandemic propaganda against minority groups and those exercising their right to protest;[42] to the complete lack of consideration of the impact on our poorest citizens of a hastily implemented draconian lockdown; to the obfuscation of facts and data and the targeting of those who sought to shed light on ground reality;[43, 44] to the utter lack of support for civil society organizations who compensated, at great personal cost, for the woeful inadequacies of our systems of public health and social protection; to the surreal phenomenon of our country's leaders competing with civil society for scarce funds[45] even as they created new hurdles to non-profits' access to resources[46]—the pandemic provided a snapshot of both, the critical value of civil society and the costs of constraining its legitimate functioning. Analysing the September 2020 amendments to the Foreign Contribution Regulation Act, for instance, the International Centre for Not for Profit Law (ICNL) observed, 'The Amendments are a disproportionate and unwarranted restriction on Indian civil society, and they have only served to debilitate the global, national, and local response to COVID-19.'

It is clear, more than ever, that the hyper-globalized, increasingly polarized world of the twenty-first century requires us to collectively design new solutions to societal challenges. As Winnie Byanyima pointed out,[47] the COVID-19 pandemic reminded us all that, 'We are not just interconnected. We are inseparable'. Civil society has demonstrated the particularly powerful role it can play in this process not just as a compensatory force for the inadequacies of State and market, but as a co-creator, an enabler and a constructive challenger, creating the political and social space for collaborations that are based on the core values of trust, service, justice and the collective good. If we are to realize the vision of our Constitution and its visionary authors, then government, business and civil society urgently need to work together to build institutional relationships based on mutual trust focused intently on the citizen Gandhi described in his talisman:

'I will give you a talisman. Whenever you are in doubt, or when the self becomes too much with you, apply the following test. Recall the face of the poorest and the weakest man [woman] whom you may have seen, and ask yourself, if the step you contemplate is going to be of any use to him [her]. Will he [she] gain anything by it? Will it restore him [her] to a control over his [her] own life and destiny? In other words, will it lead to swaraj [freedom] for the hungry and spiritually starving millions? Then you will find your doubts and your self melt away.'

Summary of Recommendations

Civil society institutions, like cooperative societies, to be a defined term in the Constitution. Directive Principles to be made a conjoint responsibility of the state and CSIs. State's role in ensuring CSIs' promotion, autonomy, democratic control and professional management, as well as its responsibility to establish mechanisms to consult, fund and collaborate with CSIs to be clearly enunciated.

Rationalize and streamline registration, clearly differentiating between types of organizations based on purpose, revenues and treatment of surplus.

Establish an independent, non-ministerial government department accountable to Parliament to serve as registrar, regulator, monitor and facilitator to the sector. Ensure national accounts and statistics measure and report civil society contribution to national income, employment and development outcomes.

Set up a civil society development fund, contributed to equally by government and civil society, to support research, capacity building and convening within civil society and between civil society and other stakeholders, and investments in civil society infrastructure.

Institutionalize participatory governance mechanisms at all levels of government and in human rights bodies as well as a parliamentary caucus focused on the sector.

Promote curriculum design, partnerships between educational institutions and civil society organizations, incentives for volunteerism and for contributions to build awareness of the sector and a vibrant civic culture. Support and recognize educational institutions that nurture talent for the sector.

Revise laws and policies placing unreasonable constraints on communication and protest offline and online. Co-create with civil society norms on protection of data, due process, proportionality and right to redress. Repeal laws that muzzle freedom of expression, assembly and association.

Promote a CSR focus on ensuring business meets its responsibilities to uphold human rights, protect the environment and comply with legal and tax obligations.

Restore tax exemptions available to charitable contributions, redefine 'charitable purpose', review 85 per cent rule for taxability of non-profit income and 5 per cent norm on overheads in CSR guidelines. Incentivize philanthropy through deductions linked to estate duty/wealth tax.

Ensure 'ease of doing civil society' and access to international resources equivalent to ease of doing business including redesign of the FCRA.

Epilogue: Repurposing the State

Gurdeep Singh Sappal

It is true that an idea can change the world. But it requires methodical and concerted effort to actualize that idea. If progressive forces are serious about checkmating the undemocratic and regressive forces that are attacking the constitutional idea of India today, we need to use all the instruments available to us. Like India's freedom fighters, we also face the full might of the State today. We do not have the luxury of waiting for a mass self-corrective to organically blossom or to hope that tried (and tired) tactics can work in restoring democratic fundamentals. Token protests, petitions, open letters, conferences and seminars in familiar haunts, social media posts, press conferences, a walkout in legislatures or sporadic rallies undoubtedly keep the flock together, but the effect of such 'spectacle politics' is limited to People-Like-Us (PLUs)[1]. These do nothing to structurally check or push back the forces uprooting India's constitutional edifice. To be successful, progressive forces need to be operationally creative and spearhead a plethora of ideological projects that *tangibly* further constitutional values. This is one step towards the solution, so we can 'rebuild the noble mansion of free India'[2].

The second step is equally crucial, and structurally more difficult to achieve. As the twelve essays in this volume attest, in the last decade, the institutions of the State have been systematically misused to further the Rashtriya Swayamsevak Sangh (RSS)'s and Bharatiya Janata Party (BJP)'s politico-ideological goals. Many stakeholders ideologically aligned to the RSS-BJP exist within the State and actively further their agenda. As and when a different political group forms a government, it will face unprecedented problems because the governance and development agenda for the nation could be subverted from within. Therefore, reclaiming and repurposing the State is of the utmost importance.

To do this, progressives need to first begin by acknowledging that any future transition will not be normal. We need to carefully rethink existing operational methodologies simply because the constitutional and institutional proprieties that existed before 2014 have been eroded irrevocably. We should not expect any quarter or nicety from the RSS-BJP, even when they go out of government. Therefore, we need to plan ahead to prepare for any eventuality and leverage this opportunity to redress long-standing structural fault lines.

First, progressive parties will need to urgently recalibrate political systems to ensure they are normatively, organizationally and programmatically working towards an ideological goal. In doing so, it is crucial to design the system to accommodate a plethora of agendas—personal and pecuniary—as well as diverse competences and skill sets. It has been argued that political organizations should not be a foil to the RSS-BJP and hence not be either streamlined or centralized. There is undoubtedly much merit in delegating operational functions to ensure programmatic vibrancy. But when it comes to governing a state or a nation, there has to be a certain degree of disaggregated control. That control should not be centralized in the Prime Minister's Office or Chief Minister's Office or any one leader either, since that inevitably leads to authoritarian, undemocratic and exclusionary practices. Various leaders should be empowered to be operationally experimental and adventurous. The prime minister or chief minister or leader should only oversee the entirety of it all, maintaining a delicate balance between all projects, intervening only when one project strays from the overall normative and political vision. The experience of the two UPA governments must be studied for reference. It practised decentralized governance, had cabinet autonomy, allowed for creative and even combative manoeuvring on policies. Such an approach delivered the longest period of peace and stability in contemporary times, along with unprecedented growth in the country. At the same time, the two UPA governments underline the stark reality that econocracy, howsoever successful in delivering peace and progress, cannot be a replacement for the political and ideological projects.

This is critical to systematize within political parties because the system has a logic to itself. It has an inbuilt pace and inertia that no individual leader (no matter how omnipotent or omnipresent) can overcome without seriously disrupting the democratic foundations of the nation. Anyone who has served within or led the system understands the complexities of managing the whole system. That is why political stakeholders need to be united in purpose and bound by a vision.

Second, in that spirit, it is critical to create an economic, social, geopolitical and cultural vision on where the nation should be heading in 100, 150 and 200 years. Only then can the political Executive start restructuring and recalibrating key cogs in the system. In doing so, it is important to remember that even though revolutions have been romanticized, change cannot come overnight because it could adversely disrupt the system. Therefore, a lot of effort and resources have to be expended to build up individual and systemic capacities, and keep nudging the nation towards the desirable goal. Grounded in decades of experience and unique vantage points, the twelve preceding essays in this volume have proffered some astute and revolutionary recommendations of reform that could propel India to even greater heights. This toolkit of statecraft reform is the starting point for creating a more responsive, just and efficient State.

Third, progressives need to accept and internalize that a political demagogue is not conducive to structural reforms—either within the State, in political organizations or in non-State organizations. Demagogues can temporarily enthral, but the nation is moving past them. Because of rapid technological changes aiding the ill-informed echo chambers and enabling rumour-mongering addressed to raise baser emotions, people get swayed by demagogues. But this phenomenon crosses a critical acceptability among the masses only if there is an ideological and organizational foundation to galvanize demagoguery and harvest its impact. To cite an obvious example, no matter how effective a demagogue the incumbent prime minister is, he could not have succeeded without the organizational, ideological and operational base of the RSS-BJP. What progressive forces need today is constitutional evangelicals, who like Mahatma Gandhi, Pt Nehru, Sardar Patel, Maulana Azad, J.B. Kriplani and Sarojini Naidu, patiently rebuild relationships with constituencies and mass organizations, establish new systems and constructively channelize both in the furtherance of our shared values.

Fourth, after we have institutionalized our hundred flowers manned by millions of our constitutional evangelicals, we need to devote considerable time and effort in synergizing the interests of multiple stakeholders with the national ideological agenda. This requires inducting many of them within political organizations so they become genuinely representative (the Raipur Declaration of the Indian National Congress gives an excellent blueprint for such a transformation, which is being effectively actualized). This also means inclusive governance and the forging of a bipartisan consensus (which necessitates not viewing political opponents as enemies). The onus is inevitably on the political Executive and a mature political leadership to groom a second and third generation set of leaders who can be bound together in a common purpose.

Fifth, it is crucial that the governing instruments of State are skilfully and efficiently managed. Towards this end, it needs to be remembered that institutions, per se, aren't designed to be innovative or disruptive. Instead they are designed to safeguard the status quo. The people trained to run institutions invariably choose bureaucratic stillness. This bureaucratic stillness may not always be an undesirable thing, as it often translates into institutional memory. An innovative, evolutionary system requires disruption tempered with institutional memory. The bureaucrats manning a system are also familiar with and control the tools that can stifle and circumscribe innovation. Ironically, the same familiarity also equips them with the knowledge to disrupt the system. So they need to be channelized with ideological clarity, with a periodic injection of fresh blood and innovation. Disruptive ideas and innovation are often individual or external interventions, but they require systemic acceptance and institutional memory to succeed. This needs to be factored in while preparing a new approach to re-establish the institutional framework in consonance with constitutional values and adept to technological changes.

Finally, in driving the nation towards a visionary normative goal, it needs to be recognized that the State perforce has to be a pragmatic organization. It has to ensure that ideological and programmatic infirmities do not impede the overall march towards the vision for and of the nation.

To do this while balancing our commitment to a liberal, secular and democratic India, we need our version of the Camelot fairy tale[3] (as exemplified in the US by Presidents John F. Kennedy and more recently, Barack Obama). After years of an authoritarian, top-down, exclusionary and ultra-conservative government that gives free rein to mobs who flout the rule of law, India is gasping for a change. But creeping concessions to regressive organizations or allowing glaring structural fault lines in the State to fester would just be an open invitation for a repeat of what India is facing today.

A lot of systematic, patient and formational work is needed to defend democracy. Both political and non-political alliances need to be formed; systems have to be re-calibrated and newly established; elections have to be won; and most of all, the system needs to be repurposed. All of this is predicated on exceptional political entrepreneurship and clarity of purpose. As Pandit Jawaharlal Nehru once said, 'The future is not one of ease or resting but of incessant striving so that we may fulfil the pledges we have so often taken and the one we shall take today.'[4]

Notes

Introduction: Uniting the Nation: Re-engineering India's Hardware and Software

1. Byock, Ira, *The Best Care Possible: A Physician's Quest to Transform Care through the End of Life*, (USA: Avery, Penguin Group, 2012).
2. Aristotle, *The Politics* (Penguin, 2000).
3. That M.K. Gandhi defined as self-determination and self-development.
4. Dusza, K., 'Max Weber's Conception of the State', *International Journal of Politics, Culture, and Society*, *3*(1), 71–105, 1989. Retrieved 29 March 2021 from http://www.jstor.org/stable/20006938.
5. The Constitution is understood as a set of fundamental principles or established precedents according to which a state is governed.
6. For example, India makes a drastic departure from the UK. British parliamentary sovereignty formally flows from the Crown and not the body of people. Given British democracy is both nominally and concretely the servant of the Crown, there is no formal notion of popular sovereignty.
7. Quoted in 'Tryst with Destiny' speech, made on 15 August 1947, https://thewire.in/history/india-at-75-jawaharlal-nehru-tryst-with-destiny-full-text; last accessed on 10 April 2023 at 14.46 hours.
8. Ibid.
9. Nussbaum, Martha, *Political Emotions: Why Love Matters for Justice* (Cambridge, Massachusetts: Belknap Press of the Harvard University Press, 2013).

10. Ambedkar, B.R., 'Prospects of Democracy in India', 1956, https://velivada.com/2015/02/07/what-are-the-prospects-of-democracy-in-india-by-dr-b-r-ambedkar/; last accessed on 14 April 2022 at 14.16 hours.

11. Ambedkar B.R., 'Riddles in Hinduism', *Writings and Speeches Vol. 4*, Government of Maharashtra, https://www.mea.gov.in/Images/attach/amb/Volume_04.pdf; last accessed on 14 April 2021 at 14.23 hours.

12. The interpretation of Article 21 was expanded to include the right to live with dignity by the Supreme Court in *Maneka Gandhi v. Union of India*, AIR 1978 SC 597.

13. Thus anticipating Sen's assertion that the State must expand people's capabilities (their real freedoms), and opportunities to achieve states of being that they valued; Sen, Amartya and Nussbaum, Martha, *The Quality of Life* (Oxford University Press, 1993), p. 30.

14. Ambedkar B.R., 'Annihilation of Caste', in *Writings and Speeches of Babasaheb Ambedkar, Volume III*, Government of Maharashtra, 1936, pp. 102 and 107.

15. Harrison, S.S., 'The Challenge to Indian Nationalism', *Foreign Affairs*, 34(4), 1956, pp. 620–36.

16. Quoted in Béteille, Andre, 'Constitutional Morality', *Economic and Political Weekly*, Vol. 43, No. 40, 2008, pp. 35–42. *JSTOR*, http://www.jstor.org/stable/40278025; last accessed on 10 April 2023 at 14.57 hours.

17. Sreevatsan, Ajai, 'British Raj Siphoned out $45 Trillion from India: Utsa Patnaik', *LiveMint*, 21 November 2018, https://www.livemint.com/Companies/HNZA71LNVNNVXQ1eaIKu6M/British-Raj-siphoned-out-45-trillion-from-India-Utsa-Patna.html; last accessed on 2 April 2021 at 16.30 hours.

18. Yadav, Yogendra, 'India's First Republic Is All but Dead. We the People Need to Shape the Second One', ThePrint, 26 January 2022, https://theprint.in/opinion/indias-first-republic-is-all-but-dead-we-the-people-need-to-shape-the-second-one/813003/; last accessed on 29 January 2022.

19. Deshpande, Pushparaj, 'Recreating the Congress Movement', *Economic and Political Weekly, 49*(32), 2014, pp. 23–25. Retrieved 2 April 2021, from http://www.jstor.org/stable/24480781.

20.   Deshpande, Pushparaj, 'The War Within: A Hindu Rashtra vs
      Constitutional India', Scroll.in, 26 November 2015, https://
      scroll.in/article/771765/the-war-within-a-hindu-rashtra-vs-
      constitutional-india; last accessed on 2 April 2021 at 16.17 hours.
21.   The Sangh Parivar refers to the collection of right-wing organizations
      affiliated to the RSS. These include the political party Bharatiya
      Janata Party, the Vishva Hindu Parishad, a students' union named the
      Akhil Bharatiya Vidyarthi Parishad (ABVP), a militant organization
      named Bajrang Dal that forms the youth wing of the Vishva Hindu
      Parishad (VHP), and the workers' union Bharatiya Kishan Sangh. It
      also includes a number of informally affiliated outfits.
22.   On the one hand, the RSS bitterly denounced the new Indian
      Constitution as foreign and swore not to abide by it. On the other
      hand, in response to the Hindu Reform Bills, 'in a single year, 1949,
      the RSS organised as many as 70 meetings in Delhi where effigies
      of Prime Minister Nehru and Law Minister Ambedkar were burnt'
      (Guha, Ramchandra, 'Reforming the Hindus', *The Hindu*, 18 July
      2004, http://www.thehindu.com/thehindu/mag/2004/07/18/
      stories/2004071800120300.htm; last accessed on 24 March 2021.
23.   Golwalkar, M.S., *We or Our Nationhood Defined*, (Nagpur: Bharat
      Publications, 1939), p. 38.
24.   Two articles in RSS's mouthpiece *Organiser* (on 30 November 1949
      and 25 January 1950) demanded that instead of the Constitution,
      the *Manumsriti* be enacted as the law of the land. The 30 November
      editorial argued, 'The worst thing about the new constitution of
      Bharat is that there is nothing Bhartiya about it . . . there is no mention
      of the unique constitutional development in ancient Bharat . . . To
      this day his (Manu's) laws as enunciated in the Manusmriti excite
      the admiration of the world and elicit spontaneous obedience and
      conformity. But to our constitutional pundits that means nothing.'
25.   Golwalkar, M.S., *We or Our Nationhood Defined*, pp. 15–16.
26.   Ibid, pp. 23–24.
27.   Ibid., p. 26.
28.   Ibid, pp. 54–55.
29.   Savarkar, V.D., *Essentials of Hindutva*, retitled as *Hindutva: Who
      Is a Hindu?*, published by V.V. Kelkar, Jagathitechu Press, 1923,

https://archive.org/details/hindutva1923/page/n1/mode/2up; last accessed on 19 August 2023 at 22.30 hours).

30.   Ibid, p.88.

31.   'India Has the Longest Running Fascist Movement in the World—The RSS', Interview with Benjamin Zachariah, Partha P. Chakrabartty, Wire.in, https://thewire.in/politics/benjamin-zachariah-fascism-sangh-parivar; last accessed on 3 April 2021 at 19.15 hours.

32.   The RSS's oath of loyalty that members have to take states: 'I take the oath that I will always protect the purity of Hindu religion, and the purity of Hindu culture . . . And I will keep this vow for as long as I live.' Interestingly, even though the Sangh formally distances itself from Golwalkar's *We or Our Nationhood Defined*, it does not disassociate itself from Golwalkar's 1966 book *Bunch of Thoughts* (published by Vikram Prakashan), which also expresses similar ideas.

33.   Prologue by M.S. Aney, Golwalkar, M.S. *We or Our Nationhood Defined*, p. 33.

34.   Dhinga, Sanya, 'RSS-Backed IAS Institute Has Been Quietly Grooming 'Nationalist' Civil Servants since 1986', ThePrint, 16 September 2020, https://theprint.in/india/education/rss-backed-ias-institute-has-been-quietly-grooming-nationalist-civil-servants-since-1986/503660/, last accessed on 6 April 2021; Guha, Ramchandra, 'Gandhi Said RSS Was "Communal with a Totalitarian Outlook"—And That's Still True', 20 December 2020, Scroll.in, https://scroll.in/article/981781/ramachandra-guha-gandhi-said-rss-was-communal-with-a-totalitarian-outlook-and-thats-still-true; last accessed on 6 April 2021; Bal, Hartosh Singh, 'The Takeover: How the RSS is Infiltrating India's Intellectual Spaces', *Caravan*, 25 February 2018, https://caravanmagazine.in/reportage/how-rss-infiltrating-india-intellectual-spaces, last accessed on 7 April 2021; Jha, Sanjay K., 'Call to Reclaim Gandhian Institutions from Socialists and Sanghis', the *Telegraph*, 28 December 2020, https://www.telegraphindia.com/india/call-to-reclaim-gandhian-institutions-from-socialists-and-sanghis/cid/1801859, last accessed on 7 April 2021, at 14.28 hours.

35.   Ibid.

36. Betancourt, R. and Gleason, S., 'The Allocation of Publicly-Provided Goods to Rural Households in India: On Some Consequences of Caste, Religion and Democracy', *World Development* 28(12), 2000, pp. 169–82.

37. Despite reservation in government services, only 11.5 per cent of the A class administrative positions in India are occupied by Dalits, while 95 per cent of Dalits are clustered in grades C and D in what can only be characterized as *inclusionary exclusion;* Deshpande, Pushparaj, 'Revisiting Ambedkar, Gandhi and India's Unfinished War', The Wire, 14 April 2016, https://thewire.in/politics/revisiting-ambedkar-gandhi-indias-unfinished-war.

38. Scheduled Castes (SC) and Scheduled Tribes (ST) candidates are routinely excluded from employment in the private sector since applicants are purposefully scrutinized through the lens of caste (to sift out SC candidates). Similarly, a first-of-its-kind survey on the social profiles of 315 senior decision-makers in thirty-seven newspapers and television channels found that 90 per cent of the decision-makers in the English language print media and 79 per cent in television were upper caste. Not a single one of these 315 was from the SC/ST communities.

39. Roy, Arundhati, 'The Doctor and the Saint' (Introduction) in Ambedkar, B.R., 'Annihilation of Caste' (New Delhi: Navayana, 2014), p. 33; Thorat, S. and Senapati, C., 'Reservation in Employment, Education and Legislature—Status and Emerging Issue', Indian Institute of Dalit Studies, Working Paper Series, Vol. II, No. 05; Department Related Parliamentary Standing Committee on Personnel, Public Grievances, Law and Justice, Twenty-First Report, 17 August 2007; 'Upper Castes Dominate National Media, Says Survey in Delhi', *The Hindu*, 5 June 2006; Singh, D., 'Development of Scheduled Castes in India: A Review', *Journal of Rural Development*, 28 (4), 2009, p. 533; Thorat, S.K., *Dalits in India: Search for a Common Destiny* (New Delhi: Sage, 2009).

40. Bhagwat, Mohan, *Yashasvi Bharat* (New Delhi: Prabhat Prakashan, 2021), p. 205.

41. Deshpande, Pushparaj, 'The Battle for India's Soul', in Rathore, Aakash Singh and Nandy, Ashis, *Vision for a Nation: Paths and Perspectives* (New Delhi, Penguin India, 2020).

42. Ministry of Social Justice and Empowerment, 'Baba Saheb—Emancipator of the Downtrodden', Press Information Bureau, 6 December 2006, https://pib.gov.in/newsite/erelcontent.aspx?relid=22891.

43. In *The Discovery of India*, Nehru recounts an incident that explains his conception of Bharat Mata. Nehru writes that as he moved across India meeting people, he would often be greeted with the slogan '*Bharat Mata ki Jai*' and he would ask who was this Bharat Mata. His audience, Nehru wrote, would be bewildered and seek an answer from Nehru himself. Nehru would explain that 'Bharat Mata was essentially these millions of people.' 'You are parts of this Bharat Mata,' Nehru would tell his listeners, 'you are in a manner yourselves Bharat Mata.' And Nehru recalled, 'As this idea slowly soaked into their brains, their eyes would light up as if they had made a great discovery'; Mukherjee, Rudrangshu, 'Who is Bharat Mata—On History, Culture and the Idea of India: Writings by and on Jawaharlal Nehru: Nehru's Idea of India', *The Hindu*, 10 August 2019, https://www.thehindu.com/books/books-reviews/who-is-bharat-mata-on-history-culture-and-the-idea-of-india-writings-by-and-on-jawaharlal-nehru-review-nehrus-idea-of-india/article28939684.ece; last accessed on 9 April 2021 at 11.57 hours).

44. Agrawal, Purshottam, 'Who is Bharat Mata: On History, Culture and the Idea of India: Writings by and on Jawaharlal Nehru' (New Delhi: Speaking Tiger Publishing, 2019).

45. Nussbaum, Martha, *Political Emotions: Why Love Matters For Justice*.

46. Odgers, W., 'A Defence of Rousseau's Theory of the Social Contract', *Journal of the Society of Comparative Legislation, 16*(2), 322–32, 1916; Retrieved 2 April 2021, http://www.jstor.org/stable/752430.

47. Rukmini S., 'Young India Is Conservative: Opposed to Homosexuality, Likes to Marry Within Their Caste, Wants a Government Job', 4 April 2017, https://www.huffingtonpost.in/2017/04/04/young-india-is-conservative-opposed-to-homosexuality-likes-to_a_22025362/; 'Attitudes, Anxieties and Aspirations of India's Youth: Changing Patterns', Centre for the Study of Developing Societies (CSDS) and Konrad Adenauer

Stiftung (KAS), 3 April 2017, https://www.lokniti.org/content/CSDS-KAS-Youth-Study-2016-17.

48. 'Religion in India: Tolerance and Segregation', Pew Research Center, Washington, 2021, https://www.pewforum.org/2021/06/29/religion-in-india-tolerance-and-segregation/, last accessed on 29 July 2021 at 11.58 hours).

49. Varshney, Ashutosh, 'What Does It Mean to Be Indian?', the *Indian Express*, 26 July 2021, https://indianexpress.com/article/opinion/columns/hindu-nationalism-indian-nationhood-diversity-7421980/; last accessed on 29 July 2021 at 12.24 hours.

50. This has been famously characterized as the 'thali' theory of Indian nationalism. 'Like a thali, we are a collection of different items in different bowls; since we are in different dishes we don't necessarily flow into each other, but we belong together on the same platter and combine on your palate to give you a satisfying repast'; Tharoor, Shashi, 'Mohan Bhagwat's Idea of India Is Not a Thali of Identities but a Khichdi', ThePrint, 27 September 2018, https://theprint.in/opinion/mohan-bhagwats-idea-of-india-is-not-a-thali-of-identities-but-a-khichdi-shashi-tharoor/125168/, last accessed on 29 July 2021 at 12.29 hours.

51. Nandy, Ashis, 'Theories of Oppression and another Dialogue of Cultures', Volume XLVII, No. 30, *Economic and Political Weekly*, Mumbai, 2012.

52. Ibid.

53. Heller, Patrick, 'Parties, Civil Society and Democratic Deepening: Comparing India, Brazil and South Africa', Studies in India Politics, 11 (1) pp. 10–26, 2023.

54. For years after Independence, the Congress Party was able to sustain and capitalize on the set of functional networks of numerous socio-economic groups it had established during the freedom struggle. These were mediated and managed by a managerial set of politicians at the panchayat, block, district, state and national levels. Internal party elections played a crucial role in managing and more importantly, accommodating dissent within this system. This plurality made the party infinitely more representative and the legitimacy of the party was premised on the consensus thus built.

55. 'The 2019 Global Multidimensional Poverty Index (MPI)', United Nations Development Programme, http://hdr.undp.org/en/2019-MPI, last accessed on 3 April 2021 at 00.24 hours.

56. 'BJP Ideology Appeals to the Middle Class Because of Its Own Anxieties: Sociologist Yogendra Singh', Interview with Ajaz Ashraf, Scroll.in, 5 May 2016, https://scroll.in/article/806994/interview-the-bjps-ideology-appeals-to-the-middle-class-because-of-its-own-anxieties, last accessed on 3 April 2021 at 00.19 hours.

57. Heller, Patrick (2023): 'Parties, Civil Society and Democratic Deepening: Comparing India, Brazil and South Africa'.

58. Synder, Timothy, *On Tyranny: Twenty Lessons from the Twentieth Century* (New York: Tim Duggan Books, 2017).

59. Deshpande, Pushparaj, 'The Battle for India's Soul', 2020.

60. Reich, Wilhelm, 'The Mass Psychologe of Fascism' (New York: Organe Institute Press, 1946).

61. '"Kejriwal Knew IAC Movement Was Propped Up by BJP-RSS", Says Prashant Bhushan', *Wire.in*, 25 September 2020, https://thewire.in/politics/prashant-bhushan-arvind-kejriwal-upa-iac-bjp-rss; last accessed on 3 April 2021 at 17.24 hours.

62. Deshpande, Pushparaj, 'Is Democracy Around the World Devouring Itself?', The Wire, 20 September 2019, https://thewire.in/rights/is-democracy-around-the-world-devouring-itself.

63. *Gleichshaltung,* euphemistically translated as coordination, was a process by which the Nazi Party established total control of the State in Germany.

64. Khaitan, Tarunabh, 'Killing a Constitution with a Thousand Cuts: Executive Aggrandizement and Party-State Fusion in India', *Law and Ethics of Human Rights*, Vol. 14, No. 1, 2020, pp. 49–95, https://doi.org/10.1515/lehr-2020-2009, last accessed on 18 November 2021; O'Brien, Derek, 'The BJP Is Killing Our Institutions', The Wire, 18 February 2018, https://thewire.in/government/bjp-killing-institutions, last accessed on 18 November 2021; Vanaik, Achin, 'How Does the BJP Control Educational Institutions in India?', NewsClick, 23 October 2017, https://www.newsclick.in/how-does-bjp-control-educational-institutions-india, last accessed on 18 November 2021; Guha, Ramchandra, 'Gandhi Said RSS Was

"Communal with a Totalitarian Outlook"—And That's Still True', *Scroll.in*,; Bal, Hartosh Singh, 'The Takeover: How the RSS is Infiltrating India's Intellectual Spaces', *Caravan*; Jha, Sanjay K., 'Call to Reclaim Gandhian Institutions from Socialists and Sanghis', the *Telegraph*, 28 December 2020, https://www.telegraphindia.com/india/call-to-reclaim-gandhian-institutions-from-socialists-and-sanghis/cid/1801859, last accessed on 7 April 2021 at 14.28 hours.

65. Varma, Subodh, 'How Modi Government is Destroying Key Indian Institutions', NewsClick, 27 October 2018, https://www.newsclick.in/how-modi-government-destroying-key-indian-institutions, last accessed on 7 April 2021 at 18.29 hours.

66. Heinrich Knirr, colour poster with a portrait of Hitler and the Nazi slogan 'Ein Volk, ein Reich, ein Führer', 1935, United States Holocaust Memorial Museum, https://collections.ushmm.org/search/catalog/irn516176, last accessed 10 April 2023 at 15.28 hours.

67. 'India Has the Longest Running Fascist Movement in the World—The RSS', Interview with Benjamin Zachariah, Partha P. Chakrabartty, Wire.in.

68. Saikia, Arunabh, '"They Are Polarising India": Ex RSS Worker on Why He Filed Affidavit Claiming VHP, RSS Set Off Bombs', The Scroll, 2 September 2022, https://scroll.in/article/1031927/they-are-polarising-india-ex-rss-worker-on-why-he-filed-affidavit-claiming-vhp-rss-set-off-bombs; last accessed on 17 April 2023 at 19.05 hours.

69. 'Peoples' Chargesheet on Five Years of NDA Rule (2014–19)', Jan Sarokar–Peoples' Agenda, 2019; Thapar, Karan, 'Budget to Widen K-Shaped Recovery, Polarise India v Bharat', The Wire, https://thewire.in/economy/watch-pronab-sen-says-budget-to-widen-k-shaped-recovery-polarise-india-v-bharat-doubts-2-lakh-cr-capex; last accessed on 4 February 2022 at 12.37 hours); 'Budget 2022: A Pathbreaking Document, but for Wrong Reasons', *Policy Circle*, 8 February 2022, https://www.policycircle.org/opinion/budget-2022-anti-poor/; last accessed on 15 February 2022 at 09.26 hours.

70. The NDA government has proposed to sell national assets including 31 airports, 23 ports, 26,700 kms of highways (20 per cent of the

nation's road length), 400 railway stations, 1400 kms of rail lines as well as the entirety of the Konkan railway, four heritage hill railways and the dedicated freight corridor. It is also privatizing banks and partially privatizing the Life Insurance Corporation.

71. There has been a 28 per cent annual rise in sedition cases between 2014 and 2020; quoted in 'A Decade of Darkness—The Story of Sedition in India', Article 14, https://sedition.article-14.com; last accessed on 4 February 2020 at 12.00 pm.

72. 'Autocratization Turns Viral: Democracy Report 2021', V-Dem Institute, University of Gothenburg, https://www.v-dem.net/files/25/DR%202021.pdf; last accessed on 7 April 2021 at 19.00 hours; Alam, Mahtab, 'India's "Extraordinary" Laws Need to Be Revoked, Not Revamped', The Wire, 18 February 2021, https://thewire.in/rights/uapa-sedition-psa-nsa-extraordinary-laws; last accessed on 7 April 2021 at 18.45 hours.

73. 'The State of the World's Human Rights 2017/18: India', Amnesty International, 22 February 2018, https://amnesty.org.in/publications/amnesty-international-report-2017-2018-india/, last accessed on 9 July 2019 at 18.15 hours.

74. 'Freedom in the World 2019: India', Freedom House, https://freedomhouse.org/report/freedom-world/2019/india, last accessed on 9 July 2019 at 20.56 hours.

75. Ibid.; 'India Has Launched a Sharp Assault on Press Freedom – But Independent Media Is Determined to Resist', Kavitha Iyer, Scroll.in, 15 February 2021, https://scroll.in/article/986981/as-more-indians-turn-to-independent-media-for-news-press-freedom-faces-sharp-attacks, last accessed on 7 April 2021 at 19.00 hours.

76. Ahmad, Mudasir 'BJP Leader in Front, Hindu Ekta Manch Waves Tricolour in Support of Rape Accused in Jammu', The Wire, 17 February 2018, https://thewire.in/politics/hindu-ekta-manch-bjp-protest-support-spo-arrested-rape-jammu, last accessed on 9 July 2019; Shuja-ul-Haq, 'Kathua Rape Case: 2 BJP Ministers Attend Rally in Support of Accused', India Today, 4 March 2018, https://www.indiatoday.in/india/story/kathua-rape-case-2-bjp-ministers-attend-rally-in-support-of-accused-1181788-2018-03-04, last accessed on 9 July 2019 at 19.22 hours.

77. Chander, Mani, 'The Rise of India's Police State: Shadowy New Agencies With Shadowy Powers', Article 14, 7 December 2021, https://www.article-14.com/post/the-rise-of-india-s-police-state-shadowy-new-agencies-with-shadowy-powers-61aed9b1b6796, last accessed on 4 February 2022; Shakhavat, Devendra, 'Police & Govt Ally With Hindu Groups Intimidating, Attacking Christians in MP, 0.29% of State Population', Article 14, 3 February 2022, https://www.article-14.com/post/police-govt-ally-with-hindu-groups-intimidating-attacking-christians-in-mp-0-29-of-state-population-61fb458cf16f5; last accessed on 4 February 2020.

78. Inamdar, Nikhil, 'Covid Accelerates India's Millionaire Exodus', British Broadcasting Corporation, 13 April 2021, https://www.bbc.com/news/world-asia-56659615, last accessed on 5 November 2021 at 13.24 hours.

79. Ganguly, Meenakshi, 'Dissent Is "Anti-National" in Modi's India', Human Rights Watch, 13 December 2019, https://www.hrw.org/news/2019/12/13/dissent-anti-national-modis-india,last accessed on 11 April 2023 at 21.58 hours.

80. Including the Government of the National Capital Territory (Amendment) Bill, which gives greater powers to a lieutenant governor nominated by the Union government over the elected Delhi Assembly; the numerous Love Jihad laws in effect banning inter-faith marriages, thereby violating the Constitution, etc.

81. Menon, Amarnath K., 'How the Right to Information Act Is Being Steadily Scuttled', *India Today*, 24 October 2021, https://www.indiatoday.in/india-today-insight/story/how-the-right-to-information-act-is-being-steadily-scuttled-1868754-2021-10-24, last accessed on 5 November 2021 at 13.32 hours.

82. Ibid.

83. 'Number of CAG Reports on Centre Down by 75% Over the Last Five Years: RTI', The Wire, 7 March 2021, https://thewire.in/government/cag-reports-down-modi-government-nda-upa-rti; last accessed on 5 November 2021 at 13.29 hours.

84. Mahaprashasta, Ajoy, 'Why Opposition's Claim of Central Agencies Being Misused Rings True', The Wire, 5 September 2019, https://

thewire.in/politics/chidamabaram-shivakumar-arrest-central-agencies, last accessed on 6 November 2021; Raj, Kaleeswaram, 'Rule of Law Fails, Politics Gains', *the Deccan Herald*, 18 April 2021, https://www.deccanherald.com/specials/sunday-spotlight/rule-of-law-fails-politics-gains-975643.html, last accessed on 6 November 2021 at 13.40 hours.

85. Sircar, Jawahar, 'Picking, Kicking and Wrecking: Subjugation of the Bureaucracy in the Modi Regime', The Wire, 7 September 2021, https://thewire.in/government/bureaucracy-modi-government, last accessed on 10 April 2021 at 14.21 hours.

86. Bhat Naseer Ahmad, Bazila Shameem, and Nisha Yadav, 'Downward Spiral in Civil Service Anonymity and Neutrality: An Analysis of Indian Bureaucracy during Rise of Chauvinism and Right-Wing Nationalism', *Palarch's Journal of Archaeology of Egypt/Egyptology*, 17 (7), 2020.

87. Ruparelia, Sanjay, 'Minimum Government, Maximum Governance: The Restructuring of Power in Modi's India', *South Asia: Journal of South Asian Studies*, 38:4, 2015.

88. Tocqueville, Alexis de, *Democracy in America*, Project Gutenberg, https://www.gutenberg.org/files/815/815-h/815-h.htm; last accessed on 4 April 2021 at 12.53 hours.

89. Ibid.

90. 'India Is No Longer a Democracy but an 'Electoral Autocracy': Swedish Institute', The Wire, 11 March 2021, https://thewire.in/rights/india-no-longer-democracy-electoral-autocracy-v-dem-institute-report-bjp-narendra-modi, last accessed on 8 November 2021 at 17.07 hours).

91. 'Democracy under Siege', Freedom House, https://freedomhouse.org/report/freedom-world/2021/democracy-under-siege, last accessed on 9 November 2021 at 17.00 hours.

92. 'Democracy Index 2020: In Sickness and in Health?', The Economist Intelligence Unit, https://www.eiu.com/n/campaigns/democracy-index-2020/?utm_source=economist-daily-chart&utm_medium=anchor&utm_campaign=democracy-index-2020&utm_content=anchor-1, last accessed on 8 November 2021 at 17.10 hours.

93.   Sherman, Taylor C., 'A Man of His Time', *The Caravan*, 1 May 2023, https://caravanmagazine.in/history/nehru-modi-today; last accessed on 10 May 2023 at 12.18 hours.

94.   Srivastava, Amitabh, 'Why Engineered Defections Are a Revolting Strategy', *India Today*, 23 April 2021, https://www.indiatoday. in/india-today-insight/story/why-engineered-defections-are-a-revolting-strategy-1844404-2021-08-23, last accessed on 10 April 2023 at 16.34 hours.

95.   'For the BJP, Battle for a State Does Not Stop at Elections', the *Times of India*, 4 July 2022, http://timesofindia.indiatimes.com/ articleshow/92581135.cms?utm_source=contentofinterest&utm_medium=text&utm_campaign=cppst; last accessed on 10 April 2023 at 16.37 hours.

96.   Jha, Manoj, and Pushparaj Deshpande, 'Suspending MPLADS Funds for Coronavirus Crisis Is Another Stab at Indian Democracy', ThePrint, 24 April 2020, https://theprint.in/opinion/suspending-mplads-for-coronavirus-stab-at-indian-democracy/407935/, last accessed on 10 April 2023 at 16.16 hours.

97.   Gandhi, Varun, 'Why Is There No Debate in Parliament?', *the Indian Express*, 20 April 2022, https://indianexpress.com/article/opinion/ columns/why-is-there-no-debate-in-parliament-lok-sabha-monsoon-session-bills-7877230/, last accessed on 10 April 2023; O'Brien, Derek, 'The Ordinance Raj of the Bharatiya Janata Party', *Hindustan Times*, 11 September 2020, https://www.hindustantimes. com/analysis/the-ordinance-raj-of-the-bharatiya-janata-party/ story-NlVvn0pm6updxwYlj0gSvJ.html, last accessed on 10 April 2023; Singhvi, Abhishek Manu, and Jaiveer Shergill, 'The Government and Bjp Have Consistently Undermined Parliament', the *Times of India*, 18 January 2021, https://timesofindia.indiatimes. com/blogs/voices/the-government-and-bjp-have-consistently-undermined-parliament/, last accessed on 10 April 2023 at 16.29 hours.

98.   Sircar, Nilanjan, 'Corporate-Controlled Capitalism in India', *Seminar Magazine*, Vol. No. 749, January 2022, https://www.india-seminar.com/semsearch.htm, last accessed on 15 February 2022 at 09.19 hours.

99. Kant, Krishna, 'Profit Concentration in India Inc Rises amid Private Sector Growth', *Business Standard News,* 25 November 2021, https://www.business-standard.com/article/companies/profit-concentration-in-india-inc-rises-amid-private-sector-growth-121112500070_1.html, last accessed on 5 February 2022; Mukherjea, Saurabh, and Harsh Shah, 'India's Top 20 Leviathans: Awe-Inspiring Dominance', *Marcellus,* 2021, https://marcellus.in/blogs/indias-top-20-leviathans-awe-inspiring-dominance/, last accessed on 5 February 2022 at 20.54 hours.

100. Hall, Peter A., and David Soskice (eds.), *Varieties of Capitalism: The Institutional Foundations of Comparative Advantage* (Oxford and New York: Oxford University Press, 2001).

101. An electoral bond is a financial instrument for making donations to political parties. It is like a promissory note that can be bought by any Indian citizen or company incorporated in India from select branches of State Bank of India. The citizen or corporate can then donate the same to any eligible political party of his/her choice anonymously.

102. 'In 2019–20, BJP Got 76% of Total Electoral Bonds; Congress Got 9%: Report', The Wire, 10 August 2021, https://thewire.in/politics/bjp-congress-electoral-bonds-2019-20-donations-political-parties, last accessed on 5 February 2022 at 21.03 hours.

103. 'BJP Got 78% of Donations to National Parties', *The Hindu,* 27 February 2020, https://www.thehindu.com/news/national/bjp-got-78-of-donations-to-national-parties/article30935574.ece, last accessed on 5 February 2022 at 21.07 hours.

104. Rajhansa, Nandita and Saurabh Mukherjea, 'India's 20 Largest Profit Generators Are Earning 80% of the Nation's Profits', The Wire, 12 January 2023, https://thewire.in/economy/winner-takes-all-in-indias-new-improved-economy; last accessed on 2 September 2023 at 11.52 hours.

105. Himanshu, 'India's Slow but Sure De-industrialisation Is Worrying", LiveMint, 15 June 2023, https://www.livemint.com/opinion/columns/indias-manufacturing-sector-faces-worsening-decline-implications-for-growth-employment-and-income-11686851477882.html; last accessed on 2 September 2023 at 11.56 hours.

106. Weber, Isabella M. and Evan Wasner, 'Sellers' Inflation, Profits and Conflict: Why Can Large Firms Hike Prices in an Emergency?', *Review of Keynesian Economics*, Vol. 11, No. 2, Summer 2023, pp. 183–213, https://www.elgaronline.com/view/journals/roke/11/2/article-p183.xml?tab_body=abstract; last accessed on 3 September 2023 at 14.39 hours).

107. Vyas, Mahesh, 'Sticky Inflation at Elevated Levels', Centre for Monitoring Indian Economy, 27 February 2023, https://www.cmie.com/kommon/bin/sr.php?kall=warticle&dt=20230224190212&msec=206, last accessed on 11 April 2023 at 14.22 hours.

108. 'Budget 2022: A Pathbreaking Document, but for Wrong Reasons', *Policy Circle*, 8 February 2022., https://www.policycircle.org/opinion/budget-2022-anti-poor/, last accessed on 15 February 2022 at 09.26 hours.

109. Report No. 5 of 2022 (Indirect Taxes—Goods and Services Tax), Comptroller and Auditor General of India, https://cag.gov.in/uploads/download_audit_report/2022/3-%20Chapter-1-062f0e3be7c82f0.00161787.pdf; last accessed on 3 September 2023 at 12.13 hours.

110. 'Summary of the Economic Survey 2022-'23', Press Information Bureau, 31 January 2023, https://static.pib.gov.in/WriteReadData/userfiles/file/EconomicSurvey2023Q44O.pdf; last accessed on 3 September 2023 at 14.51 hours.

111. Vyas, Mahesh, 'Unemployment Rate Falls, but Still Too High', Centre for Monitoring Indian Economy, 6 February 2023, https://www.cmie.com/kommon/bin/sr.php?kall=warticle&dt=20230206145531&msec=156, last accessed on 11 April 2023 at 14.15 hours.

112. Goyal, Malini, 'SMEs Employ Close to 40% of India's Workforce, but Contribute Only 17% to GDP', the *Economic Times*, 9 June 2023, https://economictimes.indiatimes.com/small-biz/policy-trends/smes-employ-close-to-40-of-indias-workforce-but-contribute-only-17-to-gdp/articleshow/20496337.cms?utm_source=contentofinterest&utm_medium=text&utm_campaign=cppst; last accessed on 3 September 2023 at 12.08 hours.

113. Roy, Esha, 'Oxfam Report: In 2021, Income of 84 Per Cent Households Fell, but Number of Billionaires Grew', *Indian Express*, 17 January 2022, https://indianexpress.com/article/india/oxfam-report-2021-income-households-fell-7726844/, last accessed on 15 February 2022 at 09.41 hours.

114. 'Household Debt Increased on an Average by 1.5X between 2012 & 2018', SBI Research, State Bank of India, 15 September 2021, https://sbi.co.in/documents/13958/10990811/150921-Ecowrap_20210915.pdf/58b316c8-9f60-a119-65d0-bb89c41fd561?t=1631765892649, last accessed on 11 April 2023 at 14.27 hours.

115. Pisharody, Rahul, 'Civil Society, the New Frontiers of War, Can Be Manipulated to Hurt a Nation's Interests: Ajit Doval', *Indian Express*, 12 November 2021, https://indianexpress.com/article/cities/hyderabad/ajit-doval-nsa-warfare-civil-society-7619555/, last accessed on 17 April 2023 at 17.24 hours.

116. 'FCRA Licences of 6,677 NGOs Cancelled in 5 Years: Govt', *Indian Express*, 7 December 2022, https://indianexpress.com/article/india/fcra-licence-of-6677-ngos-cancelled-in-5-years-govt-8311630/, last accessed on 17 April 2023 at 17.37 hours.

117. Narayan, Khushboo, 'Past Records under I-T Scanner, over 2 Lakh NGOs, Trusts Set to Register Again', *Indian Express*, 20 February 2020, https://indianexpress.com/article/india/past-records-under-i-t-scanner-over-2-lakh-ngos-trusts-set-to-register-again-6276693/, last accessed on 17 April 2023 at 17.39 hours.

118. Pisharody, Rahul, 'Civil Society, the New Frontiers of War, Can Be Manipulated to Hurt a Nation's Interests: Ajit Doval', *Indian Express*, 12 November 2021, https://indianexpress.com/article/cities/hyderabad/ajit-doval-nsa-warfare-civil-society-7619555/, last accessed on 3 September 2023 at 14.56 hours.

119. Kapur, Devesh and Pratap Bhanu Mehta, *Rethinking Public Institutions in India* (New Delhi: Oxford University Press, 2017), pp. 2–3.

120. Brødsgaard, Kjeld Erik, 'Can China Keep Controlling Its SOEs?', *The Diplomat*, 5 March 2018, https://thediplomat.com/2018/03/can-china-keep-controlling-its-soes/, last accessed on 8 November

2021; McGregor, Richard, 'How the State Runs Business in China', the *Guardian*, 25 July 2019, https://www.theguardian. com/world/2019/jul/25/china-business-xi-jinping-communist-party-state-private-enterprise-huawei, last accessed on 8 April 2021 at 13.07 hours.

121. Bahl, Raghav, 'How to Quickly Privatise 300 PSUs Without Selling a Single Share!', The Quint, 25 February 2021, https://www.thequint.com/voices/opinion/raghav-bahl-on-alternative-privatisation-model-maruti-disinvestment-modi-govt-air-india-psu-banks, last accessed on 7 April 2021 at 15.40 hours.

122. 'National Monetisation Pipeline | Here's the Breakup of the Govt's Big Privatisation Push', *The Hindu*, 24 August 2021, https://www.thehindu.com/business/Economy/national-monetisation-pipeline-heres-the-breakup-of-the-govts-big-privatisation-push/article36075874.ece, last accessed on 10 April 2023 at 15.32 hours.

123. Kelkar, Vijay, and Ajay Shah, *In Service of the Republic* (Penguin Allen Lane, 2019).

124. 'Minimum Government, Maximum Governance', Narendra Modi, 14 May 2014, https://www.narendramodi.in/minimum-government-maximum-governance-3162, last accessed on 11 April 2023 at 14.40 hours.

125. Goel, Samiksha, 'The Doctor-Population Ratio in India Is 1:1456 against WHO Recommendation', the *Deccan Herald*, 31 January 2020, https://www.deccanherald.com/business/budget-2020/the-doctor-population-ratio-in-india-is-11456-against-who-recommendation-800034.html, last accessed on 8 November 2021 at 13.15 hours.

126. 'Judge-Population Ratio Stood at 21.03 Judges per Million People in 2020: Law Minister', the *Economic Times*, 5 August 2021, https://economictimes.indiatimes.com/news/india/judge-population-ratio-stood-at-21-03-judges-per-million-people-in-2020-law-minister/articleshow/85072861.cms, last accessed on 8 November 2021 at 13.24 hours.

127. 'India's Student-Teacher Ratio Lowest among Compared Countries, Lags behind Brazil and China', *India Today*, 14 July

2019, https://www.indiatoday.in/education-today/news/story/
india-s-student-teacher-ratio-lowest-lags-behind-brazil-and-
china-1568695-2019-07-14, last accessed on 8 November 2021 at
13.28 hours.

128. Ghosh, Abantika, '1 Doctor for 1,511 People, 1 Nurse for 670—
COVID Exposes India's Healthcare "Fault Lines"', ThePrint, 11
February 2021, https://theprint.in/health/1-doctor-for-1511-
people-1-nurse-for-670-covid-exposes-indias-healthcare-fault-
lines/602784/, last accessed on 9 November 2021 at 13:30 hours.

129. 'Hannah Arendt', Yasemin Sari, *Philosophy Now*, 2014, https://
philosophynow.org/issues/100/Hannah_Arendt, last accessed on
10 April 2023 at 15.37 hours.

130. Cherry, Kendra, 'Milgram's Experiments and the Perils of Obedience',
Very Well Mind, 12 May 2021, https://www.verywellmind.
com/the-milgram-obedience-experiment-2795243, last accessed
on 8 November 2021; Cherry, Kendra, 'The Asch Conformity
Experiments', Very Well Mind, 30 April 2020, https://www.
verywellmind.com/the-asch-conformity-experiments-2794996,
last accessed on 8 November 2021 at 13.41 hours.

131. The Milburn and Asch experiments were a series of social
psychology experiments that found that a large number of study
participants administered fatal electric shocks to subjects upon the
instruction of authority figures. These participants suspended their
conscience and value systems just because they were instructed to
do so. Incidentally, the shocks themselves were not real but the
participants did not know that until after the experiments were
completed.

132. 'Foreign Ministry Spokesperson Zhao Lijian's Regular Press
Conference on July 28, 2021', https://www.fmprc.gov.cn/mfa_
eng/xwfw_665399/s2510_665401/t1895706.shtml, last accessed
on 5 August 2021 on 5 August 2021.

133. Cohen, Stephen Philip, *The South Asia Papers: A Critical Anthology of
Writings* (New Delhi: HarperCollins Publishers India, 2016).

134. Ibid.

135. Huning, Wang, 'The Structure of China's Changing Political
Culture', translated by David Ownby, 1988, https://www.

readingthechinadream.com/wang-huning-ldquothe-structure-of-chinarsquos-changing-political-culturerdquo.html; last accessed on 12 October 2021 at 19.15 hours.

136. Deshpande, Pushparaj, 'The Future of Progressive Politics in India', *Economic and Political Weekly*, Volume 55, Issue No. 14, 4 April 2020.

137. Ibid.

138. Mukherjee, Rudrangshu, 'Who is Bharat Mata—On History, Culture and the Idea of India: Writings by and on Jawaharlal Nehru: Nehru's Idea of India', *The Hindu*.

139. Quoted in 'The Future of Progressive Politics in India', *Economic and Political Weekly*, Vol. 55, Issue No. 14, 4 April 2020, https://www.epw.in/engage/article/future-progressive-politics-india, last accessed on 10 April 2023 at 15.58 hours.

140. Paine, Thomas, 'The American Crisis (1776-1783)', Bill of Rights Institute, https://billofrightsinstitute.org/primary-sources/the-american-crisis, last accessed on 10 April 2023 at 16.01 hours.

The Cabinet: A Check on Authoritarianism

1. Constituent Assembly Debates (C.A. Deb.). Vol. VII; pp. 32–33.
2. Ibid.
3. Constituent Assembly Debates (C.A. Deb.). Vol. VII; pp. 32–33.
4. Pylee, M.V., India's Constitution, S. Chand, 16th ed., p. 122.
5. Lok Sabha Debates, Vol. 9, Issues 6–10, p. 2704.
6. Ibid.
7. C.H. Alexandrowicz, *Constitutional Developments in India* (Bombay: Oxford University Press, 1957).
8. Ibid.
9. Sisson, Richard, 'Prime Ministerial Power and the Selection of Ministers in India: Three Decades of Change', *International Political Science Review*, Vol. 2, No. 2 (1981), pp. 140–44, https://www.jstor.org/stable/1600871, last accessed on 13 April 2019, at 13.04 hours.
10. Note to Mahatma Gandhi, 6 January 1948, *Selected Works of Jawaharlal Nehru*, Second Series, Vol. 5, p. 473.

11. Sisson, Richard, 'Prime Ministerial Power and the Selection of Ministers in India: Three Decades of Change', *International Political Science Review*.

12. Ibid.

13. Note by Aiyar, 8 October 1951, Prasad: Correspondence and Select Documents, Vol. 14, pp. 286–87.

14. Kumarasingham, Harshan, 'Indian Version of First Among Equals—Executive Power during the First Decade of Independence', Modern Asian Studies, Cambridge University Press, Vol. 44, No. 4 (July 2010), p. 715, https://www.jstor.org/stable/40664944, last accessed on 28 April 2019 at 18.44 hours.

15. Correspondence between Matthai and Nehru in Gopal's *Selected Works of Jawaharlal Nehru*, Second Series, Vol. 14, part 2, pp. 227–50.

16. Nehru to Patel, 25 May 1950 in Gopal's *Selected Works of Jawaharlal Nehru*, Second Series, Vol. 14, part 2.

17. Ibid, p. 144.

18. Barbieri, Cristina, 'The Cabinet: A Viable Definition and its Composition in View of a Comparative Analysis, Government and Opposition', Vol. 48, No. 4 (October 2013), p. 529, https://www.jstor.org/stable/10.2307/26350309, accessed on 19 April 2019 at 17.25 hours.

19. The AICC and the Congress Ministries, *The Leader*, 8 November 1937, reprinted in the Unity of India, London, 1941, pp. 78–85.

20. Hardgrave, R. L., 'The Congress in India—Crisis and Split, *Asian Survey, 10*(3), 1970, pp. 256–62, https://doi.org/10.2307/2642578.

21. Ibid.

22. *U.N. Rao vs Indira Gandhi*, 17 March 1971, AIR 1971 SC 63.

23. Kumarasingham, Harshan, 'Indian Version of First Among Equals—Executive Power during the First Decade of Independence', p. 710.

24. Johari, J.C., *Indian Polity: A Concise Study of the Indian Constitution, Government and Politics* (New Delhi: Lotus Press, 2004, p. 80).

25. Ibid.

26. Kavanagh, D., *British Politics: Continuities and Change* (London and New York, NY: Oxford University Press, 2000, p. 253).

27. EGoM and GoMs were responsible for investigating and reporting as well as taking decisions in specified matters. Both EGoMs and GoMs were stipulated under the Government of India's Transaction of Business Rules 1961, which at para 6 (4) provides that 'ad hoc

Committees of Ministers including Group of Ministers may be appointed by the Cabinet, the Standing Committees of the Cabinet or by the Prime Minister for investigating and reporting to the Cabinet on such matters as may be specified, and, if so authorised by the Cabinet, Standing Committees of the Cabinet or the Prime Minister, for taking decisions on such matters'.

28. 'Government Abolishes All GOMs and EGOMs for Greater Accountability and Empowerment', Prime Minister India's Office, Government of India, 31 May 2014, https://www.pmindia. gov.in/en/news_updates/government-abolishes-all-goms-and-egoms-for-greater-accountability-and-empowerment/?tag_term=goms&comment=disable; last accessed on 8 October 2023 at 12.01 hours.

29. Ibid.

30. Calamur, Krishnadev, 'An Unexpected Stop in Pakistan', *The Atlantic*, 25 December 2015, https://www.theatlantic.com/international/archive/2015/12/modi-in-lahore/421923/; last accessed on 25 September 2023 at 20.23 hours.

31. '"Howdy, Modi!": Trump Hails Indian PM at "Historic" Texas Rally', British Broadcasting Corporation, 23 September 2019, https://www.bbc.com/news/world-us-canada-49788492; last accessed on 18 October 2019 at 12.00 hours.

32. Holland, Steve, and Alasdair Pal, '"Namaste Trump"': Modi Holds Huge Rally for President's Visit', Reuters, https://www.reuters.com/article/us-india-usa-trump-idUSKCN20I0B6; last accessed on 25 February 2020 at 12.00 hours.

33. Jha, Prashant, 'End of the Madhesi Blockade: What It Means for Nepal', *Hindustan Times*, 6 February 2016, https://www.hindustantimes.com/opinion/end-of-the-madhesi-blockade-what-it-means-for-nepal/story-JixO1gsdWLprj8Lc6G0hQL.html; last accessed on 15 September 2023 at 20.05 hours.

34. Vora, Anchal, 'Modi's China Policy Is a Failure', *Foreign Policy*, 18 January 2023, https://foreignpolicy.com/2023/01/18/modis-china-policy-is-a-failure/; last accessed on 25 August 2023 at 19.46 hours.

35. Sisson, Richard, 'Prime Ministerial Power and the Selection of Ministers in India: Three Decades of Change', *International Political Science Review*.

36. Ibid.

37. Ibid.

38. Kaarbo, Juliet, 'Coalition Cabinet Decision Making: Institutional and Psychological Factors', *International Studies Review*, Vol. 10, No. 1, Mar., 2008, p. 78, https://www.jstor.org/stable/25481930, last accessed on 16 April 2020 at 11.45 hours.

39. Ahluwalia, Montek, *Backstage: The Story behind India's High Growth Years* (Rupa Publications, 2020).

40. Ahluwalia, Montek, *Backstage: The Story behind India's High Growth Years*.

41. 'Farm Bills: "Centre Did Not Consult Us, but It Should at Least Talk to Farmers", Says SAD Chief', Scroll.in, 22 September 2023, https://scroll.in/latest/973760/farm-bills-centre-did-not-consult-us-but-it-should-at-least-talk-to-farmers-says-sad-chief; last accessed on 27 September 2023 at 12.17 hours.

42. 'Bjp Did Not Follow Coalition "Dharma", Claims JD(U) Chief Lalan Singh', ANI, 12 August 2022, https://theprint.in/politics/bjp-did-not-follow-coalition-dharma-claims-jdu-chief-lalan-singh/1079910/; last accessed on 27 September 2023; 'Manipur Polls: BJP Has Not Followed Coalition Dharma, Says Conrad K. Sangma', ET Bureau, 19 February 2022, https://economictimes.indiatimes.com/news/elections/assembly-elections/manipur/manipur-polls-bjp-has-not-followed-coalition-dharma-says-conrad-k-sangma/articleshow/89673222.cms?from=mdr; last accessed on 27 September 2023.

43. Khare, Harish, 'After Seven Years of Modi and Shah, the RSS's Fall from Grace is Total and Complete', The Wire, 3 June 2021, https://thewire.in/politics/rss-mohan-bhagwat-bjp-modi-covid-19; last accessed on 27 September 2023 at 20.23 hours.

44. Jawaharlal Nehru, Speeches, Vol. 4, Publications Division, Government of India, pp. 54–55 and 60.

Enhancing Peoples' Rights and Freedoms: The NAC Revisited

1. The National Common Minimum Programme (NCMP) of the Government of India was a document outlining the minimum

objectives of the United Progressive Alliance (UPA) government in India, whose principal partners included the INC, RJD, DMK, NCP, PMK, TRS, JMM, LJP, MDMK, AIMIM, PDP, IUML, RPI (A), RPI (G) and KC(J). The NCMP in 2004 strived to strengthen 'secular and progressive forces for parties wedded to the welfare of the farmers, agricultural labour, weavers, workers and weaker sections of society, [and] for parties irrevocably committed to the well being of the common man across the country'.

2. Gupta, Barun Das, 'Jawaharlal Nehru: The Architect of Modern India', *Mainstream*, Vol. LII, No 23, 31 May 2014.

3. Some of the twenty-nine sub-committees included Manufacturing and Industries, Labour, Currency and Banking, Crops: Planning and Production, Power and Fuel, General Education, Technical Education and Development Research, Rural and Cottage Industries, Industrial Finance, Land Policy, Agricultural Labour and Insurance, National Housing, etc.

4. The members of the NAC included Anu Aga, Aruna Roy, Ashis Mondal, A.K. Shiva Kumar, Deep Joshi, Farah Naqvi, Harsh Mander, Jean Drèze, J.P. Narayanan Madhav Gadgil, Mihir Shah, Mirai Chatterjee, M.S. Swaminathan, Narendra Jadhav, Dr N.C. Saxena, Pramod Tandon, Ram Dayal Munda and Virginius Xaxa.

5. The NAC's internal procedures provided for details on how these consultations were to be carried out. Section 6, Consultations, NAC Procedures, 5 July 2010.

6. The NAC's website is no longer accessible after the NDA government came into office. The address was nac.nic.in.

7. Section 1, Guiding Principles, NAC Procedures, 5 July 2010.

8. Section 9, Petitions, NAC Procedures, 5 July 2010.

9. Section 5.15, Working Groups, NAC Procedures, 5 July 2010; Section 8.5, Follow-up Action on NAC Recommendations, NAC Procedures, 5 July 2010.

10. Prime Minister Manmohan Singh's address to the nation on 24 June 2004.

11. Some of the other pro-people issues that the NAC took up over the course of its tenure included natural resource management, including revitalization of agriculture; the development of Scheduled

Castes and Scheduled Tribes; welfare of minorities; the Prevention of Communal Violence Bill; poverty alleviation and employment generation, land rights and land reforms, right to education; welfare of disadvantaged children; health security and medical insurance; social security and safety net for the disadvantaged groups; urban poverty; development of the North-East Region; governance and accountability issues; gender issues; renewal of the handloom sector; eco-restoration and increasing forest cover; climate change initiatives through national missions; innovations in science and technology and taking it to the grassroots; Millennium Development Goals (MDGs); cooperative reforms; policy on internal displacement due to conflict; strengthening the Integrated Child Development Services, and flagship programmes such as Bharat Nirman, Sarva Shiksha Abhiyan, National Rural Health Mission, Jawaharlal Nehru National Urban Renewal Mission, Scheduled Tribes and Other Traditional Forest Dwellers (Recognition of Forest Rights) Act, 2006, etc.

12. 'Peoples' Monitoring of the RTI Regime in India, 2011-2013' by RaaG and CES, 2014; cited in Report Card of Information Commissions in India 2021–22, Satark Nagrik Sangathan (https://snsindia.org/wp-content/uploads/2022/12/Report-Card-2022.pdf; last accessed on 31 March 2023 at 11.33 a.m.).

13. Mann, Neelakshi and Pande, Varad, 'MG-NREGA Sameeksha', Ministry of Rural Development, 2012 and MGNREGA, Report to the People, Ministry of Rural Development, February 2014.

14. Ibid.

15. Ibid.

16. Rajya Sabha, Unstarred Question No.2703, dated 12 August 2015.

17. FRA Status Report, May 2015, Ministry of Tribal Affairs.

18. Editorial (2015): 'Splendid Decade, but Miles to Go', The Hindu, 16 December, http://m.thehindu.com/opinion/editorial/human-development-index-splendid-decade-but-miles-to-go/article7992807.ece; last accessed on 17 December 2015 at 19.30; Jahan, Selim, 'Human Development Report 2015, UNDP, 2015, http://hdr.undp.org/sites/default/files/2015_human_development_report.pdf; last accessed on 17 December 2015 at 19.35.

19. Stiglitz, Joseph, 'Keynote Address, Annual World Bank Conference on Development Economics 1997', Wider Annual Lectures 2, World Bank, 1998.

20. Chomsky, Noam, *Profit over People: Neoliberalism and Global Order* (New York: Seven Stories Press, 1999).

21. Trivedi, Divya, 'Where Would the Proposed Forest Conservation Rules Leave Forest Dwellers?', *Frontline*, 24 July 2022, https://frontline.thehindu.com/environment/snatch-and-grab-proposed-forest-conservation-rules-2022-dilute-rights-of-forest-dwellers/article65661818.ece; last accessed on 29 March 2023 at 13.57 hours.

22. 'The Role of Independent Institutions in Protecting and Promoting Constitutional Rights', Prashant Bhushan and Anjali Bharadwaj, in *We The People: Establishing Rights and Deepening Democracy*, edited by Nikhil Dey, Aruna Roy and Rakshita Swamy, Rethinking India series, Penguin (2020).

23. Union Budget Documents, Government of India.

24. 'Cash Transfer of Food Subsidy Directly into the Bank Account of PDS Being Implemented on a Pilot Basis in Three UTs—Chandigarh and Puducherry since September, 2015 and Urban Areas of Dadra and Nagar Haveli since March, 2016', Press Information Bureau, Ministry of Consumer Affairs, Food and Public Distribution, 30 March 2022, https://pib.gov.in/PressReleaseIframePage.aspx?PRID=1811483#:~:text=The%20Direct%20Benefit%20Transfer%20(DBT,(vi)%20promote %20financial%20inclusion.

25. S.O. 371(E), Notification, Ministry of Consumer Affairs, Food and Public Distribution, 8 February 2017, https://egazette.nic.in/WriteReadData/2017/174131.pdf.

26. 'Aadhaar and Food Security in Jharkhand: Pain Without Gain?', *Economic and Political Weekly*, 16 December 2017.

27. 'Making Aadhaar-Based Payments Compulsory for NREGA Wages Is a Recipe for Disaster', Jean Drèze, The Wire, 16 February 2023, https://thewire.in/rights/aadhaar-payments-compulsory-nrega; last accessed on 31 March 2023 at 15.30 hours.

28. '18 States yet to Receive ₹4,700 crore in MGNREGS wages from Union Government', *The Hindu*, 27 December 2022, https://www.thehindu.com/news/national/18-states-yet-to-receive-

4700-crore-in-mgnregs-wages-from-union-govt/article66310110. ece; last accessed on 31 March 2023 at 15.33 hours.

29. Dashboard, Mahatma Gandhi National Rural Employment Guarantee Act, Ministry of Rural Development, last accessed on 11 February 2022, https://ruraldiksha.nic.in/RuralDashboard/MGNREGA_New.asp x.

30. Report No. 20, Critical Evaluation of Mahatma Gandhi National Rural Employment Guarantee Act, Standing Committee on Rural Development, 2021–22, http://164.100.47.193/lsscommittee/Rural%20Development%20 and%20Panchayati%20Raj/17_Rural_Development_and_Panch ayati_Raj_20.pdf.

31. 'Democratising Lawmaking: The Tale of Pre-Legislative Consultation Policy', MediaNama, 15 August 2019, https://www.medianama.com/2019/08/223-democratising-lawmaking-the-tale-of-pre-legislative-consultation-policy/; last accessed on 31 March 2023 at 16.46 hours.

32. 'Sonia Gandhi Writes on Budget 2023–24: A Silent Strike on the Poor', *Indian Express*, 6 February 2023, https://indianexpress.com/article/opinion/columns/sonia-gandhi-writes-on-budget-2023-24-a-silent-strike-on-the-poor-8425947/; last accessed on 31 March 2023 at 15.47 hours.

33. Ibid.

34. Ibid.

Reimagining Parliament: Hopes and Perils

1. Quoted in Granville Austin, *The Indian Constitution: Cornerstone of a Nation* (Oxford: Clarendon Press, 1966), p. 1.

2. Somnath Chatterjee, quoted in 'Valedictory References in the 14th Lok Sabha', https://eparlib.nic.in/bitstream/123456789/722920/1/11265.pdf, last accessed on 29 March 2023.

3. Christophe Jaffrelot and Sanjay Kumar, *Rise of the Plebeians? The Changing Face of Indian Legislative Assemblies* (New Delhi: Routledge India, 2009), pp. 5–9.

4. Niraja Gopal Jayal, 'The Rival Representative Claims of Parliament and Civil Society in India' in Sudha Pai and Avinash Kumar *The*

Indian Parliament: A Critical Appraisal (New Delhi: Orient Blackswan, 2014), pp. 334–340.

5. Ibid.
6. Suhas Palshikar, 'The State's Strong Arm', *Indian Express*, Saturday 12 August 2023.
7. Niraja Gopal Jayal, 'The Rival Representative Claims of Parliament and Civil Society in India', pp. 334–340.

The Centrality of Coalitions to Statecraft

1. Yechury, Sitaram, 'Advance, Not Retreat', *Hindustan Times*, 6 March 2011, https://www.hindustantimes.com/india/advance-not-retreat/story-Ip8eXFfhN8rBh8CwQxLliJ.html; last accessed on 18 August 2023 at 20.52 hours).
2. Patel, Sujata, 'Class Conflict and Workers Movement in Ahmedabad Textile Industry, 1918–23', *Economic and Political Weekly*, Vol. 19, No. 20/21, 1984, pp. 853–64, http://www.jstor.org/stable/4373280; last accessed on 19 August 2023 at 11.09 hours).
3. Chandra, Bipan, *History of Modern India,* (New Delhi: Orient Blackswan, 2009).
4. Ibid.
5. Ibid.
6. Kochanek, Stanley A., 'Briefcase Politics in India: The Congress Party and the Business Elite', *Asian Survey*, Vol. 27, No. 12 (1987), pp. 1278–301, https://doi.org/10.2307/2644635; last accessed on 19 August 2023 at 11.17 hours).
7. Kothari, Rajni, 'The Congress "System" in India', *Asian Survey*, Vol. 4, No. 12 (1964), pp. 1161–73, https://doi.org/10.2307/2642550; last accessed on 19 August 2023 at 11.19 hours).
8. Arora, Balbeer, 'The Political Parties and the Party System', in Hasan, Zoya (ed.), *The Emergence of New Coalitions in Parties and Party Polices in India*, (New Delhi: Oxford University Press, 2002); Arora, Balbeer, 'Negotiating Differences: Federal Coalitions and National Cohesion', in *Transforming India*, ed. Francine R. Frankel, Zoya Hassan, Rajeev Bhargava and Balveer Arora (Oxford India, 2000).

9.   Arora, Balbeer, 'Negotiating Differences: Federal Coalitions and National Cohesion', in *Transforming India*, ed. Francine R. Frankel, Zoya Hassan, Rajeev Bhargava and Balveer Arora, (Oxford India, 2000).

10. In 1986, India signed a Rs 1437-crore deal with Swedish arms manufacturer AB Bofors for the supply of 400 Howitzer guns for the army. A year later, a Swedish radio channel alleged that the company had bribed top Indian politicians and defence personnel to secure the contract. The scandal rocked the Rajiv Gandhi-led government in the late 1980s. However, in 2005, the Delhi High Court had rejected the allegations in the CBI case related to the Bofors scam.

11. The Mandal Commission was established in 1979 by the Janata Party government with aim of identifying socially or educationally backward classes of India. In 1980, based on its rationale that OBCs identified on the basis of caste, social and economic indicators made up 52 per cent of India's population, the commission's report recommended that members of OBCs be granted reservations up to 27 per cent of jobs under the Central government. Despite the report being submitted in 1980, the V.P. Singh government announced its decision to execute the recommendations in August 1990, leading to widespread student protests across India. Reservations were extended to higher education institutions in 2006 under Dr Manmohan Singh.

12. In the confidence vote that followed, the V.P. Singh government lost—142 to 346.

13. The L.K. Advani-led Rath Yatra started from Somnath to Ayodhya, expressly for a Ram temple at the disputed site at Ayodhya starting on 25 September 1990. It led to communal tensions and the Babri Masjid demolition. It remains a polarizing episode in Indian history.

14. In 1993, Prime Minister P.V. Narasimha Rao's minority government survived the motion in the house by a mere fourteen votes.

15. In July 1993, four Jharkhand Mukti Morcha (JMM) members of Parliament along with seven members of a breakaway faction of the Janata Dal (A) were allegedly paid at least Rs 8.7 crores to ensure the survival of the P.V. Narasimha Rao government.

16. On 6 December 1992, the RSS and its affiliates, the Vishwa Hindu Parishad (VHP), organized a rally involving 1,50,000 VHP and RSS-BJP supporters at the site of the disputed structure. It included speeches by RSS, BJP and VHP leaders. In this heightened situation, a communal mob demolished the Babri Masjid.

17. The United Front was a coalition of thirteen political parties formed after the 1996 general elections. The coalition formed two governments, under prime ministers H.D. Deve Gowda and I.K. Gujral between 1996 and 1998.

18. In the 1996 general elections, the BJP was the single-largest party with 161 seats, followed by Congress with 140. The President invited the BJP to form the government, and Atal Bihari Vajpayee took oath on 15 May 1996, in the hope that regional parties would lend their support to the government in forming a majority. That, however, did not happen.

19. National Common Minimum Programmes of the UPA Government, 2004, Ministry of Information and Broadcasting, Government of India.

20. 'Why Ethnic Violence in India's Manipur Has Been Going On for Three Months', Al Jazeera, 9 August 2023, https://www.aljazeera.com/news/2023/8/9/why-ethnic-violence-in-indias-manipur-has-been-going-on-for-three-months; last accessed on 19 August 2023 at 22.34 hours.

21. Khan, Khadija, 'PM Modi Pushes for Uniform Civil Code: How It Can Impact Different Communities', the Indian Express, 2 July 2023, https://indianexpress.com/article/explained/explained-law/pm-modi-pushes-for-uniform-civil-code-how-it-can-impact-different-communities-8689361; last accessed on 19 August 2023 at 22.39 hours.

22. Sahay, Anand K., 'Ahead of the 2024 Elections, the BJP-RSS Is Setting the Ideological Stage', The Wire, 14 August 2023, https://thewire.in/politics/setting-of-the-ideological-stage-before-the-election; last accessed on 19 August 2023 at 22.44 hours.

23. Mehra, Ajay K., 'The Uses (and Abuses) of Investigative Agencies', The Wire, 12 November 2022, https://thewire.in/government/cbi-nia-enforcement-directorate-use-abuse; last accessed on 19 August 2023 at 22.48 hours.

24. Deuskar, Nachiket, 'Raj Bhavans Turn BJP Office Extensions? Why Governors Are Increasingly Combative in Non-BJP States', *Scroll,* 14 January 2023, https://scroll.in/article/1041818/raj-bhavans-turn-bjp-office-extensions-why-governors-are-increasingly-combative-in-non-bjp-states; last accessed on 19 August 2023 at 22.51 hours.

25. Sharma, Richi, and Manish Ananda, 'Passing Bills Without Discussion Recipe for Bad Laws, Invites Judicial Intervention', the *New Indian Express,* 5 August 2023, https://www.newindianexpress.com/nation/2021/aug/05/20-bills-passed-in-monsoon-session-without-debate-2340403.html; last accessed on 19 August 2023 at 23.00 hours.

26. Deshpande, Pushparaj, 'The Sengol Issue: Instead of Placing Symbols, PM Modi Needs to Restore Parliament's Legitimacy'', The Wire, 25 May 2023, https://thewire.in/politics/sengol-new-parliament-inauguration-modi; last accessed on 19 August 2023.

27. M.S. Golwalkar writes, 'Hindusthan is the land of the Hindus and is the terra firma for the Hindu Nation alone to flourish upon . . .' in M.S. Golwalkar, *We or Our Nationhood Defined,* (Nagpur: Bharat Publications, 1939), https://sanjeev.sabhlokcity.com/Misc/We-or-Our-Nationhood-Defined-Shri-M-S-Golwalkar.pdf; last accessed on 19 August 2023 at 23.19 hours)

Reimagining, Reforming and Transforming India's Judiciary

1. The Statement proceeds to refer to the Supreme Court's interpretation of the right to freedom of speech and expression, including that of the press and the right to practise any profession or to carry on any occupation, trade or business.

2. Justice A.N. Ray was appointed Chief Justice of India (1973) superseding three judges senior to him (1973). Similarly, Justice M.H. Beg was appointed Chief Justice of India (1977) superseding Justice H.R. Khanna who was the lone dissenter in the infamous *ADM Jabalpur versus Shivkant Shukla* case relating to preventive detention.

3. Through its decision in the ADM Jabalpur case, the Supreme Court emasculated the fundamental right of personal liberty during the Emergency, though guaranteed by our Constitution.

4. The decision in *Bandhua Mukti Morcha versus Union of India* gave freedom to a few thousand bonded labour. The Supreme Court described the bonded labour system as one in which a person can be 'bonded to provide labour to another for years and years until an alleged debt is supposed to be wiped out which never seems to happen during the life time of the bonded labourer.'

5. Class-action litigation is not unknown in common law countries, including India. Our Code of Civil Procedure has recognized representative suits for over a century. Such suits are nothing but class-action litigation, which is no different from public interest litigation. There is, however, a very significant distinction that must be appreciated, and this relates to access to justice. It is, and always has been, practically unthinkable (for example) that bonded labour can approach a constitutional court to exercise their constitutional right to be relieved from the curse of bonded labour. Similarly, it is and always has been practically unthinkable (again for example) that slum dwellers or residents of footpaths as in the case of *Olga Tellis versus Bombay Municipal Corporation* can approach a constitutional court against arbitrary eviction from what they called their home.

6. The Supreme Court was clear, and there are a large number of decisions in this regard, that no court, not even the Supreme Court, can interfere in an investigation by a duly authorized agency. So, while monitoring the investigations, the Supreme Court did not interfere in the actual investigation itself.

7. Convention on the Elimination of Discrimination against Women.

8. Parliament did nothing to enact legislation to implement the Convention despite Article 51 of our Constitution, which requires the State, as a directive principle of state policy, to endeavour to foster respect for international law and treaty obligations in the dealings of organized peoples with one another.

9. Issues of unemployment, food security, housing, patriarchy, dowry demands and so on continue to plague our society.

10. Providing for the operation of a legal system that promotes justice on the basis of equal opportunity, particularly providing free legal aid by suitable legislation or schemes.

11. The law provides for free legal assistance for those who do not have the financial capacity to obtain legal advice or access courts and authorities. More importantly, it ensures and guarantees free legal assistance to, among others, prisoners, both under-trial and convicted, women and children, persons with disabilities and citizens belonging to Scheduled Castes and Scheduled Tribes.

12. Since 1995, only 15 million people have been provided legal services and advice by the Legal Services Institutions established, quoted in https://www.indiaspend.com/indias-legal-aid-system-needs-more-female-paralegals-monitoring/.

13. Several other deficiencies were highlighted leading me to believe in compulsory social audits.

14. The NALSA website shows that in 2019, only 19.5 per cent of pre-litigation cases were disposed of by national lok adalats. Similarly, in pending cases (referred by the courts to the national lok adalats) only 35.7 per cent cases were disposed of. https://nalsa.gov.in/statistics/national-lok-adalat-report/national-lok-adalat-2019/disposal-of-national-lok-adalat-held-on-14-12-2019-for-all-types-of-cases.

15. Just to cite one example, rapacious mining activity brought in royalties for the State and money bags for the leaseholders while causing distress not only to thousands but also the environment.

16. Briefly, the Chief Justice and two senior judges of the high court constitute a high court collegium and recommend candidates to the Supreme Court for appointment as high court judges. The Chief Justice of India and two senior judges of the Supreme Court constitute the Supreme Court collegium. The Supreme Court collegium considers the recommendation of the high court collegium and forwards its views, if in the affirmative, to the Government of India for issuance of a warrant of appointment by the President. A larger Supreme Court collegium of the Chief Justice of India and four senior judges constitute a collegium for recommending the appointment of judges to the Supreme Court. A Memorandum of Procedure is followed by all concerned and this is available at: https://doj.gov.in/appointment-of-judges/memorandum-procedure-appointment-supreme-court-judges.

17. Up to 1990, over 90 per cent of all the judges of the Supreme
     Court were either Brahmins or from what were termed 'forward
     castes'. There have been 243 judges appointed to the Supreme
     Court.

18. A recommendation from the community had a long-term impact in
     that the appointee would go on to become the Chief Justice of the
     high court. So, that high court would always have as a Chief Justice
     a member of a particular community.

19. There is now a possibility of a female Chief Justice of India in
     2027.

20. Court News, Vol. I, Issue No. 4, October–December 2006, https://
     main.sci.gov.in/pdf/CourtNews/2006_issue_4.pdf.

21. Ecourts Services, https://ecourts.gov.in/ecourts_home/.

22. Increase in the pendency of cases has resulted in an increase in the
     number of under-trial prisoners (accused prisoners awaiting trial).
     Seven in 10 of the 4,78,600 people in Indian jails are under-trial,
     according to the 2019 National Crime Records Bureau data (August
     2020). From 2002–19, nearly two in three (64 per cent) under-
     trials on average were from the Scheduled Castes (21.7 per cent),
     Scheduled Tribes (12.3 per cent), and Other Backward Classes
     (30 per cent). More than one in five (21.5 per cent) under-trials
     were Muslim.

23. This was based on the number of cases instituted and the number of
     cases disposed of by judges.

24. I would describe him as the 'thirty-fifth judge' of the Supreme
     Court.

25. For example, cases relating to preventive detention, electoral bonds,
     Kashmir, freedom of speech and expression and so on.

26. One judge praised the prime minister before an international
     audience as a versatile genius and an internationally acclaimed
     visionary. Another described him as the most popular, loved, vibrant
     and visionary leader. Was this necessary?

27. The patron-in-chief of the National Legal Services Authority
     is none other than the Chief Justice of India and the executive
     chairperson is usually the senior-most judge of the Supreme
     Court. The governance structure is the same for the State Legal

Services Authorities, with the Chief Justice of the high court as the patron in chief and the senior-most judge of the high court as the executive chairperson. Under the guidance of such distinguished judges, paralegal volunteers can make an enormous contribution to providing legal services at the grassroots level.

28. They are described as the 'torch bearers of the Legal Services Institutions at the ground level', and include housewives, students, teachers, doctors, professionals and retired personnel.

29. Building Better Courts: Surveying the Infrastructure of India's District Courts, Vidhi Centre for Legal Policy supported by Tata Trusts.

30. *All India Judges Association versus Union of India*, MANU/SC/0980/2020. I have not taken into consideration the North-eastern states, Jammu and Kashmir and Delhi.

31. Published by Tata Trusts in collaboration with six organizations.

32. IndiaSpend, 'Inadequate Budget for Judiciary Crippling Reforms, Hurting Growth: Report', *Business Standard*, 9 January 2020, https://www.business-standard.com/article/economy-policy/inadequate-budget-for-judiciary-crippling-reforms-hurting-growth-report-119120400323_1.html, accessed on 13 June 2021.

33. The intention was to establish 2500 gram nyayalayas by 2017. However, less than 400 gram nyayalayas were established, and recent studies have indicated that a little over 200 of them are functional.

34. Lawyers tend to believe that if cases are settled out of court, they will face an alarming drop in revenue and anecdotally, that is one of the reasons for rejecting alternative dispute resolution systems by them as a class. The thrust and parry goes on, but mediation is the way forward.

35. A visit to any observation home for children or Juvenile Justice Board in the country will expose you to the pathetic state of affairs.

36. The Bangalore Principles of Judicial Conduct, 2002, https://www.unodc.org/pdf/crime/corruption/judicial_group/Bangalore_principles.pdf.

37. Measures for the Effective Implementation of the Bangalore Principles of Judicial Conduct, 21 and 22 January 2010, https://www.yargitay.gov.tr/documents/bangaloreetigi.pdf.

The Partisan Role of Governors in New India

1. Sir Muhammad Saleh Akbar Hydari, a career Indian Civil Service officer, was appointed as the last governor of Assam on 4 May 1946.
2. Singh, K.P., 'The Governor in the Constituent Assembly', *The Indian Journal of Political Science, 26*(4), (1965), pp. 37–44, http://www.jstor.org/stable/41854120; last accessed on 24 November 2021.
3. Dr B.R. Ambedkar's intervention in Constituent Assembly Debates, 1 June 1949, Part I, https://indiankanoon.org/doc/1648960/, last accessed on 24 November 2021.
4. Ibid.
5. Ibid.
6. Jawaharlal Nehru's intervention in the Constituent Assembly Debates, 31 May 1949, Part I, https://indiankanoon.org/doc/1158142/, last accessed on 24 November 2021.
7. Singh, K.P., 'The Governor in the Constituent Assembly', *The Indian Journal of Political Science*.
8. Mahatma Gandhi in *Harijan* (21 December 1947); quoted in 'Why We Need Governors', Gopalkrishna Gandhi, *The Kashmir Monitor*, 7 July 2018, https://www.thekashmirmonitor.net/why-we-need-governors/, last accessed on 23 November 2021.
9. Quoted in 'Custodians of the Republic', Gopalkrishna Gandhi, *The Seminar*, Volume 717, May 2019, https://www.india-seminar.com/2019/717/717_gopalkrishna_gandhi.htm, last accessed on 24 November 2021.
10. Articles 155 and 156, Chapter II, part VI of the Indian Constitution.
11. Report of the Sarkaria Commission, Inter-State Council Secretariat, Ministry of Home Affairs, Government of India, http://interstatecouncil.nic.in/report-of-the-sarkaria-commission/, last accessed on 25 November 2021.
12. Ibid.
13. 'Supreme Court Restores Congress Government in Arunachal Pradesh', *The Wire*, 13 July 2016, https://thewire.in/law/arunachal-pradesh-supreme-court, last accessed on 27 November 2021.
14. *Nabam Rebia and Bamang Felix vs Deputy Speaker*, Arunachal Pradesh (2016), 8 SCC 1.

15. *Satpal vs State of Haryana*, AIR 2000 SC 1702.

16. 'Uttarakhand HC quashes President's Rule', *The Hindu*, 16 April 2016, https://www.thehindu.com/news/national/other-states/uttarakhand-presidents-rule-high-court-pained-at-centres-behaviour/article8503518.ece, last accessed on 27 November 2021.

17. 'I didn't expect BJP to form the government', Interview with Governor Mridula Sinha, Yogesh Naik, *Mumbai Mirror*, 16 March 2017, https://mumbaimirror.indiatimes.com/mumbai/other/i-didnt-expect-bjp-to-form-the-government/articleshow/57660607.cms?utm_source=contentofinterest&utm_medium=text&utm_campaign=cppst, last accessed on 25 March.

18. Quoted in 'From Goa to Manipur, Modi's Governors Have Sabotaged Democracy', Rajeev Dhawan, *The Wire*, 23 March 2017, https://thewire.in/politics/modis-governors-goa-manipur, last accessed on 25 March 2023.

19. *Rameshwar Prasad vs Union of India* (2006) case.

20. Krishnadas Rajagopal, 'Conduct Maharashtra Floor Test on Nov. 27, Supreme Court Tells Governor', *The Hindu,* 26 November 2019, https://www.thehindu.com/news/national/sc-orders-maharashtra-floor-test-on-nov-27/article61614592.ece, last accessed on 20 July 2019.

21. Quoted in Punchhi Commission, Inter-State Council Secretariat, Ministry of Home Affairs, Government of India, http://interstatecouncil.nic.in/report-of-the-commission-on-centre-state-relations/, last accessed on 28 November.

22. Punchhi Commission, Inter-State Council Secretariat, Ministry of Home Affairs, Government of India, http://interstatecouncil.nic.in/report-of-the-commission-on-centre-state-relations/, last accessed on 28 November.

23. Sarkaria Commission, Para 4.6.03.

24. *Mahatma Gandhi—The Last Phase*, Vol. II (1958), p. 65.

25. *B.K. Manish & Ors. vs. State of Chhattisgarh & Ors.* judgment and order dt. 12 March 2013 in WP (PIL) 23 of 2012, Bilaspur High Court.

26. 'Report of MPs and Experts to make recommendations on the salient features of the law for extending provisions of the

Constitution (73rd) Amendment Act, 1992, to scheduled areas', 1994, p.14, http://www.odi.org.uk/projects/00-03-livelihood-options/forum/sched-areas/about/bhuria_report.html; last accessed on 28 November 2021.

27. 'Government to Set Up National Tribal Advisory Council', Press Information Bureau, Release ID 130055, 29 October 2015, https://pib.gov.in/newsite/PrintRelease.aspx?relid=130055; last accessed on 28 November 2021.

28. PM Nehru, quoted in Sarkaria Commission, Para 4.6.03.

29. Punchhi Commission, Inter-State Council Secretariat, Ministry of Home Affairs, Government of India, http://interstatecouncil.nic.in/report-of-the-commission-on-centre-state-relations/, last accessed on 28 November.

30. Ibid.

Election Commission: The Bedrock of a Democracy

1. As per the provision of Article 324 of the Constitution, 'the power of superintendence, direction and control of elections to parliament, state legislatures, the office of president of India and the office of vice-president of India shall be vested in the Election Commission'.

2. Election Expenditure Reports, Association for Democratic Reforms, https://adrindia.org/content/election-expenditure-report; last accessed on 15 July 2023 at 12.33 hours).

3. The high court restricted the scope of the EC inquiry in the Narottam Mishra case, *Dr Narottam Mishra vs Election Commission Of India And . . .* on 18 May 2018: 'This aspect is crucial because the Election Commission's remit cannot ordinarily extend to judging content of speech; it is only to adjudge whether the election expenses incurred by the candidate or someone on her or his behalf, under her or his authority have been accounted under Section 77'.

4. Announced in the 2017 Union Budget, electoral bonds are interest-free bearer instruments used to donate money anonymously to political parties. A bearer instrument does not carry any information about the buyer or payee and the holder of the instrument (which is the political party) is presumed to be its owner.

5. 'EC Opposes Stay on Electoral Bonds as SC Reserves Order on Plea to Restrain Fresh Sales', The Wire, 24 March 2021, https://thewire.in/law/election-commission-electoral-bonds-supreme-court-adr-plea; last accessed on 15 July 2023.
6. A political action committee (PAC) is a mechanism to pool campaign contributions from members and donate those funds to campaigns for or against candidates, ballot initiatives or legislation.
7. Constituent Assembly of India Debates (Proceedings), Vol. III, 16 June 1949, https://loksabha.nic.in/writereaddata/cadebatefiles/C16061949.pdf, last accessed on 14 September 2023 at 12.25 hours.
8. 'The ECI Cannot Be a Super Government', P.D.T. Achary, The Hindu, 19 April 2021.

India's Fading Federal Institutions

1. Thomas Isaac, T.M., R. Mohan and Lekha Chakraborty, *Challenges to Indian Fiscal Federalism* (New Delhi: LeftWord Books, 2019), p. 23.
2. 'It shall be the duty of the Commission to make recommendations to the President as to (a) The distribution between the Union and the States of the net proceeds of taxes which are to be, or may be, divided between them under this Chapter and the allocation between the States of the respective shares of such proceeds; (b) The principles which should govern the grants-in-aid of the revenues of the States out of the Consolidated Fund of India; (bb) The measures needed to augment the Consolidated Fund of a State to supplement the resources of the Panchayats in the State based on the recommendations made by the Finance Commission of the State; (c) The measures needed to augment the Consolidated Fund of a State to supplement the resources of the Municipalities in the State based on the recommendations made by the Finance Commission of the State; or (d) Any other matter referred to the Commission by the President in the interests of sound finance.'
3. Thomas Isaac, T.M., R. Mohan and Lekha Chakraborty, *Challenges to Indian Fiscal Federalism* (New Delhi: LeftWord Books, 2019), p. 23.
4. Clauses [(bb)] and [(c)] of Article 280, Constitution of India.

5.   Gulati, I.S., and K.K. George, *Essays in Federal Financial Relations* (New Delhi: Oxford & IBH Publishing Company Pvt. Ltd, 1988).

6.   Thomas Isaac, T.M., R. Mohan and Lekha Chakraborty, *Challenges to Indian Fiscal Federalism* (New Delhi: LeftWord Books, 2019), p. 24.

7.   Ibid., p. 61.

8.   Ibid., p. 62.

9.   Ibid., p. 56.

10.   'Note of Dissent by Dr Amaresh Bagchi', Report of the 11th Finance Commission, pp. 09–10, https://fincomindia.nic.in/writereaddata/html_en_files/oldcommission_html/fcreport/notedes.pdf; last accessed on 25 April 2021 at 16.44 hours.

11.   'Report of the Twelfth Finance Commission (2005–2010)', https://fincomindia.nic.in/ShowContent.aspx?uid1=3&uid2=0&uid3=0&uid4=0&uid5=0&uid6=0&uid7=0; last accessed on 25 April 2021 at 17.55 hours.

12.   Thomas Isaac, T.M., R. Mohan and Lekha Chakraborty, *Challenges to Indian Fiscal Federalism* (New Delhi: LeftWord Books, 2019), p. 78.

13.   Terms of Reference, 15th Finance Commission, https://fincomindia.nic.in/writereaddata/html_en_files/fincom15/TermsofReference_XVFC.pdf; last accessed on 25 April 2021 at 15.25 hours.

14.   Gulati Institute of Finance and Taxation, *Seminar Report—Additional Terms of Reference of the 15th Finance Commission: Implications of the States*, Thiruvananthapuram, 2019; Thomas Isaac, T.M., 'An Open Letter to Finance Ministers', *The Hindu*, 14 May 2018, https://www.thehindu.com/opinion/op-ed/an-open-letter-to-finance-ministers/article62111604.ece, last accessed on 14 September 2023 at 12.54 hours); Thomas Isaac, T.M., 'Centre Must Not Micromanage Finance Commission', *Business Standard*, 14 July 2018, https://www.business-standard.com/article/economy-policy/centre-must-not-micro-manage-finance-commission-kerala-fm-thomas-isaac-118071400772_1.html., last accessed on 14 September 2023 at 12.52 hours; Finance Department, Government of Kerala, *Memorandum Presented to the Fifteenth Finance Commission*. Thiruvananthapuram, 2018.

15. Patnaik, Prabhat, 'End of Planning Commission?', *Economic and Political Weekly*, Vol. 49, No. 29, 19 July 2014.

16. 'Amit Shah's Ministry of Cooperation an Assault on Federalism', News Minute, Sarita Balan, 13 October 2021, https://www. thenewsminute.com/article/amit-shah-s-ministry-cooperation-assault-federalism-thomas-isaac-interview-156464; last accessed on 21 April 2022 at 22.30 hours.

17. Joseph. K.J and Anithakumary, L., 'India's GST Paradigm and the Trajectory of Fiscal Federalism: An Analysis with Special Reference to Kerala', *The Indian Economic Journal* (2023), 71(1), pp. 187–2004.

18. 'People's Planning is Revolution: Interview with Thomas Issac', Jishnu E.N., *Mathrubhumi*, 3 August 2021, https://englisharchives. mathrubhumi.com/features/web-exclusive/janakeeyassothranam-25th-anniversary-1.5880586; last accessed on 20 April 2022 at 18.30 hours.

Re-Empowering the People: Strengthening India's Information Commissions

1. Cited in 'Welcome Address of the Hon'ble Chief Information Commissioner, Shri Wajahat Habibullah', Third Annual Convention on RTI and its Ramifications for Good Governance, Central Information Commission, November 2008, https://cic. gov.in/sites/default/files/CIC-Speech.pdf.

2. 'Indians File 6 Million RTI Requests a Year. Some Died for Their Efforts', NDTV, 14 September 2017, https://www.ndtv.com/ india-news/indians-file-6-million-rti-requests-a-year-some-died-for-their-efforts-1750156.

3. The position of collector, as the name implies, was instituted by Raja Todar Mal, head of Mughal imperial finance, in the sixteenth century to collect land revenue, mainstay of the Empire under the name amal guzar.

4. Sebastian Morris, 'The Challenge to Governance in India', *India Infrastructure Report 2002* (New Delhi: Oxford University Press, 2002), Ch 2, p. 19.

5.	Which includes, but is not limited to, enhanced investments in healthcare, better organization of healthcare services, the prevention of diseases and promotion of good health through cross-sectoral actions, access to technologies, developing human resources, encouraging medical pluralism and building knowledge base.

6.	Tweet by Jairam Ramesh, 5 July 2021, https://twitter.com/Jairam_Ramesh/status/1411981389184917504?s=20; last accessed on 15 July 2023 at 12.44 hours.

7.	On the basis of the report of the Bhuria Committee submitted in 1995, the Parliament enacted the Panchayats (Extension to Scheduled Areas) Act, 1996 (PESA) to extend Part IX of the Constitution with certain modifications and exceptions to the Schedule V areas. At present, Schedule V areas exist in ten states, namely, Andhra Pradesh, Chhattisgarh, Gujarat, Himachal Pradesh, Jharkhand, Madhya Pradesh, Maharashtra, Odisha, Rajasthan and Telangana.

8.	'India in Growth Recession; Extreme Centralisation of Power in PMO Not Good: Rajan', PTI, 8 December 2019, https://timesofindia.indiatimes.com/business/india-business/india-in-growth-recession-extreme-centralisation-of-power-in-pmo-not-good-rajan/articleshow/72423425.cms.

9.	Section 2 (f), Right to Information Act.

10.	'Finance Ministry Rejected Highest Number of RTI Applications in the Year Demonetisation Was Implemented: CIC Report', the *New Indian Express*, 16 March 2018, https://www.newindianexpress.com/nation/2018/mar/16/finance-ministry-rejected-highest-number-of-rti-applications-in-the-year-demonetisation-was-implemen-1788228.html.

11.	'RBI Refuses to Disclose Information on Wilful Defaulters under RTI Act, Cites National Security', *India Today*, 29 November 2018, https://www.indiatoday.in/india/story/rbi-refuses-to-disclose-information-on-wilful-defaulters-under-rti-act-cites-national-security-1399160-2018-11-29.

12.	'PMO Denies RTI Plea Seeking Info on PM-CARES', *The Hindu*, 16 August 2020, https://www.thehindu.com/news/national/pmo-denies-rti-plea-seeking-info-on-pm-cares/article32369180.ece.

13. '10% EWS Quota: Govt Refuses to Share Details of Decision Making Process under RTI', *Outlook India*, 10 February 2019, https://www.outlookindia.com/website/story/india-news-10-ews-quota-govt-refuses-to-share-details-of-decision-making-process-under-rti/325227.

14. 'Electoral Bonds: CIC Says Revealing Names of Donors Not in Public Interest, Violates RTI', the *Indian Express*, 23 December 2020, https://indianexpress.com/article/india/electoral-bonds-cic-says-revealing-names-of-donors-not-in-public-interest-violates-rti-7115866/.

15. 'Declassification of All Netaji Files Is the Only Way to Stop Propagation of Fantasies as Fact', Sugata Bose, Scroll.in, 24 September 2025, https://scroll.in/article/757426/declassification-of-all-netaji-files-is-the-only-way-to-stop-propagation-of-fantasies-as-facts; last accessed on 15 July 2023 at 12.50 hours.

16. Prime Minister's Inaugural Address at the 7th Annual Convention of Central Information Commission, Central Information Commission, https://cic.gov.in/sites/default/files/2012/PMspeech.pdf.

17. *Report of People's RTI Assessment 2008*, RTI Assessment and Analysis Group (RaaG) and National Campaign for People's Right to Information (NCPRI), October 2009, https://snsindia.org/wp-content/uploads/2018/10/RAAG-study-executive-summary.pdf.

18. Arun Jaitley was, in fact, law minister when India adopted the Freedom of Information Act in 2002.

19. 'Government is Promoting a Culture of Secrecy, Undermining Legislation Such as RTI', Christophe Jaffrelot, 24 September 2020, Carnegie Endowment for International Peace, https://carnegieendowment.org/2020/09/24/government-is-promoting-culture-of-secrecy-undermining-legislation-such-as-rti-pub-82786; last accessed on 12 July 2021.

20. 'As RTI Act Completes 17 Years, Huge Backlog of Pending Cases May Undo its Effectiveness', Gursimran Kaur Bakshi, *NewsClick*, 13 October 2022, https://www.newsclick.in/RTI-Act-Completes-17-Years-Huge-Backlog-Pending-Cases-May-Undo-Effectiveness.

21. 'Report Card on the Performance of Information Commissions ("ICs") in India, 2020', Satark Nagrik Sangathan (SNS) and Centre for Equity Studies (CES), October 2020.

22. Ibid.

23. 'Eighty-Six RTI Activists Have Been Murdered, 170 Have Been Physically Assaulted and 183 Cases of Threats or Harassment Have Been Registered', The Wire, 6 February 2021, https://thewire.in/rights/maharashtra-dubious-distinction-highest-attacks-rti-activists-chri-report; last accessed on 15 July 2023 at13.37 hours).

24. https://egazette.nic.in/WriteReadData/2014/159420.pdf.

25. *Chief Information Commissioner vs High Court of Gujarat and Anr*, Civil Appeal No. (S). 1966–1967 OF 2020 (Arising out of SLP© No.5840 of 2015).

26. '"Abuse" of RTI Has Led to "Paralysis and Fear" among Officials, Says CJI Bobde, *The Hindu*, 16 December 2019, https://www.thehindu.com/news/national/abuse-of-rti-has-led-to-paralysis-and-fear-among-officials-says-cji-bobde/article30320357.ece.

27. 'Is Right to Information Regime Losing Steam in its 16th Year?', Commonwealth Human Rights Initiative, 1 November 2021, http://attacksonrtiusers.org/Home/InTheNews/19; last accessed on 12 June 2021.

28. Central Public Information Officer, *Supreme Court of India vs Subhash Chandra Agarwal*, Civil Appeal No. 10044 of 2010, 13.11.2019.

29. *Subhash Chandra Agrawal vs Supreme Court of India* CIC Appeal No. CIC/WB/A/2009/000529, dated 24.11.2009.

30. Circular No. 5/52/2016-IAR, dated 5 January 2021, Administrative Reforms Department, Government of Haryana, https://cdnbbsr.s3waas.gov.in/s3f80ff32e08a25270b5f252ce39522f72/uploads/2021/02/2021021065.pdf; last accessed on 12 July 2021.

31. Gandhi, M.K., *Panchayat Raj* (Navjivan Publishing House: Ahmedabad), pp. 8–9.

Patronage and Professionalism in the Indian Bureaucracy

1. World Economic Forum 2021: Global Gender Gap Report 2021 Insight Report March, Geneva.

2. IFPRI, 2020: Global Hunger Index: IFPRI, Bonn.

3. Human Development Index, UNDP, https://hdr.undp.org/data-center/human-development-index#/indicies/HDI.

4.   Saxena, Naresh Chandra, *What Ails the IAS & Why It Fails to Deliver: An Insider's View* (Sage, 2019).

5.   At the bureaucratic level, India's administration and policymaking is largely controlled by members of the Indian Administrative Service (IAS). Their initial recruitment is fair and on merit, and the cream of the nation joins the service.

6.   Appu, P.S., 'The All India Services: Decline, Debasement and Destruction', *Economic and Political Weekly*, 26 February 2005; Gill, Kaveri, *A Primary Evaluation of Service Delivery under the National Rural Health Mission (NRHM): Findings from a Study in Andhra Pradesh, Uttar Pradesh, Bihar, and Rajasthan.* Working Paper 1/2009-PEO, Planning Commission; Keefer, P., and S. Khemani, *Democracy, Public Expenditures, and the Poor,* World Bank Policy Research Working Paper, 3164, Washington, D.C.: World Bank, 2012.

7.   Lant Pritchett. *Is India a Flailing State?: Detours on the Four Lane Highway to Modernization,* HKS Faculty Research Working Paper Series RWP09-013, John F. Kennedy School of Government, Harvard University, 2009.

8.   Jaffrelot, Christophe, Atul Kohli, and Kanta Murali, eds. *Business and Politics in India: Modern South Asia* (New York: Oxford University Press, 2019).

9.   Administrative Reforms Commission, '*Fifth Report of the Second Administrative Reforms Commission.* New Delhi: Government of India, 2008.

10.   GOI, Government of India, Department of Administrative Reforms, Civil Service Day 2009, Panel Discussion, Theme Papers, 2009.

11.   Rule 11, Central Civil Services (Conduct) Rules, 1964.

12.   Wade documents that the cost of getting transferred to a desired post in the cadre of superintendent engineer in the Irrigation Department in Odisha was forty times the average monthly salary for the position. Such exorbitant sums can only be garnered by pre-transfer or post-transfer rent-seeking, as well as shady deals.

13.   http://darpg.gov.in/darpgwebsite_cms/Document/file/Decision10.pdf, and http://darpg.gov.in/darpgwebsite_cms/Document/file/decision15.pdf.

14. Deshmukh, B.G., *A Cabinet Secretary Looks Back* (New Delhi: Harper Collins Publishers India, 2004).

15. World Health Statistics 2020: Monitoring Health for the SDGs, World Health Organization, https://iris.who.int/bitstream/hand le/10665/332070/9789240005105-eng.pdf.

16. 'India's Shortage of Doctors, Nurses May Hamper COVID-19 Response', *India Spend*, 27 March 2020, https://www.indiaspend. com/indias-shortage-of-doctors-nurses-may-hamper-covid19- response/#:~:text=As%20India%20continues%20its%20 Fight,norm%20(3%20per%201%2C000.

17. Beschel Jr, R.P., 'Civil Service Reform in India: Perspectives from the World Bank's Work in Three States', *State-Level Reforms in India: Towards More Effective Government*, (2003), pp. 233–55.

18. Union Budget and Economic Surveys, https://www.indiabudget. gov.in/previous_union_budget.php.

19. UNICEF, 2007. Evaluation of ICDS in Bihar, Patna.

20. UNICEF, 2009. Evaluation of programmes in Jharkhand, Ranchi.

21. Saxena, Naresh, 'Disruptive Technologies and SDGs', https:// www.academia.edu/35054729/Disruptive_Technologies_.

22. 'Why Is India Not Doing Well in Social Sector?', *Inclusion*, 1 October 2016, https://inclusion.in/opinion/2016/10/why-is- india-not-doing-well-in-social-sector/.

23. Pandey, Priyanka, Sangeeta Goyal, Venkatesh Sundararaman, 'Community Participation in Public Schools: The Impact of Information Campaigns in Three Indian States', The World Bank South Asia Region, Human Development Department, November 2008, https://documents1.worldbank.org/curated/ pt/735071468051274602/pdf/WPS4776.pdf.

24. The *Economic Times*, 11 February 2008.

25. Jaffrelot, Christophe, *Modi's India: Hindu Nationalism and the Rise of Ethnic Democracy* (Princeton University Press, Princeton, 2021); Ahmed, Ali, 'The Indian Muslim Security Predicament', 2022, https://d1wqtxts1xzle7.cloudfront.net/63821370/The_ Muslim_Security_Predicament20200703-13340-hsalxc-libre. pdf?1593808595=&response-content-disposition=inline%3B+filen ame%3D; Jayal, Niraja Gopal, *Re-forming India*, Viking, 2019.

26. Sircar, Jawhar, 'IAS and Bureaucracy: All the Prime Minister's Men', the *New Indian Express*, 17 March 2021.

27. Soz, Salmaan Anees. 'The Great Disappointment: How Narendra Modi Squandered a Unique Opportunity to Transform the Indian Economy', (Delhi, India: Penguin Ebury Press, 2019); Tharoor, Shashi, *The Paradoxical Prime Minister* (Delhi, India: Aleph Book Company, 2018); Tiwari, Ramesh. C., *The Rise of NaMo in New India* (New Delhi: India High Brown Scribes Publications, 2021):

28. Vaishnav, Milan, 'Religious Nationalism and India's Future', Carnegie Endowment for International Peace, 4 April 2019, https://carnegieendowment.org/2019/04/04/religious-nationalism-and-india-s-future-pub-78703.

29. 'Should an IAS Officer Be Free to Air Views on Social Media or Is It Unbecoming Behaviour?', ThePrint, 11 July 2018, https://theprint.in/talk-point/should-ias-officers-be-free-to-air-views-on-social-media-or-is-it-unbecoming-conduct/81599/.

30. Kohli, Karnika, 'Modi Government Has Different Benchmarks for IAS Officers in Different States', The Wire, 13 July 2018, https://thewire.in/government/ias-sanjay-dixit-shah-faesal.

31. Bhat, Naseer Ahmad, Bazila Shameem, Nisha Yadav, 'Downward Spiral in Civil Service Anonymity and Neutrality: An Analysis of Indian Bureaucracy during the Rise of Chauvinism and Right-Wing Nationalism', *Palarch's Journal of Archaeology of Egypt/Egyptology* (2020), 17(7); Vaishnav, Milan, and Saksham Khosla, 'The Indian Administrative Service Meets Big Data', Carnegie Endowment for International Peace, 1 September 2016.

32. Werleman, C.J., 'Rising Violence against Muslims in India Under Modi and BJP Rule', *Insight Turkey* Vol. 23, No. 2 (2021), pp. 39–49.

33. That is also why the BJP government has deliberately undermined minority interests by championing the abrogation of Article 370, the Citizenship Amendment Act and the National Register of Citizens, the anti-conversion and Love Jihad laws, etc.

34. Kumar, Dr Ramesh, 'Indian Politics and Modi: A Millennium Overview', *The Journal of Oriental Research*, Chennai, September 2021, ISSN: 0022-3301.

35. Teltumbde, A., 'The New Normal in Modi's Men', *Economic and Political Weekly* (2018), *53*(31), pp. 10–11.

36. Guha, Ramachandra, 'The Delhi Police Degrades Democracy', NDTV.com, 2020, https://www.ndtv.com/opinion/the-perversions-of-justice-in-delhi-by-ramachandra-guha-2259035.

37. Anderson, Edward, and Christophe Jaffrelot, 'Hindu Nationalism and the "Saffronisation of the Public Sphere": An Interview with Christophe Jaffrelot', *Contemporary South Asia* (2018), 26(4): 468–82.

38. Deepankar Basu, *Dominance of Majoritarian Politics and Hate Crimes against Religious Minorities in India, 2009–2018*, UMass Amherst Economics Working Papers, 2 December 2019), retrieved from https://scholarworks.umass.edu/econ_workingpaper/272/?_gl=1*15pg818*_ga*MTIwNDM1NTU5OC4xNjIxMjQ2MDEw*_ ga_21RLS0L7EB*MTYyMTI0NjAwOS4xLjEuMTYyy MTI0NjA0MC4w&_ga=2.74270162.1360997307. 1621246010-1204355598.1621246010.

39. Alavi, Mariyam and Srinivasan Jain, 'Documents Planted On Computers: New Report After Stan Swamy's Death', NDTV, 6 July 2021, https://www.ndtv.com/india-news/arsenal-consulting-report-stan-swamy-others-said-evidence-was-fabricated-new-report-backs-that-2480532.

40. Varshney, Ashutosh, 'Modi Consolidates Power: Electoral Vibrancy, Mounting Liberal Deficits', *Journal of Democracy*, Volume 30, Number 4, October 2019; Ruparelia, Sanjay, *Detours on the Four Lane Highway to Modernization*, HKS Faculty Research Working Paper Series RWP09-013, John F. Kennedy School of Government, Harvard University, 2015.

41. Gupta, Shishir, 'Behind PM Modi's Stinging Critique of the IAS, a Jan Meeting Holds the Clue', *Hindustan Times*, 17 February 2021, https://www.hindustantimes.com/analysis/behind-pm-modi-s-stinging-critique-of-bureaucracy-a-jan-meeting-holds-the-clue-101613466487000.html.

42. A study (Worsdell, T. and Shrivastava, K., 2020, 'Locating the Breach: Mapping the Nature of Land Conflicts in India', New Delhi: Land Conflict Watch) shows that 2.1 million hectares of

land is locked in land conflicts, affecting the lives and livelihoods of 6.5 million people. Rs 13.7 trillion of committed, earmarked and potential investments were found embroiled, and in 104 cases, the dispute has been going on for at least two decades. In another 149 conflicts, the case has remained unresolved for at least a decade. The Government of India's law on land acquisition enacted in 2013 has some good features, such as a high compensation and consent clause, but it has many negative clauses, and a close examination of the new Act reveals that acquisition of even one acre of land would take at least three to four years.

43.   Similarly, many other programmes suffer from design flaws, as with the ICDS, which has not yet succeeded in making a significant dent in reducing child malnutrition as the programme has placed priority on food supplementation rather than on nutrition and health education interventions, and it targets children mostly after the age of three when malnutrition has already set in. The GoI should discourage the distribution of manufactured 'ready-to-eat' food, as it leads to greater corruption at the ministerial level, but unfortunately the GoI has actually encouraged this. ICDS should learn from the success of the freshly cooked mid-day meals programme that runs fairly well even in states not known for efficiency. However, the present government has not given priority to improving the design of these programmes and instead blames the bureaucracy.

44.   'New Proposal on Service Allocation Designed to Create a Loyal Bureaucracy?', *Business Standard*, 20 August 2019, https://www.business-standard.com/article/current-affairs/new-proposal-on-service-allocation-designed-to-create-a-loyal-bureaucracy-118052100131_1.html.

45.   Sardar Patel's observations in the Constituent Assembly, quoted in Refurbishing of Personnel Administration, Second Administrative Reforms Commission.

46.   Central Civil Services (Pension) Amendment Rules, dated 31 May 2021, https://timesofindia.indiatimes.com/india/government-broadens-rules-that-bar-retired-officials-from-publishing-sensitive-information/articleshow/83179380.cms.

47. The RTI was designed to undo the culture of secrecy institutionalized by the colonial Official Secrets Act, 1923, by compelling departments to provide official information in the form of records or documents to citizens when specific requests were made.

48. M. Sridhar Acharyulu, 'How the RBI Dodged RTI Appeals for Minutes of Meeting on Demonetisation', The Wire, 13 March 2019, https://thewire.in/political-economy/rbi-minutes-demonetisation-rti; 'Finance Ministry Rejected Highest Number of RTI Applications in the Year Demonetisation was Implemented: CIC Report', New Indian Express, 16 March 2018, https://www.newindianexpress.com/nation/2018/mar/16/finance-ministry-rejected-highest-number-of-rti-applications-in-the-year-demonetisation-was-implemen-1788228.html.

49. Sircar, Jawhar, 'Picking, Kicking and Wrecking: Subjugation of the Bureaucracy in the Modi Regime', The Wire, 7 September 2020.

50. Ibid.

51. Chatterjee, E. 'New Developmentalism and its Discontents: State Activism in Modi's Gujarat and India', Development and Change (2020).

52. 'Fewer Bureaucrats Opting for Centre at Senior Management Grades, Shows Data', 18 March 2021, https://www.business-standard.com/article/economy-policy/fewer-bureaucrats-opting-for-centre-at-senior-management-grades-shows-data-121031701413_1.html.

53. Deshpande, Pushparaj, 'The Battle for India's Soul', in Vision for a Nation, eds, Aakash Singh Rathore and Ashis Nandy, (Penguin Random House India, 2020).

An Agenda for Policy Reform for Civil Society in India

1. Mahajan, Vijay, 'India's Constitution Needs to Recognize Civil Society', India Development Review, https://idronline.org/indias-constitution-needs-to-recognise-civil-society/.

2. 'There Is More to Democracy than Elections', Neera Chandoke, the Tribune, https://www.tribuneindia.com/news/comment/there-is-more-to-democracy-than-elections-316544.

3.   *The Future Role of Civil Society*, World Economic Forum, 2013, https://www3.weforum.org/docs/WEF_FutureRoleCivilSociety_ Report_2013.pdf.

4.   The Future of Civil Society, World Economic Forum, World Scenario series, https://www3.weforum.org/docs/WEF_Future RoleCivilSociety_Report_2013.pdf.

5.   Bhandari, Sekhri, Maheshwari, Aggarwal, 'The Use and Misuse of Section 144 CrPC', SSRN: https://papers.ssrn.com/sol3/papers. cfm?abstract_id=4389147.

6.   'Five Years in a Row: India Is 2022's Biggest Internet Shutdowns Offender', https://www.accessnow.org/press-release/keepiton-internet-shutdowns-2022-india/.

7.   ITUC Global Rights Index 2022; https://www.globalrightsindex. org/en/2022/countries/ind.

8.   I. Srinath, *COVID-19, Corporatisation and Closing Space: The Triple Threat to Civil Society in India*, LSE Working Paper Series 2022, // www.lse.ac.uk/international-development/Assets/Documents/ PDFs/Working-Papers/WP206.pdf.

9.   U. Anand, 'India Has 31 Lakh NGOs, More than Double the Number of Schools', the *Indian Express*, https://indianexpress. com article/india/india-others/india-has-31-lakh-ngos-twice-the-number-of-schools-almost-twice-number-of-policemen/.

10. Income Tax Department, Government of India, https:// incometaxindia.gov.in/Pages/utilities/exempted-institutions.aspx.

11. Home Ministry, Government of India: https://fcraonline.nic.in/ fc_dashboard.aspx.

12. UN-DESA Survey of Civil Society Organizations, https://www. un.org/en/ecosoc/qcpr/pdf/cso_survey_annex_8_june_2012.pdf.

13. Dadrawala, N., *Analysis of the Current Legal Framework For Civil Society In India*, https://www.icnl.org/wp-content/uploads/Legal-Framework-for-Civil-Society-in-India-Dadrawala-vf.pdf.

14. Charity Commission for England and Wales, Government of the United Kingdom, https://www.gov.uk/government/ organisations/charity-commission.

15. Australian Not-for-Profit and Charities Commission, Government of Australia, https://www.acnc.gov.au.

16. Regulatory Frameworks for India's Voluntary Sector, Centre for Social Impact and Philanthropy, Ashoka University, https://csip.ashoka.edu.in/research-and-knowledge/.

17. Ramon Magsaysay Award Foundation, https://www.rmaward.asia/awardees/1/year/india/area/issue/sort.

18. '"Solar Mamas" Power Up Women's Development', M. Iqbal, The Hindu, https://www.thehindu.com/specials/women-in-action/solar-mamas-power-up-womens-development/article20016526.ece.

19. 'How Was Child Helpline International Founded?', Child Helpline International, https://childhelplineinternational.org/about/history/.

20. 'India's Million Missions: 75 Years of Service Toward Nation-Building'; https://www.guidestarindia.org.in/SiteImages/Indias MillionMissions.pdf.

21. Freedom in the World, Freedom House, https://freedomhouse.org/country/india/freedom-world/2023.

22. Index on Censorship, Modi's India: The Age of Intolerance, https://www.indexoncensorship.org/2023/03/modis-india-the-age-of-intolerance/.

23. United States Commission on International Religious Freedom, India—USCIRF—Recommended for Countries of Particular Concern, https://www.uscirf.gov/sites/default/files/2022-04/2022%20India.pdf.

24. CIVICUS Monitor: India, https://monitor.civicus.org/country/india/.

25. RSF—Reporters Without Borders, World Press Freedom Index, https://rsf.org/en/country/india.

26. V DEM Democracy Report 2020, https://www.v-dem.net/documents/14/dr_2020_dqumD5e.pdf.

27. V DEM Democracy Report 2023, https://www.v-dem.net/documents/29/V-dem_democracyreport2023_lowres.pdf.

28. 'Remembering Gauri Lankesh: A Hope, a Possibility, a Lesson', Shivasundar; The Wire, https://thewire.in/rights/remembering-gauri-lankesh-lesson.

29. Sahoo. N., 'Mounting Majoritarianism and Political Polarization in India', Carnegie Endowment for International Peace, https://carnegieendowment.org/2020/08/18/mounting-majoritarianism-and-political-polarization-in-india-pub-82434.

30. Kiai, Maina, 'India: Special Rapporteur's Legal Analysis Argues Restrictions on Foreign Funding Contrary to International Law', http://freeassembly.net/news/india-fcra-info-note/.

31. Biswas, Sayantani, 'IPC to Bharatiya Nyaya Sanhita 2023: "Subversive activities" replaces "sedition" | Key Changes, Mint, 11 August 2023, https://www.livemint.com/politics/policy/ipc-to-bharatiya-nyaya-sanhita-2023-subversive-activities-replaces-sedition-key-changes-11691746691991.html.

32. Sheth, A., Batabyal, J., Nundy, N., Misra, A., Pal, P., *India Philanthropy Report 2023*, https://www.bain.com/insights/india-philanthropy-report-2023/.

33. Doing Good Index, Centre for Asian Philanthropy and Society, https://caps.org/work/our-research_doing-good-index-2018.

34. 'Giving Civil Society the Right Response', Charities Aid Foundation International, https://www.cafonline.org/international-giving/global-responses-to-covid-19.

35. Section 11 (1) Income Tax Act, https://incometaxindia.gov.in/Pages/i-am/trust.aspx?k=Exemptions

36. Impact of Finance Act, 2023 on Charitable Trust and Institution Referred to in Section 12AA or 12AB or Clause (23C) of Section 10 of the Act, 1961, https://taxguru.in/income-tax/impact-finance-act-2023-charitable-trust-institution.html.

37. Charitable purpose of advocacy; (incomplete)

38. Kiai, Maina, 'The Clampdown on Resourcing: Comparing Civil Society and Business' *State of Civil Society Report 2015*, http://civicus.org/images/SOCS2015_ESSAY12_ClampdownOnResourcing.pdf.

39. 'India: FCRA Amendment 2020 will undermine the work of Civil Society', International Commission of Jurists, https://www.icj.org/india-fcra-amendment-2020-will-undermine-the-work-of-civil-society/.

40. https://www.corporatewatch.in/statusofcorporateresponsibility 2020.

41. 'Rebuilding Regions in Times of Crises: The Future of Europe and the "Voice" of Citizens', Lorenzo Fioramonti, *Open Democracy*, 18 July 2012, https://www.opendemocracy.net/en/rebuilding-

regions-in-times-of-crises-future-of-europe-and-voice-of-citizens/.

42. 'Centre Using COVID as Excuse to Quell Protest against Farm Laws: Farmer Leaders', H. Sabarwal, *Hindustan Times,* https://www.hindustantimes.com/india-news/centre-using-covid-as-excuse-to-quell-protest-against-farm-laws-farmer-leaders-101618850461291.html.

43. 'Dr Gagandeep Kang Who Cast Aspersions on Indigenously Made COVID-19 Vaccines Is an Anti-Modi Dhruv Rathee Fan: Details', *OpIndia,* https://www.opindia.com/2021/01/dr-gagandeep-kang-indigenously-made-covid-19-vaccines-pm-modi/.

44. 'India Arrests Dozens of Journalists in Clampdown on Critics of COVID-19 Response', the *Guardian,* https://www.theguardian.com/global-development/2020/jul/31/india-arrests-50-journalists-in-clampdown-on-critics-of-covid-19-response.

45. A. Marfatia, 'In Charts: How the PM-Cares Fund Is Hurting India's NGOs', *Scroll.in,* https://scroll.in/article/966746/in-charts-how-pm-cares-fund-is-hurting-non-profits-in-india.

46. 'How FCRA Inhibits "Giving" to India', Centre for Advancement of Philanthropy, https://capindia.in/how-fcra-inhibits-giving-to-india/.

47. Opening remarks by UNAIDS Executive Director Winnie Byanyima at the High-Level Meeting on AIDS, https://www.unaids.org/en/resources/presscentre/featurestories/2021/june/20210608_opening-remarks-unaids-executive-director-hlm.

Epilogue: Repurposing the State

1. Deshpande, Pushparaj, 'What Are the Ideological Projects Progressive Indians Stand for?', The Wire, 18 April 2023, https://thewire.in/politics/what-are-the-ideological-projects-progressive-indians-stand-for; last accessed on 22 August 2023 at 20.45 hours.

2. 'India Discovers Herself Again: The Full Text of Jawaharlal Nehru's "Tryst With Destiny" Speech', reproduced in the Wire, 15 August 2022, https://thewire.in/history/india-at-75-jawaharlal-nehru-tryst-with-destiny-full-text; last accessed on 22 August 223 at 19.38 hours.

3.   Hunter Harris, 'The Real Story of the *Life* Magazine 'Camelot' Interview in *Jackie*', The Vulture, 5 December 2016, https://www.vulture.com/2016/12/jackie-life-camelot-interview-theodore-white.html; last accessed on 22 August 2023 at 19.25 hours.

4.   'Civil Disobedience Alone Can Defend India's Soul in Such Times', The Wire, 21 December 2019, https://thewire.in/politics/anti-caa-protests-civil-disobedience; last accessed on 22 August 2023 at 20.02 hours.

About the Contributors

Mallikarjun Kharge is the current president of the Indian National Congress and the Leader of the Opposition (Rajya Sabha) since December 2022. Previously, he served as the leader of the Congress Party (Lok Sabha) and Union minister for Railways, Labour and Employment. He has held a host of portfolios in the government of Karnataka (including the Home, Revenue, Rural Development, Industries and Education departments) and served as the Leader of Opposition in the Karnataka Assembly. Winning a record ten consecutive elections, he has also been the general secretary of the All India Congress Committee and the president of the Karnataka Pradesh Congress Committee. He is also the founder-chairperson of the Siddharth Vihar Trust.

Sonia Gandhi is the current chairperson of the Congress Parliamentary Party. She also served as the chairperson of the United Progressive Alliance from 2004, the president of the Indian National Congress (INC) between 1998 and 2017, and the Leader of the Opposition (Lok Sabha) from 1999 to 2003. Under her presidency, the INC formed two Union governments at the Centre and multiple state governments. She also served as the chairperson of the National Advisory Council (NAC) from 2004 to 2006 and from 2010 to 2014. The NAC spearheaded several progressive legislations, including the Right to Information Act, the National Food Security Act, the Mahatma Gandhi National Rural Employment Guarantee Act and the Right to Education Act. She has served as a member of Parliament since 1999. She has also edited *Freedom's Daughter: Letters Between Indira Gandhi and Jawaharlal Nehru 1922–39* (1989), *Rajiv's World: Photographs by Rajiv Gandhi* (1995) and *Rajiv* (1994).

Mohammad Hamid Ansari served as Vice-President of India from 2007 to 2017. In a diplomatic career spanning thirty-eight years, he served as the permanent representative of India to the United Nations between 1993 and 1995, and Indian ambassador to Australia, Afghanistan, Iran and Saudi Arabia. Later, he was chairman of the National Commission for Minorities from 2006 to 2007. He was also the vice-chancellor of Aligarh Muslim University from 2000 to 2002. He is the author of *Travelling through Conflict: Essays on the Politics of West Asia* (2008) and the editor of *Iran Today: Twenty-Five Years after the Islamic Revolution* (2005).

Sitaram Yechury is General Secretary of the Communist Party of India (Marxist) and a member of the Politburo of the CPI(M) since 1992. Previously, he was a member of Parliament, Rajya Sabha from West Bengal from 2005 to 2017. He was the elected president of the JNU Students' Union (1977–78) and the Joint Secretary of the Students Federation of India (SFI) since 1978. In 1984, he was invited to the Central Committee of the CPI(M). He was elected to the Central Committee in the CPI(M) XII Congress in 1985, to the Central Secretariat at the XIII Congress in 1988 and to the Polit Bureau at the XIV Congress in 1992. He has authored numerous books including *What Is This Hindu Rashtra?: On Golwalkar's Fascistic Ideology and the Saffron Brigade's Practice* (1993), *Pseudo Hinduism Exposed: Saffron Brigade's Myths and Reality* (1993), *Caste and Class in Indian Politics Today* (1997), *Socialism in a Changing World* (2008) and *Modi Government: New Surge of Communalism* (2014).

Madan Lokur served as a judge of the Supreme Court of India. He is currently a judge of the non-resident panel of the Supreme Court of Fiji, the first Indian judge to become a judge of a foreign country. He is also a former chief justice of the Andhra Pradesh High Court and Guwahati High Court, and a judge of the Delhi High Court. He was a member of the Mediation & Conciliation Project Committee

of the Supreme Court of India and was also the judge in charge of the
e-committee of the Supreme Court of India.

Margaret Alva served as the Governor of Goa, Gujarat, Rajasthan
and Uttarakhand at various times between 2009 and 2014. She was
formerly the minister of state in the Ministry of Parliamentary Affairs,
and Department of Personnel, Public Grievances and Pensions. She
has served five terms as a member of Parliament. She was the United
Progressive Alliance's official candidate for the post of the Vice-
President of India in 2022. She was awarded the Kannada Rajyotsava
Award, the second-highest civilian honour of Karnataka.

Ashok Lavasa served as former vice-president of Asian Development
Bank (ADB). Prior to this, he was the election commissioner of India
from 2018 to 2020. He served for nearly four decades as an Indian
Administrative Service officer and was the Union Finance Secretary,
Secretary for Environment and Climate Change and Secretary for Civil
Aviation. He also served as Additional Secretary and Special Secretary
for Power. He led India's official delegation for climate change
negotiations at the COP 21, Paris. He has received the International
Alumnus Impact Award from Southern Cross University, Australia, in
2019. He has authored An *Uncivil Servant* (2006) and *An Ordinary Life:
Portrait of an Indian Generation* (2021).

Dr T.M. Thomas Isaac is a member of the central committee of
the Communist Party of India (Marxist), and served as the minister
for finance and coir of the Kerala government (2006 to 2011 and
2016 to 2021). He represented the Alappuzha constituency in the
Kerala Legislative Assembly. During his tenure as a member of the
Kerala State Planning Board, he was in charge of peoples planning
in Kerala. He was also a professor at the Centre for Development
Studies, Thiruvananthapuram, and has published a number of articles
and books, including *Science for Social Revolution: The Experience of Kerala
Shastra Sahithya Parishad* (1989), *Democracy at Work in an Indian Industrial
Cooperative: The Story of Kerala Dinesh Beedi* (1998), *Modernisation and
Employment: the Coir Industry in Kerala* (1992) and *Building Alternatives:
The Story of India's Oldest Construction Workers' Cooperative* (2017).

Wajahat Habibullah served as the first chief information commissioner of India. He was also the chairperson of the National Commission for Minorities. He was an officer of the Indian Administrative Service (IAS) from 1968, serving as Secretary in the Ministry of Panchayati Raj and Consumer Affairs. He was also director, Shastri National Academy and secretary, Rajiv Gandhi Foundation. He received the Rajiv Gandhi Award for Excellence in Secularism and the Gold Medal for Distinguished Service, Governor of Jammu and Kashmir. He has written *My Kashmir: Conflict and the Prospects for Enduring Peace* (2008) and *My Years with Rajiv: Triumph and Tragedy* (2020).

Dr Naresh Chandra Saxena served as Secretary of the Planning Commission, Government of India. He also worked as Secretary, Ministry of Rural Development, and Secretary, National Minorities Commission. He was a member of the National Advisory Council from 2004 to 2008 and 2010 to 2014. During 1993 –96, he was director of the Lal Bahadur Shastri National Academy of Administration, Mussoorie, and the Asian Development Bank Institute, Tokyo, from 2002 to 2004. He has chaired several government committees, such as women's land rights, identification of poor families, implementation of the Forest Rights Act, the joint review mission on elementary education and bauxite mining in Orissa. He has written *What Ails the IAS and Why It Fails to Deliver* (2019).

Prof. Ingrid Srinath was the director of the Centre for Social Impact and Philanthropy at Ashoka University. She has served as CEO with CRY (Child Rights and You), secretary general at CIVICUS, executive director of CHILDLINE India Foundation and CEO of HIVOS India. She was a member of SEBI's technical committee on the Social Stock Exchange and of NITI Aayog's sub-committee on the voluntary sector, and has served on multiple non-profit boards. In 2021, Prof. Ingrid received the Distinguished Alumnus Award from her alma mater, IIM Calcutta, in recognition of her contributions to civil society and philanthropy.